W9-CCY-225

S-40

THE *New*
MINIATURE SCHNAUZER

The Breed Since
CH. DOREM DISPLAY

CH. SKYLINE'S BLUE SPRUCE

The sire of 55 champions, carries several hundred lines to this breed's great *Super Sire*, **CH. DOREM DISPLAY**, pictured on the preceding page. Although thirty years and many, many generations separate these outstanding sires, note the striking resemblance. Note also the resemblance between **Blue Spruce** and . . .

CH. RAMPAGE'S REPRESENTATIVE,

pictured on the opposite page. He is clearly the sire of the 1990s, having recorded 45 champion get through 1996, at just seven years of age.

THE *New*
MINIATURE SCHNAUZER
by DAN KIEDROWSKI

Second Edition ——————— First Printing

1997

HOWELL BOOK HOUSE

Howell Book House
A Simon & Schuster Macmillan Company
1633 Broadway
New York, NY 10019

Copyright © 1997, 1986 by Howell Book House

All rights reserved. No part of this book may be reproduced,
stored in retrieval system or transmitted in any form or by any
means, electronic or mechanical, photocopying, recording, or
otherwise without permission in writing from the publisher. No
patent liability is assumed with respect to the use of the information contained herein. Although every precaution has been taken
in preparation of this book, the publisher and author assume no
responsibility for errors or omissions, Neither is any liability
assumed for damages resulting from the use of the information
contained herein. For information, address Howell Book HOuse,
1633 Broadway, 7th Floor, New York, NY 10019-6785

MACMILLAN is a registered trademark of Macmillan, Inc.

ISBN 0-87605-241-3

Library of Congress Cataloging-in-Publication Data is
available from the Library of Congress

Manufactured in the United States of America
99 98 97   9 8 7 6 5 4 3 2

Book Design: Dan Kiedrowski
Cover Design: Heather Kern

Dan Kiedrowski with the late Ch. Regency's Right On Target, the breed's all-time top producing sire of 78 champions. Target was bred and owned by Beverly Verna (Regency).

About the Author

DAN KIEDROWSKI has enjoyed a vicarious love affair with the Miniature Schnauzer for more than half of his lifetime. His introduction to the breed came in 1955, through an association with Chris and Bob Snowdon of the Glenshaw Kennels.

In 1960 he began publishing the monthly breed magazine, *Schnauzer Shorts,* and continues to do so after more than three decades. Since 1962 he has broadened his scope as publisher of the monthly group magazine, *Terrier Type,* producing between them over 2,500 pages annually.

An accomplished artist, Mr. Kiedrowski fills his spare time painting and sculpting.

Judging became a natural by-product of his total involvement in dogs, although AKC rulings limit this to Sweepstakes classes in the United States. Members of the American Miniature Schnauzer Club have five times honored him as their selection of Sweepstakes judge for their National Specialty (a gap of five years must intervene between nominations). In addition, he has judged Sweepstakes classes for many regional clubs from coast to coast, some of them many times.

Today he is considered one of the world's most respected Miniature Schnauzer authorities.

Contents

Acknowledgements

THE WRITING OF THIS BOOK would not have been possible without the assistance given from the by breeders throughout the world who furnished pictures and information on their dogs.

The breed's early history was so well documented in the late Anne Eskrigge's breed classic, *The Complete Miniature Schnauzer* (Howell Book House), all that was necessary was a condensation of the highlights, as most real students of the breed will have this fine effort in their personal libraries.

So much is owed to the late John Knight who devised a system to rate show dogs according to the numbers defeated in breed competition only. To this day it is still known as the Knight System, and has been taken up by countless other breed statisticians over the years. More importantly, John developed a unique system which delineates lines of champion descent so that a complete picture of many generations can be drawn from any producer of note. These have been a frequent feature in *Schnauzer Shorts*, and this system, too, has been taken up by other breed historians in providing similar records on top producers.

The chapters on the breed outside the United States required many sources. Our sincere thanks especially to Dr. Martin DeForest and Catherine McMillan of Canada, Peter Newman of England and Joan Lamping of Australia, each doing yeoman service in providing information on activities in these countries. Marcia Feld was instrumental in gathering information on European and South African activities.

The many dog show photographers over the years have contributed much in depicting the changes in the breed visually from its earliest to latest stages in both type and presentation. The handsome photos by the late Rudolph Tauskey and William Brown show the wonderful Dorem and Phil-Mar dogs in all their glory. More recently, John Ashbey, Martin Booth, William Gilbert, Joan Ludwig, Evelyn Shafer, Missy Yuhl and others have contributed much to making this book a visual pleasure.

Last but far from least, our thanks to Denis Shaw for his monumental effort in achieving and presenting the host of drawings depicting breed type and grooming. They are truly wonderful.

The foregoing are but a few of those who aided in this work, as will be seen by references to others in the course of the book.

As is inherent in any book of this nature, many people and many dogs, unfortunately, have had to go unmentioned. We are deeply indebted to all Miniature Schnauzer fanciers whose industrious efforts have advanced breed type while maintaining its unique and most satisfying character.

- DAN KIEDROWSKI

Prologue

THE PURPOSE OF THIS BOOK is to give the reader, whether a novice or seasoned breeder-exhibitor, a complete and accurate source of information on all facets of interest concerning the Miniature Schnauzer.

The last three decades have witnessed a dramatic rise in popularity for this stylish, active and intelligent breed. The challenge offered by this preferred position has been enthusiastically accepted by breed fanciers throughout the world, and we have today a much improved version, both physically and mentally—a dog for all reasons.

The Miniature Schnauzer is singularly unique in that all breeding stock throughout the world can trace its roots to one remarkably current super sire— the great CH. DOREM DISPLAY (April 5, 1945 — February 28, 1959). Therefore, every effort has been made to outline the breed from this one source, dividing it into various branches, lines and families. As many illustrations as possible have been used to more clearly delineate breed type as it has developed to the present.

You will note that statistics are liberally used to designate the producing records of the great sires and dams of the past and present. Represented are their producing records through 1996. Any male that has produced five or more champions, and any female that has produced three or more champions, is considered a Top Producer. The figure in parentheses after a dog's name will indicate the number of champions produced up to the time of publication. Example: CH. DOREM DISPLAY (42 Chs.).

Be mindful of the fact that a dozen or more new champions in the breed are finished each month, and that producing records on current sires and dams are constantly growing.

1

The Type and Character of the Miniature Schnauzer

ON APPEARANCE ALONE, the Miniature Schnauzer deserves the popularity he enjoys. It is, however, his lively, inquisitive character that launched him into the top ten ranking among all breeds in recent years. The Miniature Schnauzer is big enough to really be a dog, and small enough to share your comfortable chair. Most people will select this breed for its total livability. A good one is by nature alert, friendly, intelligent, vigorous and, most important, long-lived.

Over forty years ago, Dorothy Williams of the famed Dorem Kennel wrote the following appraisal of the breed:

The Miniature Schnauzer is of terrier outline with the same beauty of balance and with the typical style and spirit. But in all other respects, this breed has a distinct individuality from the other members of the Terrier Group. The combination of cropped ears and short tail is most unusual. Also the gray salt and pepper color is found in the Schnauzer family alone. People unacquainted with this breed often object to the bother of cropping, not realizing that the ears are healed completely in two weeks and that there is no further trouble of setting, which can go on for months in some breeds and often unsuccessfully.

Miniature Schnauzers are plucked in the same manner as wire coated terriers. But a good coat in this breed can be kept going continually without stripping down to rock bottom. Plucking is also easier as the hair comes out much more readily than other wire coats.

Miniatures have the same spirit and showmanship of most terriers, but are much more responsive to the owners' wishes and are noted for great intelligence. They do demand human companionship and have great devotion.

Miniature Schnauzers have great stamina and, in fact, will show no signs of illness until they are quite sick, and then they are fighters and will not give up. They are also easy whelpers and most careful and devoted mothers.

The responsiveness and intelligence of Miniature Schnauzers makes them ideal for obedience work, enhanced by the fact that they love to please their owners.

Four-year-old Erik Parker with Ch. Orbit's Lift Off, CDX

Four-year-old Cindy Fancy with Ch. Fancway's Voodoo Doll

Both bitches were family pets as well as top producers.

How fortunate that what was so four decades ago has, by careful breeding, been maintained.

Dogs, like people, differ greatly in character, even when they belong to the same breed. The Official Standard of the Miniature Schnauzer includes these comments regarding temperament: "The typical Miniature Schnauzer is alert and spirited, yet obedient to command. He is friendly, intelligent and willing to please. He should never be over-aggressive or timid."

For decades, breeders have given far more attention to character and temperament than what may have been suggested by the Official Standard, and have developed an all-purpose dog—a dog for all reasons.

The Schnauzer's intelligence expresses itself in many ways. One look into his face is to sense his ever-active mind and fun-loving personality.

The learning capacity of the Miniature Schnauzer is proverbial, and limited only by the patience of the teacher. The breed's performance on all levels of obedience is exceptional, and ranks among the highest in numbers of dogs that achieve obedience titles. Schnauzers learn quickly as a rule, and in time can be taught almost anything a dog is capable of learning. The only requirements are firmness, repetition, patience and, above all, *kindness.*

Frequently called "the dog with the human brain," their reasoning faculties are uncanny. Whereas most breeds think in a doggy way, Schnauzers react in a much more human fashion, and in a way we humans can better understand. Schnauzers are, in fact, pathetically dependent upon human

11

companionship and understanding. Without it they become mistrustful and dull. Once a Schnauzer makes up his mind about you and places you in his world, he seldom changes his idea of your worth. When closeness is achieved, he gives you his full devotion, and from that point on your moods and your commands are his chief concern in life.

Although Miniature Schnauzers are quick to adapt, they love a routine. The typical companion takes pride in knowing, practically before you do, what your next move will be. Heide seems to know exactly when her next walk will come, regardless of the time of day. Her mistress, a fastidious young lady, always checks her appearance at the hall mirror beforehand, and Heide always meets her at the front door.

Schnauzers have good memories and will recognize friends or former owners after a long period. As he is not a jealous dog, he will gladly share his people with others, both human and canine, and even give space to the family cat. Although not known essentially as a one-man dog, his full devotion is usually for one person, after which he includes the immediate family in various gradations of affectionate regard. Schnauzers seem to understand children, are infinitely gentle with them, and will delight them for hours with their clever antics without becoming impatient or intolerant. Children who are taught to handle them properly will particularly enjoy their whimsical character.

Miniature Schnauzers are not by nature aggressive, as are some of their terrier cousins. They should, however, be relatively fearless. Once mature, the Schnauzer has a strongly developed territorial instinct. He is an ideal guard dog as he defends vocally rather than physically. There is a meaningful difference between being quick to defend and quick to attack. A good Schnauzer will bark at anyone who may appear a threat to his home. He barks until the caller leaves, if you are not at home, or until you arrive on the scene. Once you are there, he accepts that you are in control of the situation and is silent. For all his boldness, the Miniature Schnauzer will display a natural kindness and charm for those who show themselves as friends.

Schnauzers are not random, incessant barkers. They are discriminating and intelligent guard dogs that assume this duty naturally. Too intelligent to be argumentative, they are positive thinkers, know their territorial rights, and will defend them.

Basically, the Schnauzer disposition is sweet, loving and loyal, but he is not at all subservient or overly sensitive. People who want a lie-at-your-feet type dog, or one that is aloof, would not enjoy a Miniature Schnauzer. Wanting your affection, he may climb into the middle of your newspaper or put his head under your arm with a prodding motion. It would never occur to him that you might be too occupied to pet him. A great sense of self is one of his most endearing qualities.

Schnauzers enjoy the outdoors in all kinds of weather. This need to be a part of their local surroundings should be satisfied. They enjoy long walks, and

Ch. Far Hills Magic Angel enjoying couch privileges

in pairs will run lively races with each other. Usually they like to swim, too. On the other hand, they exist quite happily on a moderate amount of exercise, and therefore are an excellent breed for the city dweller. The Schnauzer kept mostly indoors would be happiest when provided with a window or door from which to view the world outside.

Whether a dog or a bitch (female), the Miniature Schnauzer rates high as a totally reliable companion. Individual disposition is far more important than sex in a pet, both males and females being equally lovable. Many owners maintain that bitches are more affectionate, quieter, less inclined to wander and easier to train. The fact that a bitch comes in season (is breedable) twice a year, as a rule, must be considered. Confinement for two to three weeks during these periods is essential. A bitch, however, may be spayed (her reproductive organs removed), and the problem eliminated. A male may be attracted by a bitch in season at any time, and will react accordingly. He may find that a selection of potential mates live in the neighborhood, and on occasion will want to check them out if given the opportunity. Castration (removal of his reproductive organs) offers the same sense of security that spaying does for females, although comparatively few owners of males feel this more drastic measure necessary.

Miniature Schnauzers are quick to adjust to new situations, and are particularly suitable to a change of homes at any age. Many have shown that at six or seven years and beyond they will learn to enjoy completely their new family. Selecting an older dog as a pet can be just as rewarding as taking on a new puppy, as the breed's average life span is from twelve to fifteen years.

The best advice in determining the age at which to buy is to consider all the circumstances involved. If you have not had previous experience in raising a puppy, are you willing to learn? Have you the time and patience to train one? Have you the facilities? You cannot expect to train a puppy properly unless he is with you. If puddles on the floor upset you, if you are away from home most of the time, if you cannot control your small children, do not expect to successfully train a young puppy. In many cases the older dog will prove more satisfactory, particularly if he has been raised in the family, is friendly with strangers, behaves on a leash and in the car and, of course, is in good health.

A wire-coated breed such as the Miniature Schnauzer loses much of its distinction and charm if not kept in a neat, well-groomed state. This is almost a basic requirement, and only those who are conscious of these needs should consider owning a dog of the breed.

The wire hair of the Schnauzer coat is not at all like human hair. It grows for a certain period, and to a particular length, and then dies. It does not immediately shed, as in many breeds, but tends to cling half-heartedly until it is pulled out by brambles, during household play, or more specifically in the grooming process. Many owners choose to maintain their own pets, but most plan on three or four trips annually to a professional grooming shop. All will want to learn how to keep the family dog looking smart, if only between visits to a professional.

Good health and good character should always come first in selecting a companion dog, but if you are particularly conscious of the physical attributes of the breed and are interested in a future involving showing and breeding, you will want to study and understand what a good Miniature Schnauzer should look like—and why.

Why the Miniature Schnauzer Is Classified as a Terrier

The Schnauzer began his recorded history as a yard and stable dog. With a substantial infusion of cattle-droving blood, he was not only a good ratter and vermin killer but also helped herd livestock. The United States and Canada are the only countries in which the Miniature Schnauzer is classified in the Terrier Group. Throughout most of the show-giving countries worldwide, he is classified in Non-Sporting (or Utility). Originally, all three sizes, Giant, Standard and Miniature Schnauzers competed in the Working Group here, and no one seems to know how or why the move to the Terrier Group was made. In the late 1930s, the larger varieties were moved back to the Working Group while the Miniatures remained among the Terriers

In general character and type, Miniature Schnauzers do resemble terriers more closely than breeds in other Groups. In temperament, he is closer to the alert, active terrier than to gun dogs, hounds or toys. Nevertheless, a typical Miniature Schnauzer carries a dash of working temperament, and this "big dog" quality is a decided asset in making him the total companion that he is today.

Although the original intent to produce a small-scale Standard Schnauzer remains a challenge, the "terrier type" seems to have taken hold. There is ample reason for this. Judges are bound to be influenced unconsciously by a mental picture that closely relates to a terrier ideal. Sloping shoulders can easily give way to a "terrier front" with its corresponding, somewhat stilted action. Good spring of rib yields to flatter slab sides. The head becomes increasingly longer and narrower.

Using the Standard as our guide, it is clear that we have gone just about as far as we safely can in the direction of "terrier type." The challenge now is to produce a good terrier of Schnauzer type—a dog for all reasons.

Eye Diseases of the Miniature Schnauzer
by Members of the Eye Committees
of the American Miniature Schnauzer Club

Miniature Schnauzers are susceptible to many of the eye diseases and problems that occur in humans and in virtually all dog breeds. Most occur infrequently in Miniature Schnauzers.[1] The four diseases discussed here have come to the attention of breeders and/or veterinarian ophthalmologists who have conducted research into their causes. Two of the diseases have been found to be hereditary, a third appears to be so, and the cause of the fourth in unknown. Two of the problems involve cataracts (an opacity in the lens of the eye). The other two involve atrophy of the retina (the light-sensing tissue at the back of the eye).

The following sections provide a brief description of each problem, what is known about it as of publication, and how the American Miniature Schnauzer Club and individual breeders are trying to deal with it, but will not try to provide technical information on the structure of the eye or on the complexities of modes of inheritance of genetic problems. Similarly, it is beyond the scope of this discussion to describe the considerable time, effort, and money many Miniature Schnauzer breeders have devoted towards trying to find solutions to these eye diseases. All Miniature Schnauzer breeders and owners owe them a great debt.

Congenital cataracts (CC)
In the late 1950s, a veterinary student of Dr. Lionel Rubin at the University of Pennsylvania identified a form of congenital cataracts in Miniature Schnauzers which were initially called congenital juvenile cataracts (CJC). The name stemmed from the fact that the cataracts were present in fetuses and could also be seen with a relatively simple and inexpensive "slit-lamp"

---

[1] The information in this material relates to Miniature Schnauzers of show lines owned or bred by members of the American Miniatue Schnauzer Club, the Miniature Schnauzer Club of Canada, and regional Miniature Schnauzer Clubs in the United States and Canada. The authors do not have sufficient information to comment on the incidence of eye disease in show lines in other countries or in the stock of commercial kennels which produced puppies for pet stores.

examination in very young puppies as soon as the eyes were open. These cataracts are bilateral, *i.e.*, present in both eyes. They can be seen with the naked eye in some dogs as young as one or two years of age, but in many cases are not visible to the naked eye until the dog is older. In time, affected animals become virtually blind in both eyes.

Recognition of an inherited fault in a show or breeding animal inevitably affects its value as a stud dog or brood bitch, making such faults a very sensitive issue. Nonetheless, dedicated members of the AMSC, with the assistance of several veterinary ophthalmologists, implemented efforts to eliminate the problem.

The effort began in the 1960s with a series of articles alerting breeders to the problem and providing them with such information as was known. Most veterinary ophthalmologists assumed that the problem was inherited in a simple autosomal recessive[2] mode based on earlier research on similar problems in other breeds. Because information specific to CC was essential to develop a testing program, the AMSC and its members supported a research effort by Dr. Richard Donovan, a veterinary ophthalmologist in Boston, to determine the mode of inheritance of CC cataracts in Miniature Schnauzers.

In 1973, once it had been learned that CC was caused by a simple autosomal recessive gene, the AMSC board adopted a voluntary pledge by AMSC members to have dogs used for breeding and all puppies examined by a veterinary ophthalmologist and to retire from breeding any animals affected by CC or who had produced any affected puppies. The AMSC set up an Eye Committee, chaired by Jeannette Schultz, M.D. (a Miniature Schnauzer breeder and a geneticist), to work with veterinary ophthalmologists in establishing standards for test breeding to identify carriers. Based on the committee's advice, the AMSC board initiated a program to test breed clear-eyed animals to affecteds

---

[2]   A simple autosomal recessive trait is one in which the animal becomes affected with the disease only if it inherits the defective form of the gene from both parents. Such an animal is called an "affected." An animal that inherits the defective form of the gene from only one parent is clinically normal (*i.e.*, has clear eyes) and is called a "carrier." The terms "clear" and "normal" both refer to an animal that has not inherited the defective form of the gene from either parent. An affected animal will pass the defective form of the gene to all of its offspring, but only offspring who inherit the defective form of the gene from their other parent as well will be affected. On average, a carrier will pass the defective form of the gene to one half of its offspring. Clears, not having the defective form of the gene, cannot pass it to any of their offspring.

These facts are the basis for the AMSC testing program, described below, to distinguish clear-eyed animals who are clear of the defective gene from those who are carriers of the CC gene. The test involves mating the clear-eyed animal to an affected animal. If any of the puppies so produced are affected, the clear-eyed animal is a carrier. If none of the puppies are affected, the number of clear-eyed puppies will define a probability that the clear-eyed parent is normal. (All puppies so produced will be carriers.)

and thus either establish that the animal being tested was a carrier or establish a probability[3] that the animal being tested was a clear.

The testing program was feasible because the cataracts were present and identifiable in both live-born and still-born puppies. Thus, the status of puppies as affected and of older clear-eyed animals as carriers could be determined before breeding them. Most AMSC members signed the pledge and had their puppies checked and breeding stock tested. Breeders conscientiously sought "test-bred clear" stud dogs. A number of owners and breeders publicly announced that one or more of their dogs had been determined to be carriers, thus helping others assess the pedigrees of their own animals. Many others retired carrier animals from breeding.

As a result of this program, congenital cataracts have become very rare in show stock Miniature Schnauzers in the United States and Canada. Some people fear, however, that the problem may just be hidden because many fewer bitches than dogs were tested. Unless the checking of puppies and testing of breeding stock continues, CC may recur as a problem in the future.

A list of animals which have tested as "probably clear" may be obtained at mininal charge from the Chair of the AMSC's CC Committee.

Later-Onset Cataracts

In the late 1980s, the AMSC became aware of cataracts appearing in adult Miniature Schnauzers, frequently at about eighteen months to two years of age. As of early 1995, no significant research has been done on these cataracts. Most of what is known about them comes from observations by Miniature Schnauzer breeders.

The cause of these later-onset cataracts is not known with certainty, but some limited test breeding seems to indicate that the disease is genetic and follows a simple autosomal recessive pattern of inheritance. These cataracts are somewhat unusual in that the disease develops at different rates in each eye. Thus, the cataract may be larger in one eye than the other or may be visible in one eye but not the other. That, however, is not atypical of inherited cataracts.

The AMSC has been asking breeders to provide diagnoses and pedigrees of affected animals to the Later Onset Cataract Committee so that the

---

3   The percent probability that a clear-eyed tested animal is clear of the CC trait is based on the number of clear-eyed puppies — with no affected puppies — produced from a mating to an affected animal. For example, five clear-eyed puppies with no affected puppies from such a breeding establishes a 96.875% probability that the tested animal is a normal. The probability of normality increases as the number of clear-eyed puppies increases, but the test can never generate a 100% probability that the tested animal is normal. Thus, it is incorrect to assume that all animals descended from test-bred stock are clear of the CC trait. This is especially true if not all the animals in the pedigree were tested. In contrast, even one affected offspring demonstrates a 100% probability (*i.e.*, certainty) that neither parent is normal.

AMSC can monitor the frequency of the disease and gather information that may be helpful to a researcher who undertakes an investigation of the problem. Test breeding is not a viable option to eliminate the disease because of the length of time it takes for clinical signs of the disease to develop.

Current information can be obtained by contacting the chair of the AMSC's Late-Onset Cataract Committee.

Progressive Retinal Atrophy (PRA)

PRA is a gradual dying off of the light sensing organs (rods and cones) in the retina at the back of the eye. It is untreatable and results in total blindness. The first noticeable symptom is night blindness. That is followed by a gradual loss of vision until total blindness results.

Different varieties of PRA are found in varying forms in more than seventy breeds of dogs. Only one variety of the disease, called Photoreceptor Dysplasia (PD), is known to occur in Miniature Schnauzers. PD is not known to occur in any other breed.

PRA is the animal analog of Retinitis Pigmentosa in humans. As with PRA, there are many forms of Retinitis Pigmentosa. The Retinitis Pigmentosa Foundation has funded much of the basic work in PRA in dogs in the hope that information learned in research on dogs will be helpful with respect to Retinitis Pigmentosa.

Some breeds, such as Irish Setters, have early onset forms of PRA, in which the animal loses significant vision while still a puppy. In other breeds, noticeable vision loss does not occur until the animal is several years old. It was originally thought that PD was a late-onset form of PRA but it was later determined that PD is actually an early-onset disease with a very slow progression. Vision loss noticeable to the owner generally occurs at three to four years of age, but occurs earlier or later in some animals.

In the late 1980s, Dr. Charles Parshall, a veterinary ophthalmologist in private practice in Ohio; Dr. Gustavo Aguirre, a veterinary ophthalmologist then at the University of Pennsylvania; and their associates conducted a major study of PRA in Miniature Schnauzers, the results of which were published in 1991.[4] The study discovered, as mentioned above, that PD is an early-onset form of the disease with a slow progression, and that affected animals retain substantial vision even after a large percentage of the rods and cones have atrophied. The researchers concluded that PD is a simple autosomal recessive genetic disease. The number of affected dogs reported to the AMSC's PRA Committee, however, is significantly less than expected from a simple autosomal recessive disease, given the incidence of known carriers in current pedigrees. The reasons for this discrepancy are unknown at present.

---

[4] *Progress in Veterinary & Comparative Ophthalmology*, Vol. 1, No. 3, 1991, pp. 187 — 203

It was not possible to develop a test breeding program for PRA as had been done with congenital cataracts because the disease is not generally observable in young puppies.[5] In the 1980s, researchers developed the electro-retinograph (ERG) machine which held promise of detecting PRA sufficiently early to make a test breeding program feasible. The ERGs from this machine proved to be of great value in research — and the study referenced above could not have been done without them — but serious limitations precluded wide-spread use of ERG's in testing animals. First, ERG machines of the required sensitivity and quality were relatively expensive and not widely available. Second, the tests themselves were expensive because they required anesthesia of the animal being tested. Third, and most important, it required substantial expertise and experience to correctly interpret the tracings produced by the ERG machines. This was an even greater problem in Miniature Schnauzers than in some other breeds because there proved to be greater variability in normal retinas in Miniature Schnauzers than in many other breeds. Many Miniature Schnauzer breeders grew disenchanted with ERG testing after receiving different diagnoses from different practitioners. Dr. Aguirre and Dr. Parshall both believe that ERG testing is accurate when done properly and Dr. Parshall still does ERG testing on Miniature Schnauzers and on several other breeds. For current information on the availability of ERG testing, contact a veterinary ophthalmologist.

In the early 1990s, Dr. Deborah Farber and her fellow researchers at the Jules Stein Eye Institute at UCLA succeeded in isolating the defective gene that caused PRA in laboratory mice, using recombinant DNA techniques. Dr. Aguirre and his associates at the Baker Institute at Cornell University then discovered that the analogous gene in the canine genome was responsible for the form of PRA found in Irish Setters. Dr. Aguirre and his associates developed a blood test to detect the defective form of the gene. The test was made available to Irish Setter breeders in early 1994.

The new DNA test has several advantages over other types of testing. First, the blood can be drawn by a local veterinarian and shipped to the testing laboratory. There is no need to take the dog to a perhaps distant veterinary ophthalmologist. Second, the test can be done while the animal is still a puppy so that the results can be known before the animal is shown or bred. Third, no test breeding is necessary because the test will detect carriers as well as affecteds.

As soon as the AMSC learned of the success with Irish Setters, it immediately began to investigate the feasibility of research to identify the defective gene that causes PD and to develop a blood test to detect it. In June 1994, the AMSC's PRA Committee began to investigate the feasibility and cost of the research and to develop a fund-raising plan. By September 1994, the PRA Committee had determined that Dr. Aguirre's group at the Baker Institute

---

5   A few breeders report having observed night blindness in young puppies who later became blind with PRA.

affiliated with Cornell was the best qualified to conduct the research, had obtained a detailed proposal and budget from the Baker Institute, and had developed a fund-raising plan. The AMSC board then created a new Fund Raising Committee and authorized it to begin raising funds for the proposed research. The response of the AMSC members and other Miniature Schnauzer breeders and owners was overwhelming. By year-end 1994, more than $25,000 had been raised. At about the same time, the American Kennel Club announced that it was forming the AKC Canine Health Foundation and that it intended to provide significant funding for genetic research. The AMSC asked the AKC for help, specifically, to match the funds that the AMSC raised. The AKC generously agreed to do so. By the end of 1995, the AMSC had raised its entire $87,500 share of the costs of the research—an accomplishment unprecedented among breed clubs. Donations were received from more than two hundred Miniature Schnauzer clubs and breeders in the United States, Canada and Australia.

The Baker Institute hired Dr. Qi Zhang to perform the research under the guidance of Dr. Aguirre and other senior researchers at the Baker Institute. The DNA research on PD began on February 1, 1996.

Information regarding the status of the research may be obtained from the chair of the AMSC's PRA Committee.

Suddenly Acquired Retinal Dystrophy (SARD)

Like PRA, SARD causes blindness through atrophy of the retina. The symptoms are similar to those of PRA. The principal difference is in the speed at which sight deteriorates. In PRA, it normally takes about a year from the first symptoms of night blindness to total blindness. In SARD, on the other hand, it occurs in a few weeks.

Very little is known about SARD. A study on the disease was undertaken at the University of Pennsylvania, but the researchers were unable to determine the cause of the disease. It does not appear to be genetic, although a predisposition to it may be. Many of the animals that develop SARD are overweight overeaters. Many SARD-affected animals have high blood lipids. Animals tend to be six years or older when they develop SARD. Curiously, in SARD, the retina will still appear relatively normal in an ophthalmoscopic examination shortly after blindness results, whereas with PRA the retina will be seriously deteriorated before clinical signs of blindness are apparent.

Further information regarding SARD may be obtained from the chair of the AMSC's Eye Committees.

AMSC Recommendations

The AMSC's recommendations for dealing with these diseases have been embodied in an Eye Pledge which all AMSC members and applicants are asked to sign. The Eye Pledge was approved at the meeting of the AMSC board of governors on October 6, 1973. The fifth paragraph was approved by the board of governors at its meeting on March 31, 1995, at the request of the American

Kennel Club as a condition of its providing the matching funds for the PRA research project discussed above.

Each person signing the Eye Pledge promises to do the following:

1. **To make a determined effort to have slit lamp examinations of all puppies to determine the existence of congenital (juvenile) cataracts.**

2. **To retire from breeding any dam or sire that has produced a puppy with congenital cataracts or progressive retinal atrophy.**

3. **To send a report of the eye examination and pedigree of every affected Miniature Schnauzer with eye problems (and all affected litter mates as well as the total number in the litter) to whomever the AMSC board designates to collect this information and to assist concerned breeders.**

4. **To make an effort to examine yearly all show and breeding stock by a qualified ACVO.**

5. **To make a determined effort to have all breeding animals tested for the presence of the progressive retinal atrophy gene by means of a DNA test once such a test is developed and available.**

As of 1996, examination by slit lamp and ophthalmoscope costs between ten and twenty dollars per dog when done at an eye clinic held at a club meeting or show, and a little more when done at a veterinary ophthalmologist's office on an individual basis. No anesthesia is required. All that is necessary is to place dilating eye drops in the animal's eyes about twenty minutes before the examination is done.

The examination of puppies to which paragraph one of the pledge refers will detect congenital cataracts and other problems which may be evident in a young puppy. It will not detect PRA, SARD, or later onset cataracts as those do not develop until later in life. It is important to have all puppies checked — not just those being kept for show or breeding — because the presence of even one puppy affected with congenital cataracts conclusively establishes that both parents are either carriers or affecteds. Also, an examination report showing clear eyes as a puppy will aid making a definitive diagnosis of later-onset cataracts if the animal later develops cataracts.

The examinations to which reference is made in Paragraph 4 of the Pledge are designed primarily to detect PRA and later-onset cataracts, both of which may be detected by ophthalmoscopic examination before the owner will notice clinical signs. Annual testing will help distinguish between PRA and SARD because normally PRA is detectable by ophthalmoscopic examination long before the animal becomes clinically blind, whereas with SARD the retina will appear virtually normal right up until the dog becomes blind.

Finally, an animal that develops visible lesions or opacities on its eyes, or that displays difficulty in seeing, should be examined as quickly as possible by a qualified veterinary ophthalmologist.

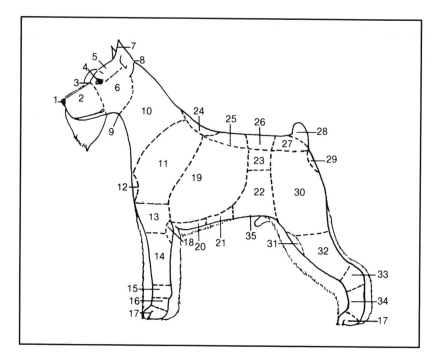

POINTS OF THE DOG
AS SHOWN ON THE MINIATURE SCHNAUZER

1 – Nose	13 – Uppe rarm	25 – Back
2 – Muzzle; foreface	14 – Forearm	26 – Loin
3 – Stop	15 – Knee	27 – Croup; rump
4 – Eye	16 – Front pastern	28 – Tail; stern
5 – Skull; forehead	17 – Foot; paw	29 – Point of buttock
6 – Cheek	18 – Elbow	30 – Thigh
7 – Ear	19 – Ribs	31 – Stifle
8 – Occiput	20 – Brisket	32 – Gaskin; second thigh
9 – Throat	21 – Abdomen; belly	33 – Hock
10 – Neck	22 – Flank	34 – Back pastern
11 – Shoulder	23 – Coupling	35 – Tuck-up
12 – Point of shoulder	24 – Withers	

LENGTH of the Schnauzer is measured from point of shoulder (12) to point of buttock (29).

HEIGHT of the Schnauzer is measured from withers (24) to ground.

LENGTH should approximate HEIGHT on the Schnauzer.

FOREQUARTERS consist of the area beginning at the withers (24) and include 11, 12, 13, 14, 15, 16 and 17.

HINDQUARTERS consist of the area beginning at the croup (27) and include 30, 32, 33, 34 and 17.

BACKLINE includes the withers, back, loin and croup.

2

What Makes a Good Miniature Schnauzer

IN ORDER TO accurately assess the physical attributes of a particular breed, early devotees found it necessary to develop a word picture that would serve as a Standard. In the early days that Standard of Perfection would more likely represent a breeder's ideal—striven for but not entirely realized. As the breed improves, through careful selection, the Standard may require revision as a particular type gains favor.

The Miniature Schnauzer Standard has had several revisions over the last half-century, the major changes relating to size. The original American Standard set a maximum shoulder height of 12 inches for both sexes. By 1934 this had been changed so that the rule read 10 1/2 to 13 1/2 inches for males and 10 to 12 1/2 inches for females, but no male was to be disqualified for oversize unless over 14 inches, and no female unless over 13 inches.

During 1956 a committee of the American Miniature Schnauzer Club (AMSC) made a study of the breed Standard and presented a revision which was accepted by a mail vote of the members and approved by the American Kennel Club (AKC) in the spring of 1957. The principal difference was again related to size, changing the minimum to 12 inches, maximum to 14 inches, and the ideal size 13 1/2 inches. In the show ring, dogs or bitches under 12 or over 14 inches were to be disqualified.

It was more than two decades later that a further revision was made. Again, a ballot noting the AMSC committee recommendations was mailed to the entire membership numbering over 500. It was necessary to have an affirmative vote of more than two-thirds of all members. It is interesting to note that all the proposed changes were approved except the one deleting the words "Ideal size to be 13 1/2 inches." This item missed being accepted by only two votes. The major change was the addition of a paragraph describing temperament. Other changes involved a clearer description of body and coat and a new paragraph on movement. These revisions were approved by the AKC in 1979. Further revisions were made in 1991, removing the "ideal size clause", and adding considerably to the descriptions of color. All revisions are included in the current Standard of Perfection which follows.

General Appearance

The Miniature Schnauzer is a robust, active dog of terrier type, resembling his larger cousin, the Standard Schnauzer, in general appearance, and of an alert, active disposition. *Faults* - Type—Toyishness, ranginess or coarseness.

Size, Proportion, Substance

Size - From 12 to 14 inches. He is sturdily built, nearly square in *proportion* of body length to height with plenty of bone, and without any suggestion of toyishness. *Disqualifications* - Dogs or bitches under 12 inches or over 14 inches.

Head

Eyes—Small, dark brown and deep-set. They are oval in appearance and keen in expression. *Faults* - Eyes light and/or large and prominent in appearance. *Ears*—When cropped, the ears are identical in shape and length, with pointed tips. They are in balance with the head and not exaggerated in length. They are set high on the skull and carried perpendicularly at the inner edges, with as little bell as possible along the outer edges. When uncropped, the ears are small and V-shaped, folding close to the skull. *Head* strong and rectangular, its width diminishing slightly from ears to eyes, and again to the tip of the nose. The forehead is unwrinkled. The *topskull* is flat and fairly long. The foreface is parallel to the topskull, with a slight stop, and it is at least as long as the topskull. The *muzzle* is strong in proportion to the skull; it ends in a moderately blunt manner, with thick whiskers which accentuate the rectangular shape of the head. *Faults* - Head coarse and cheeky. The *teeth* meet in a *scissors bite*. That is, the upper front teeth overlap the lower front teeth in such a manner that the inner surface of the upper incisors barely touches the outer surface of the lower incisors when the mouth is closed. *Faults* - Bite - Undershot or overshot jaw. Level bite.

Neck, Topline, Body

Neck strong and well arched, blending into the shoulders, and with the skin fitting tightly at the throat. *Body* short and deep, with the brisket extending at least to the elbows. Ribs are well sprung and deep, extending well back to a short loin. The underbody does not present a tucked-up appearance at the flank. The *backline* is straight; it declines slightly from the withers to the base of the tail. The withers form the highest point of the body. The overall length from chest to buttocks appears to equal the height at the withers. *Faults* - Chest too broad or shallow in brisket. Hollow or roach back. *Tail* set high and carried erect. It is docked only long enough to be clearly visible over the backline of the body when the dog is in proper length of coat. *Fault* - Tail set too low.

Forequarters

Forelegs are straight and parallel when viewed from all sides. They have strong pasterns and good bone. They are separated by a fairly deep brisket which precludes a pinched front. The elbows are close, and the ribs spread gradually from the first rib so as to allow space for the elbows to move close to the body. *Fault* - Loose elbows. The sloping *shoulders* are muscled, yet flat and clean. They are well laid back, so that from the side the tips of the shoulder blades are in a nearly vertical line above the elbow. The tips of the blades are placed closely together. They slope forward and downward at an angulation which permits the maximum forward extension of the forelegs without binding or effort. Both the shoulder blades and upper arms are long, permitting depth of chest at the brisket. *Feet* short and round (cat feet) with thick, black pads. The toes are arched and compact.

Hindquarters

The hindquarters have strong-muscled, slanting thighs. They are well bent at the stifles. There is sufficient angulation so that, in stance, the hocks extend beyond the tail. The hindquarters never appear overbuilt or higher than the shoulders. The rear pasterns are short and, in stance, perpendicular to the ground and, when viewed from the rear, are parallel to each other. *Faults* - Sickle hocks, cow hocks, open hocks or bowed hindquarters.

Coat

Double, with hard, wiry, outer coat and close undercoat. The head, neck, ears, chest, tail and body coat must be plucked. When in show condition the body coat should be of sufficient length to determine texture. Close covering on neck, ears and skull. Furnishings are fairly thick but not silky. *Faults* - Coat too soft or too smooth and slick in appearance.

Color

The recognized colors are salt and pepper, black and silver and solid black. All colors have uniform skin pigmentation, i.e., no white or pink skin patches shall appear anywhere on the dog.

Salt and Pepper

The typical salt and pepper color of the topcoat results from the combination of black and white banded hairs and solid black and white unbanded hairs, with the banded hairs predominating. Acceptable are all shades of salt and pepper, from light to dark mixtures with tan shadings permissible in the banded or unbanded hair of the topcoat. In salt and pepper dogs, the salt and pepper mixture fades out to light gray or silver white in the eyebrows, whiskers, cheeks, under throat, inside ears, across chest, under tail, leg furnishings, and inside hind legs. It may or may not fade out on the underbody. However, if so, the lighter underbody hair is not to rise higher on the sides of the body than the front elbows.

Black and Silver

The black and silver generally follows the same pattern as the salt and pepper. The entire salt and pepper section must be black. The black color in the topcoat of the black and silver is a true rich color with black undercoat. The stripped portion is free from any fading or brown tinge and the underbody should be dark.

Black

Black is the only solid color allowed. Ideally the black color in the topcoat is a true rich glossy solid color with the undercoat being less intense, a soft matting shade of black. This is natural and should not be penalized in any way. The stripped portion is free from any fading or brown tinge. The scissored and clippered areas have lighter shades of black. A small white spot on the chest is permitted, as is an occasional single white hair elsewhere on the body.

Disqualifications - Color solid white or white striping, patching, or spotting on the colored areas of the dog, except for the small white spot permitted on the chest of the black.

The body coat color in salt and pepper and black and silver dogs fades out to light gray or silver white under the throat and across the chest. Between them there exists a natural body coat color. Any irregular or connecting blaze or white mark in this section is considered a white patch on the body, which is also a disqualification.

Gait

The trot is the gait at which movement is judged. When approaching, the forelegs, with elbows close to the body, move straight forward, neither too close nor too far apart. Going away, the hind legs are straight and travel in the same planes as the forelegs.

Note: It is generally accepted that when a full trot is achieved, the rear legs continue to move in the same planes as the forelegs, but a very slight inward inclination will occur. It begins at the point of the shoulder in front and at the hip joint in the rear. Viewed from the front or the rear, the legs are straight from these points to the pads. The degree of inward inclination is almost imperceptible in a Miniature Schnauzer that has correct movement. It does not justify moving close, toeing in, crossing, or moving out at the elbows.

Viewed from the side, the forelegs have good reach, while the hind legs have strong drive, with good pickup of hocks. The feet turn neither inward nor outward. *Faults* - Single tracking, sidegaiting, paddling in front, or hackney action. Weak rear action.

Temperament

The typical Miniature Schnauzer is alert and spirited, yet obedient to command. He is friendly, intelligent and willing to please. He should never be overaggressive or timid.

Breed Standards were developed for breeders and judges as a guideline or blueprint for evaluation. Accurate assessment of your own dog or those of others requires a clear understanding of the fine points illustrated by the written words. This requires experience and does not come easily unless you are one of those rare individuals possessing a gift frequently called "an eye for a dog" — the ability to appraise the qualities of a specimen at a glance. Most of us were born without that power and must learn through constant study as well as considerable familiarity with dogs of good type.

Applying the Standard

The balance of this chapter is a point-by-point analysis of the word picture of Miniature Schnauzer perfection as outlined by the Standard. Careful study will give the reader an excellent basis for understanding the qualities that give the breed its unique "type."

The Miniature Schnauzer is a dog of normal conformation, and in basic points is similar to many other breeds. To the novice, Miniatures look much alike except for decided variations in color. Gradually, with study and experience, the differences in type become clearer and the finer points more obvious.

Since Miniature Schnauzers in the show ring are highly styled, requiring skillful grooming and presentation, those who attempt to assess their real quality must look beyond outward characteristics applied by exhibitors. Individual trimming styles can greatly affect the total picture. Our able professional handlers best exemplify this influence as they consistently have Schnauzers in the ring month after month. These handlers normally will be showing dogs of widely diverse bloodlines. The type may vary, but the handler's "stamp" will be evident, and it will cover much of the variation in type which might otherwise be obvious. The dog has not changed, only the surface qualities have been manipulated according to the individual preferences of the exhibitor. I am quite sure that were the same Schnauzer presented by one handler on one coat and by another on the next, the average breeder would not even recognize the specimen as the same individual. Has the dog changed? A different "stamp" has been placed on the outward characteristics. The dog, essentially, is the same. This is one of the reasons why "ringside judging" has its shortcomings. Any comment concerning a particular specimen should be reserved until he has been examined more closely and completely.

If we are to understand and identify correct type regardless of the stamp given the Schnauzer by his handler, we must look beyond the finishing touches which may be so skillfully applied.

Type cannot be limited to any single part of the Schnauzer, as variables are possible in all areas of his anatomy. Often a judge is faced with as many types as there are dogs in the ring. His job is to select that individual that possesses the characteristics closest to those defined by the Standard.

General Appearance

The first statement in the Official Standard of the Miniature Schnauzer attempts to give a general picture of the breed. The key phrases, "of terrier type" and "resembling his larger cousin, the Standard Schnauzer," ask the reader to have already formed impressions about these other breeds. "Without any suggestion of toyishness" also presumes previous knowledge. It is, of course, only a brief preamble to the more precise definitions that follow.

Essentially the Standard suggests a small, stylish dog of nearly square proportions with good bone and substance. Nearly square is defined by comparing the height at the withers with the length of body, the distance from the chest to the buttocks. In no way should the breed be toyish or delicate or have fine bone. A slightly made, racy look and, at the other end of the scale, a heavy, overbuilt look are considered serious faults.

No mention is made of sex characteristics, although it is accepted in most breeds that the bitch is more refined throughout. Given a male and female of equal size, make and shape, the bitch must be just as feminine as the dog (male) is masculine. A *doggy* bitch is generally coarse in head and thick in neck. A *bitchy* dog lacks strength of head for his size and substance, and may also have a less aggressive attitude. Most Standards suggest that bitches may be a little longer in loin than dogs, the neck may be lighter and more elegant, and the rump more shapely.

Size

"Size - from 12 to 14 inches. . . . dogs or bitches under 12 inches or over 14 inches to be disqualified." What could be more specific! The Standard makes a strong and solid statement in its effort to maintain this medium-sized breed.

With such a definitive statement, one might expect that breeders, exhibitors and judges would find adhering to the limits a matter of fact. Not so! If you were to ask contemporary breeders what is the most serious problem within the breed, they would unanimously say size.

In the summer of 1985, one of our more astute judges, Robert Moore, an all-arounder whose initial breed was Miniature Schnauzers, made the following plea, published in *Schnauzer Shorts:*

The time has come for the breeders and handlers to do something about the dogs that are being shown today that are entirely too tall for the Standard. At a show some time back, three of the four dogs in the open class were measured out and disqualified by me. One of these dogs had to have been at least 15 1/2 inches and had nearly finished his championship. These dogs were shown by

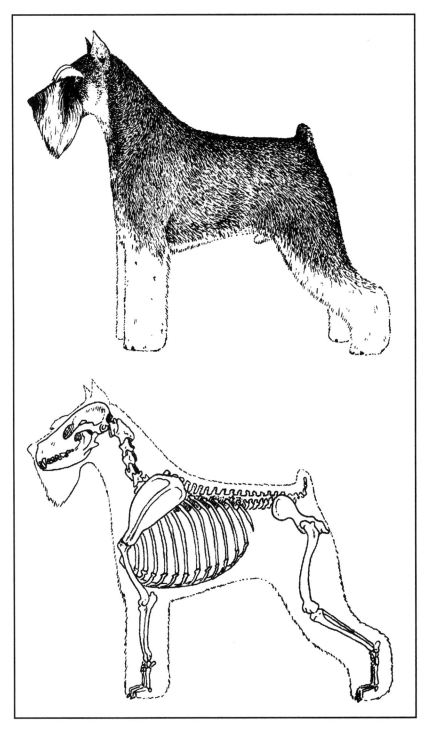

handlers who are Miniature Schnauzer breeders. Three of the four handlers thanked me for measuring the dogs out, and when asked why they showed dogs that were so large, it was explained that everyone else was showing big dogs, too.

Now is the time for breeders and handlers to get together and develop some ethics for the welfare of the breed. A breeder or a handler should not take a dog into the ring that has a disqualifying fault. Although, to my knowledge, your parent club does not promote a "Code of Ethics," this size thing is getting to be a "Moral" issue.

Over the years, many people have said that size disqualifications should be abolished. If this is done, it will not be many years until one cannot tell the difference in Miniature and Standard Schnauzers. A couple of years ago, while judging in another country, a dog was shown to me that was as big as, and coarser than Standard Schnauzers in our country. This dog was sent over by one of our leading breeders. Fortunately, he was not producing his size there, but what will this do to future generations?

Please, you breeders and handlers of the Miniature Schnauzer, do give some thought to what is happening to the breed. Get together and agree to show only dogs within the breed Standard—and prove that you care about the breed, other than today's wins, while there is still time.

It serves little purpose to ask how we got this way. The question is how can corrective actions be taken. It starts with the breeder, of course, but judges need to be better informed, and more measurements need to be taken in the show ring. Above all, exhibitors must take a firm stand on the question of size, vowing to show only those that *measure up* to Standard requirements.

External Head Characteristics

The most distinguishing characteristic of the Miniature Schnauzer is his head. The neatly cropped ears set him apart from the other members of the Terrier Group. His wedge-shaped head is accentuated by full whiskers which impart an overall rectangular look. External qualities such as ear shape, whiskers and eyebrows are manipulated by the human element, and often in such a clever way that one must all but ignore them if he is to gain a clear understanding of head type.

Fortunately, the rather "houndy" ears presently being bred can be cropped in such a way that what otherwise might be a fault can be turned into a virtue. This may not always be true, however, as many otherwise excellent specimens never see the show ring because of unsuccessful ear cropping, and those with mediocre ear crops suffer in competition.

An ear with too much bell (outer edge) left on can make the skull appear to be broader; not enough bell may accentuate cheeks that are too full and/or a skull that is too rounded. An ear that is too long gives a coarser look to an otherwise good head; too small an ear, ironically, can produce the same effect. Be sure this man-made condition is not overly influencing your evaluation of head type.

After several decades in which only cropped specimens earned titles in America, the 1980s and 90s have seen a few Miniature Schnauzers with uncropped ears become Champions of Record. In each case these individuals possessed excellent head properties, with ears that were not only small enough but well placed, well cared for in their early development, and most importantly, used well in the show ring.

Whether cropped or natural, it is the placement and carriage of the ears that must be considered as most important. Low-set and/or lazy ears detract from the look of alertness that is desired. I have seen many Schnauzers faulted, even left out of the ribbons, because of the "deadpan" expression produced by poor use of the ears.

The more obvious external head characteristics involve whiskers and eyebrows. These are placed and trimmed in a variety of ways, the object being to accentuate good qualities and give less emphasis to faults. If the longer and lighter hairs of the eyebrows are set too far back from the eyes, it can cause the skull to look shorter and broader. Eyebrows left too long, perhaps in an effort to cover a light or prominent eye, may also cause the foreface to look shorter.

The whiskers essentially play the same role and can also be manipulated and trimmed in a variety of ways. Some exhibitors simply let them grow and grow to a point where the extra length distorts whatever balance the head may have had. The object, of course, is to achieve a balanced, rectangular look that will enhance expression.

Head

The external head characteristics have little to do with head type, which is actually based on the size, shape and position of the bones and muscles of the skull and muzzle. Head balance is based on the proportions of skull length and width compared with muzzle length, width and depth. The inside corner of the eye is considered when measuring length of skull and length of muzzle (foreface). The Standard requires the foreface to be "at least as long as the top skull." A slightly longer foreface seems permissible, but a shorter foreface must be considered as less desirable.

The most common type deviations currently found on Schnauzer heads are rounded or bumpy top skulls and weak muzzles. When viewed from the side, the top of the ideal head should appear to be like two flat planes, the skull only slightly higher than the muzzle, separated by a slight stop. The most obvious deviation is a rounded top skull and prominent stop. Less obvious is a weak muzzle, lacking eye fill, as this fault can be somewhat concealed by thick whiskers. A muzzle that is dished below the eyes is a weak formation, and not worthy of a terrier.

There seems to be a tendency toward breeding narrower and longer heads, of the type found on several terrier breeds, and lacking the wedge shape described in the Standard. There are some breeders who feel that in the case of the foreface, longer is better. The nature and character of the breed would indicate otherwise, if it is to remain unique among the dogs in the Terrier Group.

The Standard is similar to many others in regard to teeth and eyes. The Miniature Schnauzer's teeth are large for the size of the dog. At the front of each jaw should be six small incisors with a canine tooth (fang) at either side. The incisors of the upper jaw should slightly overlap those of the lower jaw for a tight "scissors" bite. When the upper incisors meet the lower ones end to end, this is called a "level" bite, and should be faulted. If the upper jaw is longer, causing an "overshot" mouth, or if the lower jaw is longer, causing an "undershot" mouth, these are considered serious faults. A "wry" mouth is one in which the upper and lower jaws fail to meet in parallel alignment; it is usually the lower jaw that is affected.

Many judges will dismiss entirely any terrier that has a faulty mouth, feeling that it renders the dog unfit for the work for which it was bred. Even though no mention is made regarding the need for a full complement of forty-two teeth, many judges will penalize a dog with fewer than six incisors. Missing molar or premolar teeth are usually ignored.

The eyes are well described in the Standard, and the subject needs little clarification. They are set at the level of the stop and should be widely spaced. Eyes that are too closely set generally appear in a skull that is also too narrow. Occasionally the eyes will be too small, or "beady," and detract from the desired expression. Light and/or prominent eyes are far more common and are considered major faults.

The nose goes unmentioned, but should be black and not too small. Breeders are occasionally worried by the appearance of a partially pink nose on a puppy. Ordinarily the nose turns black by the time the puppy begins to teethe. Occasionally a mature dog will incur a seasonal change in nose color. Frequently, in winter, the nose fades slightly and has a washed-out appearance. This is a minor point and should not be penalized.

The last point is expression, and this is a combination of several factors: size, shape, color and placement of eyes; size and carriage of the ears, together with the general shape of the head. The expression of the Schnauzer is less hard-bitten than that of its many terrier cousins. It is more a sharply alert, quizzical look.

Neck

The neck consists of seven large cervical vertebrae; the first two immediately behind the head differ in shape from the others. It is the manner in which they are joined that governs the arch. The neck should be well arched and approximately equal in length to the head. An arched neck gives a flexibility to the head, allowing it to be carried high in a proud, elegant manner.

The skin fits tightly over well-developed but flat muscles which blend smoothly into the shoulders. When viewed from above, the neck is of about the same width throughout until it reaches the shoulders. Any suggestion of throatiness (dewlap) as seen in certain hound breeds is objectionable. The desired clean throat, free from folds of loose skin, is called "dry," with a "wet" throat being the houndy sort. The most objectionable variation is the "ewe neck," which sags instead of arches.

Body, Topline and Tail

The body consists of the spinal column and rib cage. The spinal column forms the topline and tail and is divided into six parts, beginning with the seven bones of the neck. The next eight bones form the withers, the next four comprise the back, followed by seven bones which form the loin. Just above the croup are the three fused bones of the sacrum, forming the base of the remaining bones of the docked tail.

The Standard calls for a straight topline, declining slightly from withers to tail. Any deviation is fairly obvious even to the untrained eye. There should be no upward arch (roach) and the muscles should give strong enough support so that the back does not sag (sway). This firm, correct topline should be evident both standing and on the move. Of the terriers that require docking, the tail of the Miniature Schnauzer is the shortest, but should always be of sufficient length to be clearly visible. The tail is docked to three joints and carried nearly perpendicular to the backline, at about one o'clock. The tail should be set on high enough that there is no dip in the topline at its base. A low-set tail is an obvious fault and is severely penalized by most terrier judges, as it prevents the dog from carrying it proudly and properly. The other extreme is called a "squirrel" tail, when carriage is almost over the back in a marked forward curve.

The remainder of the body proper is formed by the ribs. The shape of the rib cage varies tremendously in the different breeds. At one extreme is the round, full-bodied Bulldog—at the other the deep, slab-sided Greyhound or Whippet. Requirements for the Miniature Schnauzer lie somewhere in between. The ribs are long and elliptical in shape. They angle back from the spinal column, with the first five ribs being slightly flatter to allow free movement of the forelegs. They slope steeply to the sternum and brisket, extending at least to the elbow. In a mature dog, the depth of the chest should equal the length of the foreleg, from elbow to ground. There is a definite widening, or "spring," from the fifth rib to where the floating rib begins the formation of a rather short loin.

The section between the last rib and the pelvis is called the loin, or "coupling." Dogs in most breeds are shorter coupled than bitches. An overlong loin in either sex is a fault, although the bitch can be forgiven more length since she will need space in which to carry a litter. Although rounder in shape than most of the leggy terriers, the body of the Miniature Schnauzer should in no way be broad in chest or round (loaded) in shoulder. A rib cage that is too round also adds to such faults as out-at-the-elbows, bowed legs, and rolling or paddling movement. A rib cage that is too flat produces "pinched" fronts and equally untypical movement.

Forequarters

The forequarter assembly begins with the shoulder blades (scapula), which slope both to the rear and toward each other. They should be closely set at the withers, about one inch apart. A correctly placed shoulder is laid well back on the rib cage, with the point of the sternum slightly ahead of the front of the upper arm (humerus). The scapula and humerus are nearly equal in length, meeting at approximately a 90 degree angle.

The forelegs (radius and ulna) are wellboned, strong and straight. The elbows are set close to the body and point directly backwards. The pasterns are only slightly bent to assure springy action. Any looseness of elbow or pastern will negatively affect movement.

The feet are wellarched and compact, with the two center toes only just forward of the others. Thick black pads ensure that the feet will be able to cope with varied ground conditions. Deviations include the "hare" foot which is flat and long and the "splayed" foot in which the toes are spread out. Set on fairly straight pasterns, the feet should point forward, turning neither in nor out. Nails should be kept short to ensure a tight foot.

One of the most obvious deviations from correct type in today's Schnauzers has to do with incorrect shoulder angulation. The 90 degree angle is the most universally accepted formation for most of the working breeds, allowing as it does for good length of stride. When the angle is greater, and the shoulder blade more upright, the look is the "terrier front." The outline achieved can be quite elegant in a straight-shouldered dog, but he will always fail the test of movement. Straight shoulders produce a shorter stride, more typical of terriers.

Correct forehand movement depends on two basic factors. The bones must be of correct length and must form the correct angles to each other. Variation of lengths and angles account for the multitude of type deviations possible in the forequarter assembly. Any imbalance will directly affect movement.

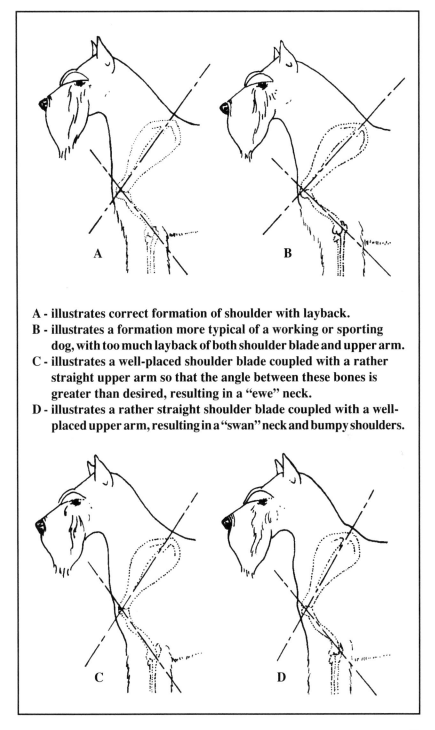

A - illustrates correct formation of shoulder with layback.

B - illustrates a formation more typical of a working or sporting dog, with too much layback of both shoulder blade and upper arm.

C - illustrates a well-placed shoulder blade coupled with a rather straight upper arm so that the angle between these bones is greater than desired, resulting in a "ewe" neck.

D - illustrates a rather straight shoulder blade coupled with a well-placed upper arm, resulting in a "swan" neck and bumpy shoulders.

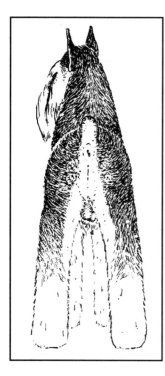

Hindquarters

The hindquarters, like the forehand, must have bone lengths and angles that complement each other. It is mainly the hindquarters that give the propulsion for movement. Historically, the well-angulated rear, which increases length of stride, was useful in the Schnauzer's work as a drover. When angulation, both front and rear, is in balance, the resulting action is very fluid and well coordinated.

Generally, the degree of hindquarter angulation, or bend of stifle, depends on how much longer the bones of the gaskin (tibia and fibula) are compared to the thigh bone (femur). When the bones are nearly equal in length, the dog will appear to be rather straight in stifle. A longer gaskin will produce proportionately more angulation.

Although the Standard makes no mention of the length of the hocks, a short hock creates better overall balance. A longer hock not only restricts rear movement but also has an adverse affect on the topline, making it high in rear.

The overlay of muscles completes the picture. Although the hindquarters are strongly muscled, they should in no way be overbuilt, as in some of the running breeds.

Viewed from behind, the hind legs are straight, in that an imaginary line drawn through the point of the buttocks, hock and foot should center all three. Weak hocks that turn in (cow-hocked) or out (open-hocked) are obvious faults. The inefficient action that either condition produces compounds the problem.

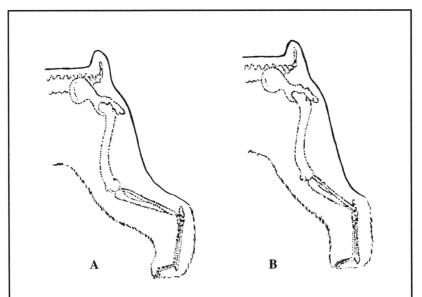

A - illustrates proper angulation, but a hock that is less than straight.
B - illustrates an assembly with a short gaskin (tibia and fibula) and the resulting lack of angulation.
C - illustrates an overangulated hindquarter assembly coupled with a less than straight hock. A dog with this assembly is commonly referred to as "sickle-hocked."
D - illustrates proper angulation, but with a steep croup, resulting in a low tail-set.

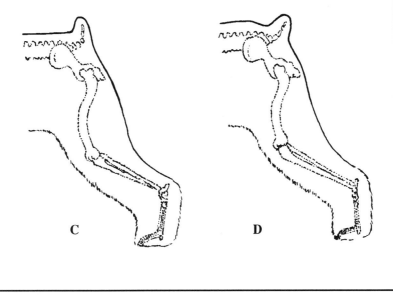

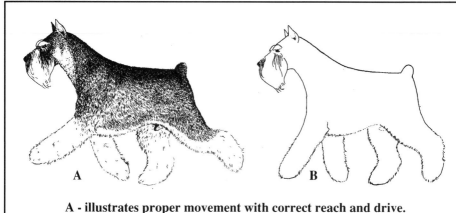

A - illustrates proper movement with correct reach and drive.
B - illustrates incorrect short stride and mincing action.

Gait

The most difficult area of the Standard to appraise accurately is movement or gait. Proper movement requires correct structure and muscle coordination. Remember that the Miniature Schnauzer is an all-purpose dog; his ancestors were drovers' dogs with the emphasis on utility of function.

All the faults of movement, such as sidegaiting, paddling or high hackney knee action cause wasted motion. It is for this reason that most Standards for "working" dogs give emphasis to gait.

The Miniature Schnauzer has a working dog gait, with forequarters and hindquarters working in such perfect harmony that the profile of the moving back appears level. The length of stride is moderate, not nearly that achieved by the German Shepherd, nor as brisk and business like as most terriers. Although not greatly extended, the gait should not be mincing, stiff or stilted. At full extension, forearm, pastern and foot should form a continuous straight line, which is maintained through the full arc of the downward swing. In traveling, the object of the foreleg is to reach as far forward as is structurally possible. Any tendency toward the high, prancing action of the Hackney Pony or the high, stiff "goose step" is totally incorrect.

Often the lift and fall of the front furnishings make it difficult to evaluate movement. Look at the feet—they should be in direct line with the points of the elbow. When a dog is out-at-the-elbow, the feet have a tendency to move towards each other (pigeon-toed). The reverse is so when the dog is "pinched" in front, the forelegs appearing to come from the same hole. The feet themselves should turn neither in nor out.

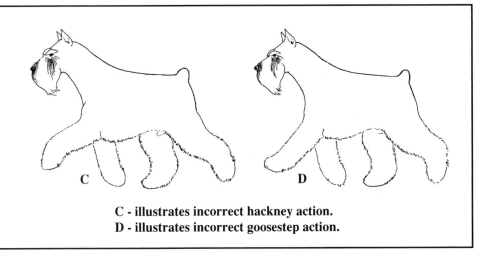

C - illustrates incorrect hackney action.
D - illustrates incorrect goosestep action.

At no time do the forelegs pull the body forward. The Miniature Schnauzer is strictly rear-drive! The hindleg swinging forward contacts the ground at approximately mid length of the body, the foot strongly pushing back and thrusting the body forward. As the leg moves beyond the line of the body, the foot is quickly lifted, creating a "snatch of hock" so desirable in achieving full extension. When viewed from the rear, the dog should be somewhat wider through the hips than he is through the shoulders, the hind legs tracking slightly outside of the front legs. The hocks are parallel when moving, and any deviation inside or outside these parallel lines is a fault.

Perhaps the best way to understand what is correct in a Miniature Schnauzer gait is to be aware of what is not. An appropriate group of illustrations is included so that this may be more easily accomplished. You must familiarize yourself with terms such as "winging", "padding", "dishing", "toeing-in" and "rope-walking" when discussing front action that is less than correct. The same is so in discussing rear movement — terms such as "cow-hocked", "open-hocked", "close", "rope-walking" and "sidewinding" will need to be understood.

Coat

The Miniature Schnauzer has a double coat, combining a hard, wiry outer coat with a dense soft undercoat. The outer coat provides weather protection; the undercoat provides warmth. Hand stripping is required to bring a dog into show condition. In the show ring the coat is required to be at least a half inch in length on the body, so that texture and color can be evaluated fairly.

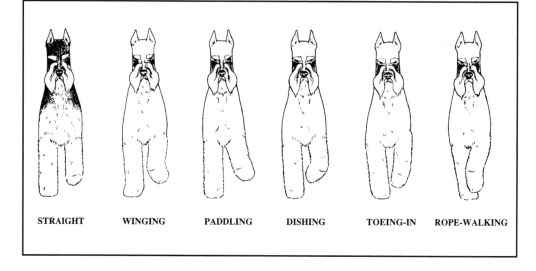

STRAIGHT   WINGING   PADDLING   DISHING   TOEING-IN   ROPE-WALKING

Some coats have a slight wave, particularly as the coat lengthens. Coats of proper texture should never curl, even when wet. An open coat, one that does not fit the body tightly, is undesirable. Although the Standard requires undercoat, the density and length must be controlled in order to keep a dog in show condition. Left unchecked, it quickly spoils body contour as well as color.

Leg hair (furnishings) should be fairly thick. Although in no way as harsh as the body coat, the furnishings may not be silky in texture. The length or fullness of beard and leg furnishings seems to be a matter of taste. The object should always be a trim, smart look, not unlike that of his terrier cousins.

Color

The acceptable colors and patterns allowed by the Standard give Miniature Schnauzers great variety. The large majority are of the distinctive and unique salt and pepper color, based on a "banded" harsh outer coat. The color is produced by each hair having three bands of light and dark shades of gray. Dark dogs will have the majority of the hair ends dark, while in the lighter colored dogs there are more lighter ends. In a true salt and pepper, each hair will be banded, not just some. Any suggestion of tan banding is permissible but should be discouraged.

Black and silvers follow the same pattern as the salt and peppers, except that the salt and pepper section must be pure black, which includes the undercoat. As with salt and peppers, the underbody hair may be lighter, or less intense, but should still be essentially black.

Black is the only solid color permitted, and must be pure in color, with no suggestion of a gray or brown tinge. Ideally, the topcoat is a rich glossy color

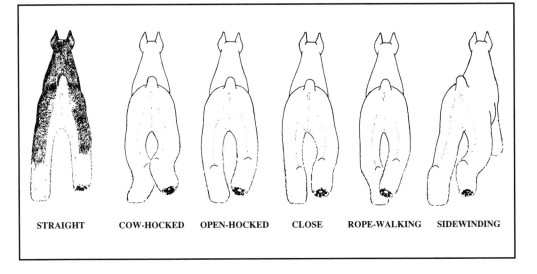

STRAIGHT   COW-HOCKED   OPEN-HOCKED   CLOSE   ROPE-WALKING   SIDEWINDING

with undercoat, furnishing and whiskers a less intense shade of black. That there will be varying shades of black is a given, and there should be no need to "alter" the color in any way. A small white breast spot is permitted.

Temperament

"Alert, spirited, obedient, friendly, intelligent," are all terms found in the paragraph on temperament, and are easily understood. They are, in fact, terms that should apply to virtually all canines that expect to be well received as human companions. Likewise, shyness or viciousness would be considered faults in any family dog.

Miniature Schnauzer temperament is less volatile than that of most of its terrier cousins. It is essentially a companion dog, with an outgoing personality that copes with all situations in a sensible and reliable way.

In the show ring, a Miniature Schnauzer is expected to display an animated, inquisitive attitude, without rowdyism or savagery, and certainly with no suggestion of meekness or shyness. Allowing for youth, inexperience or strange surroundings, a first meeting with the breed should always prove positive. In competition, they should be able to put up a good show whether facing off against another dog or just trying to please their handlers.

A final word about QUALITY and BALANCE seems appropriate here. Quality is that indefinable something that sets a dog apart from his competitors. Balance is that something that makes him appear "all-of-a-piece," both in stance and in action. Understanding all the pieces is no small feat in itself. Recognizing how and why they fit is a continuing challenge.

3
Breed Origins and Early History

$\mathbf{T}$HE MINIATURE SCHNAUZER is of German derivation, the only breed recognized in the Terrier Group without British roots. There is little data to indicate exactly how the breed originated, but it appears to be the result of considerable experimentation in Germany during the last decade of the nineteenth century.

Originally known as a Pinscher, the name Schnauzer (pronounced *Shnowtser*—the German *z* always sounds like *ts*) came from the German *Schnauze* (meaning snout), applied because of the heavy whiskers on the muzzle.

Records indicate that the Standard Schnauzer was developed first, appearing as early as 1879 in the first volume of the Pinscher-Schnauzer-Zuchtbuch (PSZ). The Pinscher-Schnauzer Klub (PSK), founded in Cologne in 1895, published the first independent Schnauzer stud book. The oldest Miniature Schnauzer registered was a black bitch, Findel, whelped in October 1888. She was of unknown parentage.

Jocco Fulda Liliput, whelped December 6, 1898, was the first Miniature Schnauzer to be registered in the PSZ. Jocco's picture appears in a book on German dogs by Emil Ilgner, published in 1902. It

Jocco Fulda Liliput

differs very little from another illustration of Fritzle, which is labeled as an Affenpinscher.

The theory regarding the origin of the Miniature Schnauzer is that the breed resulted from the crossing of Standard Schnauzers with Affenpinschers. The fact that so many of the earliest Miniatures were solid black seems to confirm the theory. Other indications point to the possibility that the black color may have been derived from the Toy Spitz, otherwise known as the Pomeranian. Ilgner's book illustrates a group of these, all blacks, owned by the Heilbronn Kennel, and Heilbronn had long been a center for black Miniature Schnauzers.

Several other breeds may have played a part in the development of the Miniature Schnauzer. It was still an experimental period at the turn of the century, with various crosses being made to improve certain characteristics. The occasional appearance of parti-colors, even today, in pure-bred litters of Miniature Schnauzers gives rise to the theory that Fox Terriers were used, even as late as the 1930s. However, the Standard for Miniature Pinschers, as late as 1924, listed parti-colors as permissible, and this may be the more likely source.

In early volumes of both German and Swiss stud books, there are several cases where puppies from the same litter are registered some as Miniature Schnauzers, some as Miniature Pinschers and even some as Affenpinschers. Individual type appears to have counted as much as did their breeding. As late

---

Prinz v. Rheinstein

as 1920, Michel Chemnitz-Plauen, registered as a Miniature Pinscher, was sired by a Miniature Schnauzer Sieger (a male German Champion) Trumpf Chemnitz-Plauen, out of a Miniature Schnauzer bitch, Resl Chemnitz-Plauen. Both parents played an important part in the breed's early development. Trumpf, whelped March 21, 1912, was a great-grandson of the most significant of the cornerstone sires, Prinz v. Rheinstein.

Whelped July 12, 1903, Prinz was bred by Herr Kissel of Frankfurt and owned by Herr Trampe of Berlin. He was described as being a very sound dog, black with yellow markings. Prinz's picture indicates a sturdier build and heavier bone than what was typical of the period.

It is to Prinz v. Rheinstein that American bloodlines owe the most, as all tail-male lines of today trace to him. Although he died at the early age of four, he left three champions, most notably Ch. Perle v.d. Goldbach, out of (ex) Nettel v.d. Goldbach, whelped December 14, 1904. Perle was bred back to her sire and produced Ch. Gift Chemnitz-Plauen, a black and tan like Prinz. All present-day male lines come through Gift, doubling the importance of his sire.

Gift, foundation sire for Herr Stocke's Chemnitz-Plauen Kennel, produced forty litters, from which came seven champion sons, one champion daughter, plus ten nonchampions who were producers. Shown under Herr Berta when six months old, Gift was described thusly in the judge's report:

An inquisitive fellow; typey, strong bone, solid if somewhat narrow front, good coat, very good in head and expression, full muzzle, luxuriant whiskers, excellent carriage and temperament.

Siegerin (female German Champion) Mirzl Chemnitz-Plauen was the only bitch among Gift's champion get. Bred to her half brother, the Gift son Ch. Fips Chemnitz-Plauen, she produced a daughter, Resl Chemnitz-Plauen, that was the granddam of Ch. Cuno v. Burgstadt, one of the most important of the early American sires.

Ch. Fips Chemnitz-Plauen, whelped June 6, 1911, was unlike his sire Gift in that he carried on through daughters rather than sons. He sired twenty-nine litters, as compared to his sire's forty. In almost all cases, the producers from Fips were strongly inbred to Gift, with several of them double granddaughters. The picture of Fips indicates that he was considerably lighter in color than his sire Gift and could be called a medium salt and pepper, probably with yellowish furnishings. His daughter Goldjungfer (Golden Girl) and son Goldjunge (Golden Boy) bore names suggesting the tawny yellow color characteristic of the breed at this point. Yellow or red was also found in many of the near descendants of Fels v.d. Goldbachhohe and Ch. Cuno v. Burgstadt, who were both unusually strong in Fips blood.

It was the Gift son Ch. Trumpf Chemnitz-Plauen who was by all odds most important. From him comes practically every male line that traces to Prinz v. Rheinstein. Trumpf's most important breedings were to the Fips daughter Motte v. Goldbachtal, from which came Linus, Heinerle and Kalle Chemnitz-Plauen, the latter a Swiss champion.

The Chemnitz-Plauen team in 1911 (from left to right): Taps Chemnitz-Plauen, Ch. Gift Chemnitz-Plauen, Ch. Fips Chemnitz-Plauen and Ch. Mirzl Chemnitz-Plauen

---

Linus was whelped in 1915, while his full brother Heinerle arrived four years later. Although not himself a champion as was Heinerle, Linus was the more successful sire of the two. It was reported that after Linus appeared on the scene, the famous Heinzelmannchen Kennel virtually scrapped their existing stock and began over again. Linus's most notable son, Bolt v. Annenhof, was whelped April 27, 1920, and sired twenty-six litters during the next nine years. Bolt's get include the double Linus grandson Fels v.d. Goldbachhohe. The Fels son Mack v.d. Goldbachhohe and daughters Ch. Lotte and Lady v.d. Goldbachhohe were cornerstones of the breed in America.

Virtually all the early American imports carried lines to Linus and Heinerle, and the most notable, Ch. Cuno v. Burgstadt, is intensely linebred through them to Gift.

Although these old-timers may seem of little consequence with the passing of time, their influence on the modern Miniature Schnauzer is immeasurable. All present day stock descends from the foregoing individuals over numerous lines. Some were so often repeated, as was Gift, that the cumulative effect cannot help but be recognizable throughout the breed's development in the United States during the past seventy years.

4
Breed Beginnings in America

DURING THE FIRST TEN YEARS of Miniature Schnauzer breeding in the United States, 108 dogs and bitches were imported from the Continent, nearly all from Germany. All the American-bred Miniature Schnauzers descend entirely from these initial imports. By 1935, the fifty-four American-bred champions finished up to that time traced to only ten of the imported dogs and eleven of the bitches.

The real beginning of the Miniature Schnauzer in America came in the summer of 1924 when Rudolph Krappatsch sent four Miniatures to Marie Slattery. They would become the foundation not only for her Marienhof Kennel but for the breed itself.

Amsel v.d. Cyriaksburg, whelped June 12, 1921, and her two puppy daughters, Lotte and Lady v.d. Goldbachhohe, whelped July 7, 1924, came across the Atlantic, along with their future mate, Mack v.d. Goldbachhohe. It is safe to say that there is no American champion today that is not descended from them thousands of times over.

Amsel was the dam of the first American-bred litter, whelped July 15, 1925, and sired by Mack. It contained Ch. Affe of Oddacre, who sired the first American-bred champion in Mrs. Slattery's Ch. Moses Taylor. Virtually all the early "firsts" would be earned by Marienhof dogs. During nearly a half century of activity, more than 100 champions would emerge, and Mrs. Slattery would earn the title of Breed Matriarch.

The Amsel daughter, Ch. Lotte v.d. Goldbachhohe, held the breed record for twenty-five years as the dam of twelve champions. Nine of these were from three litters sired by Ch. Cuno v. Burgstadt, including a record-setting litter of five that all became champions.

Two years after the untimely death of Mack in 1925, Mrs. Slattery imported the three-year-old male Cuno v. Burgstadt, who was to make breed

Ch. Amsel
v.d. Cyriaksburg
was imported in 1924
to become the breed's
matriarch in America.

Ch. Cuno
v. Burgstadt
was imported
in 1927
to become the
breed's patriarch
in America.

Litter by Flieger Heinzelmannchen out of Galloper of Marienhof, whelped March 31, 1931. First on right is Freifrau of Edgeover, and third is Fleiger of Edgeover, both future champions.

history and to have a more far-reaching effect upon the development of the breed in this country than any other imported sire. Cuno sired 14 champions, a record that only stood a few years until broken by his great-grandson Ch. T.M.G. of Marienhof.

Although he gained his American title, Cuno's record as a show dog was undistinguished. He was described as a dark salt and pepper with cream markings, short in body, with lots of beard and furnishings. The last characteristic he passed on to his get in a day when sparse whiskers and leg hair were the rule. He was an upstanding dog, but light in bone, making him appear smaller than his 12 inches at the withers. Cuno sired few litters outside of his home kennel. He was bred almost exclusively with Amsel and her daughters. Before his value was generally realized, he was killed in a dog fight with a Setter.

Shortly after Cuno's death, Leda Martin imported the breed's next significant sire, Flieger Heinzelmannchen. Mrs. Martin's specifications included small size, gray color, and a pedigree suitable for use with Cuno daughters. Herr Walther of the famed Heinzelmannchen Kennel in Germany complied with the request and Flieger arrived at Ledahof.

Leda Martin recalled Flieger as follows:

In 1930 I imported Flieger Heinzelmannchen. He died before he gained his title, but fortunately sired a few puppies. He was a lovely gray salt and pepper, and threw this color in a day when the majority of our dogs were cinnamon, black

48

and tan or black and silver, or a rather unpleasant combination of all three. He was also a very short-backed dog which at the time was not a common attribute. He threw very well-set tails in a day when most were set and carried at half-mast.

Like Mack and Cuno, Flieger's short life span allowed a limited return. He left only eight litters, from which came five champions, including four out of Galloper of Marienhof. Mrs. Martin shared in this litter, selecting and finishing Chs. Flieger and Freifrau of Edgeover. The younger Flieger was described as a small dog of good color and unusual bone, with a lovely disposition. He lived

Tom Gately with an all-champion Marienhof team consisting of *(L to R)* Porgie, Hope, Charity and Mehitabel of Marienhof III

eleven years and was a popular stud, leaving five champions plus eight nonchampions who were producers.

The breed's progress from this point forward would be based on the blending of offspring from Ch. Cuno v. Burgstadt and Flieger Heinzelmannchen. Two decades later, the breed's "super sire," CH. DOREM DISPLAY, would carry thirty-two lines to Cuno and twelve to Flieger.

Pleased with the quality Cuno was producing, and needing another stud for linebreeding, Mrs. Slattery imported the five-year-old Cuno son, Marko v. Beutenberg. He was shipped initially to Tom and Kay Gately, professional handlers at the time. The Gatelys were responsible for finishing over twenty Marienhof champions, including Marko. Tom's description of Marko gives us an impression of the breed at this time:

Marko was entirely different from anything in the breed today. He was a large dog, oversize in fact, but a true Schnauzer with small, dark, well-shaped eyes, a long head with a flat skull, strong foreface, sound running gear and a resolute disposition. Every hair was as harsh as wire, right down to the toes. His furnishings were not as profuse as those seen today—every hair was hard. His color was a dark salt and pepper, with the furnishings just slightly lighter.

Ch. Marko v. Beutenberg sired nine American champions, including three from an outstanding litter out of Mehitabel of Marienhof II. This Marienhof litter produced a number of "firsts." Ch. Mussolini of Marienhof was the first Miniature Schnauzer shown in obedience and won the Novice Class at Philadelphia in 1935. His sister, Ch. Mehitabel of Marienhof III, was the first

Ch. T.M.G. of Marienhof

uncropped Group winner and was runner-up for Best in Show in 1934. The other male, Ch. Marko of Marienhof was chosen as heir apparent and became the first American-bred to sire over ten champions. His record of 13 champions equaled the American-bred get of his grandsire, Cuno, and continued this strong tail-male line by leaving the outstanding son, Ch. T.M.G. of Marienhof.

Thomas Michael Gately's connection with T.M.G. is obvious, and his story tells so much about the times:

Some time along in the early thirties, when the depression was about at its worst, I telephoned Marie, saying that I had a customer who would pay $50 for a male puppy. I stated that I would like to make about $15, so could pay $35. She was coming to a nearby show and said she would bring a puppy along. When Marie set the puppy down in our living room, I exclaimed, "Gosh, you're not selling that pup for $35 are you?" She queried, "Don't you think he's good enough?" My response was, "Good enough I think he's just about the best Miniature Schnauzer puppy I've ever seen!" Her reply was, "All right, I'll send you another puppy, and keep this one." She kept him and named him after me.

Ch. T.M.G. of Marienhof was the leading sire of this period, producing 20 champions, a record which held until DISPLAY. Ten of T.M.G.'s eleven champion sons produced champions. His greatest influence, however, was through two breedings to Wild Honey of Sharvogue, from which fourteen puppies were produced. Eight became champions, and six left champion descendants.

The Sharvogue dogs, bred by Dr. and Mrs. Briggs, dominated the show ring between 1934 and the War years. In addition to lines from Cuno and Amsel, the Sharvogue dogs carried lines to Flieger and Freifrau, and incorporated others based on the German imports Ch. Don v. Dornbusch of Hitofa and his son Ch. Viktor v. Dornbusch.

Two of the champion males from the T.M.G. - Wild Honey breedings offer interesting comparisons. Ch. Stylobate of Sharvogue, owned by Mrs. Charles Gleason, was considered the best by many fanciers. Unfortunately, he was accidentally killed when less than three years old, shortly after going Best of Breed at Westminster in 1941. With limited use, he left five champions. The most successful mating was to Ch. Dorem Dubonnet, and included Ch. Dorem Searchlight, the dam of DISPLAY.

Ch. Sandman of Sharvogue, on the other hand, had a long career, living past fourteen years. Sandman was twice Best of Breed at Westminster and in 1946 became the first Miniature Schnauzer to place in the Group at this prestigious show. Sandman's five champions included four sons, the most successful being Ch. Tweed Packet of Wilkern (out of the DISPLAY daughter Ch. Debutante of Ledahof), the sire of 15 champions. The Sandman son Ch. Dorem Elect, out of a Dubonnet daughter, gains fame as the paternal grandsire of DISPLAY. The Sandman daughter Ch. Dorem Liberty is the dam of Ch. Enchantress, who rivals Wild Honey as the dam of eight champions. The Enchantress daughter Am. and Can. Ch. Sorceress of Ledahof, was the first to match the long-standing producing record made by Lotte.

From these beginnings emerged the basis for Dorothy Williams's dominant Dorem strain, responsible not only for the great DISPLAY but over forty homebred champions. Miss Williams purchased the bitch, Jill of Wollaton II, from the successful breeder and judge, Richard A. Kern, Jr., of the Wollaton Kennel. First bred to Ch. Jeff of Wollaton, Jill produced Dorem Diva and Dorothy's first homebred champion, Dorem Dilletante. Two years later, put to Ch. Flieger of Edgeover, Jill produced Ch. Dorem Dubonnet. Both Diva and Dubonnet were bred to Ch. Timothy of Sharvogue, strong in Flieger-Freifrau blood. Diva produced Ch. Dorem Escapade, DISPLAY's paternal granddam through her son Dorem Cockade. Dubonnet produced Elect, dam of Cockade's sire, Ch. Dorem Parade.

Intensifying the Cuno-Flieger cross, Dubonnet was then bred to Stylobate, from which came the famous "light" litter of six, including Ch. Dorem Searchlight, the dam of DISPLAY and his influential sister, Ch. Dorem Shady Lady, foundation matron for Marguerite Wolff's prolific Phil-Mar strain.

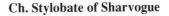

Ch. Stylobate of Sharvogue

5

The Dorem and
Phil-Mar Kennels

AMERICAN MINIATURE SCHNAUZERS are 99 percent pure
CH. DOREM DISPLAY. The breed has recorded over 5,000 American champions since the first, the imported German Siegerin, Ch. Lenchen v. Dornbusch, whelped October 17, 1920. Virtually all champions finished since the early fifties have between one and several hundred lines to DISPLAY. Few breeds can claim such a recent singular influence.

The breed's history since 1950, for all intents and purposes, can be traced exclusively through sons and daughters of DISPLAY. It is impossible to find in America an outcross to his completely dominant line.

The singular importance of DISPLAY was the result of many factors, not the least of which was the broad exposure he received at a time, after World War II, in which interest in purebred dogs was rapidly increasing. He embodied in type a more streamlined outline comparable to some of his competitors in the Terrier Group. It served him well and brought him more universal acceptance among both breeders and judges than any Miniature Schnauzer before or since.

Dorothy Williams tells it best:

As breeder of DISPLAY I would like to mention some things not generally known. Marie Mehrer of the famous Marienlust Dachshunds whelped the litter and at birth recognized an outstanding puppy. As soon as he could walk, DISPLAY showed tremendous style and always took a perfect stance. He was a balanced little show dog at all stages of puppyhood. In fact, one hardly realized that he was growing. To this day the same is true of all our best dogs. Furthermore they do not coarsen.

CH. DOREM DISPLAY winning the Terrier Group under John Marvin, handled by George Ward.

At three months DISPLAY was Best in Match at the Garden City show on Long Island, New York under Nate Levine, the well known working dog handler. Nate wanted to buy DISPLAY in spite of his feeling that he was too perfect a dog for his age.

DISPLAY was again Best in Match at a large Queensboro show under the top terrier handler, Henry Sayres. His first appearance at a point show was at Westminster 1945 at ten months of age. Harry Lumb, the great terrier judge, put him Best of Winners and then excused all the specials, except one. That one, DISPLAY's grandsire, Ch. Sandman of Sharvogue, was given the breed and went on to be the first Miniature Schnauzer to place in the Group at Westminster. DISPLAY created quite a stir and it was amazing how the news flew. When I came out of the ring the ringside was lined with terrier judges, many of whom had hardly noticed our breed before.

CH. DOREM
DISPLAY

April 5, 1945 ——————— February 28, 1959

Ch. Marko of Marienhof
Ch. T.M.G. of Marienhof
Tyranena Pansy of Marienhof
Ch. Sandman of Sharvogue
Ch. Bleuboy of Sharvogue
Wild Honey of Sharvogue
Woots of Sharvogue
Ch. Dorem Parade
Falcon of Sharvogue
Ch. Timothy of Sharvogue
Ch. Freifrau of Edgeover
Dorem Elect
Ch. Flieger of Edgeover
Ch. Dorem Dubonnet
Jill of Wollaton II
SIRE: Dorem Cockade
Ch. Flieger of Edgeover
Falcon of Sharvogue
Cairnsmuir Wistful
Ch. Timothy of Sharvogue
Flieger Heinzelmannchen
Ch. Freifrau of Edgeover
Galloper of Marienhof
Ch. Dorem Escapade
Ch. Cuno of Wollaton
Ch. Jeff of Wollaton
Ch. Jean of Wollaton
Dorem Diva
Ch. Virgo of Tassac Hill
Jill of Wollaton II
Jessie of Wollaton

Ch. Marko von Beutenberg
Ch. Mehitabel of Marienhof
Ch. Porgie of Marienhof
Abigail of Marienhof
Falcon of Sharvogue
Ch. Allsworth Gossip
Falcon of Sharvogue
Ch. Freifrau of Edgeover
Cairnsmuir Wistful
Ch. Flieger of Edgeover
Fleiger Heinzelmannchen
Galloper of Marienhof
Flieger Heinzelmannchen
Galloper of Marienhof
Ch. Virgo of Tassac Hill
Jessie of Wollaton
Flieger Heinzelmannchen
Galloper of Marienhof
Ch. Medor Strupp
Mira von Burgstadt
Falk Heinzelmannchen
Sgn. Freifrau Heinzelmannchen
Ch. Viktor von Dornbursh
Grey Girl of Marienhof
Ch. Cuno von Burgstadt
Ch. Lotte v.d. Goldbachhohe
Ch. Bodo von Schillerberg
Ch. Jemima of Wollaton
Ch. Don v. Dornbusch of Hitofa
Ch. Halowell Vega
Ch. Marko von Beutenberg
Judy of Wollaton

CH. DOREM DISPLAY

Ch. Marko von Beutenberg
Ch. Marko of Marienhof
Ch. Mehitabel of Marienhof II
Ch. T.M.G. of Marienhof
Ch. Porgie of Marienhof
Tyranena Pansy of Marienhof
Abigail of Marienhof
Ch. Stylobate of Sharvogue
Falcon of Sharvogue
Ch. Bleuboy of Sharvogue
Ch. Allsworth Gossip
Wild Honey of Sharvogue
Falcon of Sharvogue
Woots of Sharvogue
Ch. Freifrau of Edgeover
DAM: Ch. Dorem Searchlight
Falk Heinzelmannchen
Flieger Heinzelmannchen
Sgn. Freifrau Heinzelmannchen
Ch. Flieger of Edgeover
Ch. Viktor von Dornbusch
Galloper of Marienhof
Grey Girl of Marienhof
Ch. Dorem Dubonnet
Ch. Don v. Dornbusch of Hitofa
Ch. Virgo of Tassac Hill
Ch. Halowell Vega
Jill of Wollaton II
Ch. Marko von Beutenberg
Jessie of Wollaton
Judy of Wollaton

Ch. Cuno von Burgstadt
Lotte von Beutenberg
Ch. Bodo von Schillerberg
Ch. Mehitabel of Marienhof
Ch. Bodo von Schillerberg
Fritzie of Marienhof
Ch. Marko von Beutenberg
Fiffi of Marlou
Ch. Flieger of Edgeover
Cairnsmuir Wistful
Jorg von Dornbusch
Ch. Gretel of Marienhof
Ch. Flieger of Edgeover
Cairnsmuir Wistful
Flieger Heinzelmannchen
Galloper of Marienhof
Ass Heinzelmannchen
Grille Heinzelmannchen
Ass Heinzelmannchen
Elektra Heinzelmannchen
Ch. Don v. Dornbusch of Hitofa
Berwel von Dornbusch
Ch. Affe of Oddacre
Lady v.d. Goldbachhohe
Sr. Friedel von Affentor
Ch. Lennchen von Dornbusch
Ch. Viktor von Dornbusch
Sgn. Gaudi Baltischhort
Ch. Cuno von Burgstadt
Lotte von Beutenberg
Arno of Wollaton
Ch. Jemima of Wollaton

I got telephone calls and telegrams from all over the country and of course many offers to buy. Since I was working and living in New York City, I decided to sell to someone who could campaign DISPLAY properly. Mrs. Phil Meldon was chosen because she allowed me free stud services to DISPLAY for life, and agreed to let me keep him until Ch. Dorem Silverette could be mated.

The resulting litter produced Tribute. Ch. Dorem High Test had already been born from an accidental mating. Having such confidence in the Sharvogue line, I had purchased Ch. Imprudent of Sharvogue, a litter sister to Sandman, at the age of three months. She jumped into DISPLAY's pen and taught him the facts of life when the dog was only seven months. This accidental but successful mating must have been the basis for the mistaken rumor that DISPLAY himself was the result of an accidental breeding.

Mrs. Meldon took her new dog to his first show at Pocono, Pennsylvania. His trim had grown out but Edwin Sayres, Sr. spotted him in the exercise ring and asked to trim and show him. DISPLAY went through to his first of five Bests in Show. He also topped four Specialties.

But DISPLAY's greatest win was his first in the Group at Westminster in 1947 over 800 terriers. George Ward took him in only one hour after he had been engaged as handler. But this was a great showman and asked for it every minute. When gaited individually, DISPLAY went up and down the length of that Garden barking at the gallery. The next year this big little dog went second to the Best in Show-winning Bedlington, Ch. Rock Ridge Night Rocket.

Mrs. Meldon was responsible for DISPLAY's show career with the able help of Pop Sayres. Later she sold him to Shirley Angus of the Benrook Kennels. Jigger, as he was known and loved, was no longer young and spent the rest of his life under the loving care of Mrs. Angus.

DISPLAY, whelped April 5, 1945, came to the end of a full life in 1959 shortly before his fourteenth birthday. He was one of those rare individuals who are preeminent as both show winners and producers. He was not only the breed's first Best in Show winner, but his record went unchallenged for over two decades. His Westminster record is unparalleled.

As an individual, DISPLAY was about thirteen inches tall, with a short back, excellent head and neck and first-class temperament. He was a clear salt and pepper with an unusually dark undercoat, which appeared often in his get.

DISPLAY was only ten months old when his first champion son Dorem High Test was whelped. Ch. Dorem Tribute followed in July and the litter brothers Chs. Delegate and Diplomat of Ledahof in October of 1946. This at once established him as a successful sire while he was still making his big wins in the show ring.

In the early 1950s, the great impact that DISPLAY would have on the breed was just beginning to be recognized. At the same time, the force of this same gene-pool was emerging through the descendants of his full sister, Ch. Dorem Shady Lady, CD, the grand matriarch of the prolific Phil-Mar family.

Four generations of Phil-Mar champions. From left to right: Ch. Dorem Shady Lady, CD, and her daughter, Ch. Phil-Mar Gay Lady, and her son, Ch. Phil-Mar Gay Knight, and his son, Ch. Phil-Mar Bright Knight.

Shady arrived at Phil-Mar on March 14, 1949, already a champion, and at the time in whelp to Dorem Dominant. She was to be the only foundation for a breeding program that extended over three decades. There would be thirty-seven champions bearing Marguerite Anspach Wolff's illustrious Phil-Mar prefix, and all would descend from Shady.

Although a relative novice in dogs when Shady arrived, Mrs. Wolff remembers her as being very different from her famous brother.

Shady did not look like her brother—she was a short, compact and powerful bitch, excelling in rear movement. Her front was not the most desirable, but with her huge and deep chest, it was understandable that her forehand was not tightly constructed. Her major fault was that she had large, round eyes, although dark enough in color. Besides being beautiful, lovable and a wonderful mother, she was also brilliant. I took her through her CD degree after just six weeks of training—and at five years of age.

Shady's first litter at Phil-Mar contained Ch. Phil-Mar Watta Lady, plus two others that earned obedience degrees. Watta Lady was the first of a long

Ch. Phil-Mar Watta Lady

Ch. Phil-Mar Lucy Lady

Ch. Phil-Mar Lady Be Good

succession of champions that would be breeder-owner conditioned and handled to their titles.

Bred next to her uncle, Ch. Dorem Tribute, Shady again produced a litter of seven. One of them, Ch. Phil-Mar Gay Lady, became an easy champion.

Shady's final breeding was to the DISPLAY grandson, Ch. Dorem Tempo, from which came her third champion, Ch. Phil-Mar Lucky Lady. Tempo, a son of Ch. Delegate of Ledahof, would prove to be the key sire in the Phil-Mar plans for the future. Mrs. Wolfe's admiration for Tempo is made clear by the following:

I bred Watta Lady to Tempo, who for my money is one of the greatest sires of all-time. He was owned by Muriel and Jack Ainley of Connecticut. He was a terrific coated dog. Jack showed him continuously for three years, always in perfect show coat. According to Muriel, Tempo was used at stud only nine times. He produced a champion in each litter that he sired for me, including my three Best-in-Show dogs.

From the Tempo's breeding to Watta Lady came the great show bitch, Ch. Phil-Mar Lucy Lady. She was the breed's top winner in 1954, and with her second Best in Show win became one of only five bitches with multiple Bests. Lucy was also one of the few bitches to win Best of Breed at Westminster. As the dam of the outstanding show dog and top producing sire Ch. Phil-Mar Lugar (26 Chs.), her achievements and impact are rare indeed.

Each of Shady's three champion daughters became top producers in their own right. Numerically, Shady's best producing daughter was Lucky Lady with five champions, including Ch. Phil-Mar Lady Love (by Tribute), also the dam of five champions. Watta Lady produced three champions, including Lucy, who in turn

Ch. Phil-Mar Lugar

had three champion get, including Lugar. Gay Lady also produced three champions, including two top producers: Ch. Phil-Mar Gay Knight (by Tempo), sire of nine champions, and Ch. Phil-Mar Lady Be Good, dam of Ch. Perci-Bee's First Impression, sire of 15 champion get, including Lugar, who was unquestionably one of Peggy's favorites:

My most beloved Ch. Phil-Mar Lugar, twice Best in Show, is a most remarkable dog — almost perfect, he was so well balanced. Lugar was one of the best moving dogs that I bred. He had gorgeous layback of shoulder, a level topline and beautiful length of neck with an arch. Lugar showed like he owned the world — head held high, with movement like he was floating on a cloud.

In summing up nearly forty years of successful breeding, Peggy wrote:

I was fortunate to start with a high-class bitch that was a sound mover, with good topline, coat, and above all, showmanship. All of Shady's fine qualities are fused in varying degrees in all the Phil-Mar Miniature Schnauzers.

The quality that was inherent in the Dorem and Phil-Mar strains will be treated more completely as we examine the tail-male branches from DISPLAY. It is the combination of lines from DISPLAY and Shady in which the entire Delegate branch is based.

6
The Tail-Male
Branches from
CH. DOREM DISPLAY

HAVING ESTABLISHED the tight linebreeding that produced DISPLAY, let us now examine the background of his nine top producing sons, as each represents a "branch" from this single great oak.

Before considering them as individuals, an analysis of their pedigrees is essential, since each is the result of varying degrees of linebreeding on the original Cuno-Flieger cross.

Tribute, Delegate and Diplomat—this trio of sires are very nearly identical in background, being out of Spotlight daughters, and sharing the Sharvogue dogs with equal intensity.

The pedigree on Ch. Dorem Tribute shows the result of closer than half brother to half sister breeding, Spotlight and Searchlight being littermates. Ch. Dorem Silverette produced five champions by five different sires and had a profound effect on the breed, as the dam not only of Tribute but also of Ch. Dorem Tempo, who so greatly influenced the Phil-Mar family. Tribute carries five lines to Dorem's foundation bitch Jill of Wollaton II, and the same is so with the brothers, Delegate and Diplomat. Out of Ch. Enchantress, they are from Ledahof's most outstanding litter, alos including Chs. Destiny and Debutante of Ledahof. In all, Enchantress produced eight champions, including the foundation matron for the Marwyck family, Am. and Can. Ch. Sorceress of Ledahof, who gave Marian Evashwick a record-setting 13 champions, including one Canadian champion.

**Ch. Enchantress
and her daughter, Ch. Sorceress of Ledahof**

```
                Ch. Dorem Parade          Ch. Sandman of Sharvogue
        Dorem Cockade                     Dorem Elect
                Ch. Dorem Escapade        Ch. Timothy of Sharvogue
                                          Ch. Dorem Diva
```

CH. DOREM DISPLAY

```
                Ch. Stylobate of Sharvogue    Ch. T.M.G. of Marienhof
        Ch. Dorem Searchlight                 Wild Honey of Sharvogue
                Ch. Dorem Dubonnet            Ch. Flieger of Edgeover
                                              Jill of Wollaton II
```

❊ By matching the **DISPLAY** pedigree above with each of those below and on the next page, a four-generation pedigree emerges for each of his nine top producing sons.

CH. DOREM TRIBUTE

```
                Ch. Stylobate of Sharvogue    Ch. T.M.G. of Marienhof
        Dorem Spotlight                       Wild Honey of Sharvogue
                Ch. Dorem Dubonnet            Ch. Flieger of Edgeover
                                              Jill of Wollaton II
ex CH. DOREM SILVERETTE
                Ch. Timothy of Sharvogue      Falcon of Sharvogue
        Ch. Dorem Escapade                    Ch. Freifrau of Edgeover
                Ch. Dorem Diva                Ch. Jeff of Wollaton
                                              Jill of Wollaton II
```

CH. DELEGATE OF LEDAHOF and CH. DIPLOMAT OF LEDAHOF

```
                Ch. Stylobate of Sharvogue    Ch. T.M.G. of Marienhof
        Dorem Spotlight                       Wild Honey of Sharvogue
                Ch. Dorem Dubonnet            Ch. Flieger of Edgeover
                                              Jill of Wollaton II
ex CH. ENCHANTRESS
                Ch. Sandman of Sharvogue      Ch. T.M.G. of Marienhof
        Ch. Dorem Liberty                     Wild Honey of Sharvogue
                Ch. Dorem Escapade            Ch. Timothy of Sharvogue
                                              Ch. Dorem Diva
```

CH. MELDON'S RUFFIAN

```
        CH. DOREM DISPLAY                 Dorem Cockade
        Ch. Dorem Tribute                 Ch. Dorem Searchlight
                Ch. Dorem Silverette      Dorem Spotlight
                                          Ch. Dorem Escapade
ex MELDON'S MEMORIES
                Ch. Dorem High Test       CH. DOREM DISPLAY
        Meldon's Mar Mose                 Ch. Imprudent of Sharvogue
                Ch. Dorem Highlight       Ch. Stylobate of Sharvogue
                                          Ch. Dorem Dubonnet
```

☀ Virtually all of today's winners and producers trace to one or more of the above four DISPLAY sons.

CH. DOREM HIGH TEST

Ch. Marko of Marienhof	Ch. Marko von Beutenberg
Ch. T.M.G. of Mairenhof	Mehitabel of Marienhof II
Tyranena Pansy of Marienhof	Ch. Porgie of Marienhof
	Abigail of Marienhof

ex CH. IMPRUDENT OF SHARVOGUE

Ch. Bleuboy of Sharvogue	Falcon of Sharvogue
Wild Honey of Sharvogue	Ch. Allsworth Gossip
Woots of Sharvogue	Falcon of Sharvogue
	Ch. Freifrau of Edgeover

CH. MELDON'S MERIT

Ch. Norcrest Enuff	Ch. Rufus of Mairenhof
Loki of Appletrees	Desire of Marienhof
Ch. Dorem Liberty	Ch. Flieger of Edgeover
	Jill of Wollaton II

ex EXOTIC OF LEDAHOF

Dorem Spotlight	Ch. Sandman of Sharvogue
Ch. Enchantress	Ch. Dorem Dubonnet
Ch. Dorem Liberty	Ch. Sandman of Sharvogue
	Ch. Dorem Escapade

CH. BENROOK BEAU BRUMMELL

Ch. Kubla Khan of Marienhof	Ch. T.M.G. of Marienhof
Ch. Kismet of Marienhof	Ch. Kathleen of Marienhof
Ch. Neff's Mehr Licht	Eric von Neff
	Mix of Marienhof

ex CH. KAREN OF MARIENHOF II

Ch. Opal Heinzelmannchen	Balzar v.d. Zwick
McLuckie's Opal's Gal	Carmen Heinzelmannchen
Ch. Lucky of Marienhof	Ch. T.M.G. of Marienhof
	Amarantha of Ravenroyd

CH. GENGLER'S DRUM MAJOR

CH. DOREM DISPLAY	Dorem Cockade
Ch. Diplomat of Ledahof	Ch. Dorem Searchlight
Ch. Enchantress	Dorem Spotlight
	Ch. Dorem Liberty

ex SALTY IMP

Ledahof's Sentry	Falcon of Palawan
Countess Reta of Ledahof	Neff's Risque
Ch. Exclusive of Ledahof	Loki of Appletrees
	Ch. Enchantress

CH. BENROOK ZORRA

Ch. Meldon's Mignon	Ch. Dorem High Test
Ch. Benrook Basil	Ch. Dorem Highlight
Ch. Karen of Marienhof II	Ch. Kismet of Marienhof
	McLuckie's Opal's Gal

ex BENROOK BREEZIE

CH. DOREM DISPLAY	Dorem Cockade
Benrook Beegee	Ch. Dorem Searchlight
Ch. Meldon's Manana	Ch. Dorem Tribute
	Meldon's Mar-Mose

Ch. Karen of Marienhof II

The background on High Test is strictly within the same family, as his dam, Ch. Imprudent of Sharvogue, is a full sister to Stylobate and Sandman, who figure so prominently in the pedigrees of Tribute, Delegate and Diplomat.

The breeding on Ch. Meldon's Merit shows some variation from the Cuno-Flieger cross, as it introduces the import Sieger and Ch. Qualm Heinzelmannchen, the sire of Ch. Rufus of Marienhof. However, this is hardly an outcross, since Merit's dam is a double granddaughter of Ch. Dorem Liberty, making his breeding much the same as that of the Ledahof brothers.

The dam of Am. and Can. Ch. Benrook Beau Brummell, the good producer Ch. Karen of Marienhof II, brings in an additional Heinzelmannchen import through Opal, but as a double grandson of T.M.G., Karen is not an outcross either. Karen was a remarkable producer, serving as foundation for Shirley Angus's successful Benrook Kennels. Each of Karen's four champion offspring were producers of note. Her son, Ch. Benrook Buckaroo (by Tribute) is the sire of 17 champions, from which five more generations of top producing sires descend. Karen's son Ch. Benrook Basil produced Ch. Benrook Banning (9 Chs.). Karen's daughter Ch. Benrook Ben-Gay (4 Chs.) is the dam of Ch. Flirtation Walk Tiara (by DISPLAY), who in turn produced six champions as well as a daughter that produced five.

The remaining three top producing DISPLAY sons came later in his stud career and were linebred, already carrying from two to five lines from him.

Ch. Gengler's Drum Major, whelped in 1951, carried two lines to DISPLAY, one from Diplomat. Ch. Meldon's Ruffian, whelped in 1950, was out of Meldon's Memories, who carried a line to both Tribute and High Test. Most intensely linebred of all, Ch. Benrook Zorra carried five lines to DISPLAY, two from High Test and one from Tribute.

The CH. BENROOK ZORRA branch

Ch. Benrook Zorra sired six champions, all from different dams, and all located in the Midwest. None, however, were champion producers, and this "branch" from DISPLAY can be left here.

The CH. GENGLER'S DRUM MAJOR branch

Ch. Gengler's Drum Major sired seven champions, including a son, Ch. High Potentate of Gengl-Aire (out of a Drum Major daughter) with five champions. The tail-male line of top producers, however, ends here.

There are active tail-female lines stemming from Drum Major, the main family connection being through the DISPLAY daughter, Ch. Flirtation Walk Tiara. The Tiara granddaughter, Blikaywin Pixie's Peggy, bred to Potentate, produced the foundation stock for the dozen Kansho champions bred in Texas by Margaret Brown. Among the four champions sired by Mrs. Brown's multiple-Group-winning Potentate son, Ch. Winposa Arch Rival, was Ch. Kansho's Sugar Time, with four lines from Drum Major.

Sugar was selected by Carol and Gerald Somers, of Kalamazoo, Michigan, to blend with their original family based on the Drum Major granddaughter, Ch. Rosalinde von Brittanhof II. Three decades of Zomerhof champions have emerged based on the combination of Sugar and Rosalinde offspring, and the Somers are currently into their tenth generation of homebreds.

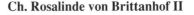

Ch. Kansho's Sugar Time   **Ch. Rosalinde von Brittanhof II**

Ch. Zomerhof's Ruffy Ringo

Mrs. Somers remembers both Rosalinde and Sugar as follows:

Rosalinde was Jerry's dog from the minute she came to live with us. She read the paper with Jerry every night, lying next to him in his big easy chair. Sugar was most appropriately named, as she was sweetness personified and loved everyone. It was a good beginning — from Rosalinde and Sugar our temperaments have been so enjoyable, and Ringo lived past fifteen. We are especially pleased with the good health and longevity within our line.

The Somers selected the Diplomat branch to complement their foundation stock, basically breeding to studs tightly linebred within this branch. Two top producing sires emerged, beginning with Ch. Zomerhof's Ruffy Ringo (7 Chs.).Their top dam is Zomerhof's Moment of Decision, dam of six champions, all by their multiple-Group-winning Am. and Can. Ch. Zomerhof's Limited Edition (20 Chs.), who carries thirty-two lines to Drum Major.

In 1994, the fiftieth and fifty-first homebred Zomerhof champions were made up, and as might be expected Ch. Zomerhof's Major Dad and his brother Ch. Zomerhof's Major League are out of Ch. Zomerhof's Junior Miss, from the combination of Limited Edition and Moment of Decision that worked so well for them.

Drum Major has his broadest extension in modern pedigrees through his son Ch. Bramble of Quality Hill. The Bramble son Ch. Wid's Von Kipper, CDX can be found behind many of today's top winners and producers, as the maternal grandsire of Ch. Sky Rocket's Uproar (35 Chs.), one of the cornerstone sires of the Ruffian branch.

Ch. Zomerhof's Limited Edition

**Ch. Dorem
High Test**

_____

The CH. DOREM HIGH TEST branch

Ch. Dorem High Test was from DISPLAY's first litter and became his first champion son. The circumstances were aptly described by Dorothy Williams (Dorem) in an earlier chapter. As the sire of 15 champions, he stands fourth among DISPLAY's nine top producing sons.

High Test was an immediate success in the show ring and as a sire. He finished at eight months and produced his first litter at ten months, out of Ch. Dorem Highlight (litter sister to DISPLAY's dam). The combination of High Test and Highlight had a great impact on the breed, producing four champions plus five others that produced champions. Foremost among them were Ch. Meldon's Mignon (5 Chs.) and Meldon's Mar Mose (3 Chs.).

The tail-male line of top producers from the High Test branch traces only two generations further, ending with Ch. Benrook Banning, a Mignon son. Banning carries two lines to High Test, the other through his maternal granddam Mar Mose. Although Banning sired nine champions, he leaves few, if any, modern descendants.

The current lines to Mignon come primarily through his son, Ch. Dody's Dimitri and two daughters, Ch. Dorem Inspiration and Ch. Phil-Mar Lady Be Good. Dimitri, in spite of his spectacular breed "first" as Best in Show at Montgomery County from the classes in 1955, was little used at stud and left only two champions. He is one of nine Dody champions bred in Maryland by Dorothy Goldsworthy, all descending from the DISPLAY daughter Ch. Benrook

Bon-Bon of Marienhof. Dimitri carries a line to three DISPLAY branches — High Test, Tribute and Merit — and figured prominently in west coast bloodlines as the sire of Ch. Minquas Alicia.

Marguerite Jones, also in Maryland, began working with Marienhof stock during the 1940s. There were ten homebred Minquas champions, nine of them descendants of the DISPLAY daughter Minquas Vivacious. Mae Dickenson's Delfin family was founded on two Minquas bitches, Ch. Minquas Athena, a Vivacious daughter, and Ch. Minquas Merry Elf, a Tweed Packet daughter. There would be twenty homebred Delfin champions, the "star" being Ch. Delfin Janus (34 Chs.).

It was the Dimitri daughter Ch. Minquas Alicia that would bring more High Test blood to the West Coast, as foundation matron for the Mutiny Kennel. Alicia gave them five champions, including Ch. Mutiny Coquette, foundation matron for the California-based Windy Hills (see DIPLOMAT branch).

Ch. Meldon Mignon's daughter Ch. Dorem Inspiration is the key behind all the top producing Helarry dogs (see RUFFIAN branch), through the Inspiration son Ch. Dorem Choice Play. The foundation matron at Helarry, Helarry's Delsey, is a Choice Play granddaughter. He is also the great-grandsire of yet another Helarry matron, Ch. Dorem Symphony II. Choice Play's litter sister, Dorem My Play, can be found in the Michigan-based Budhof, Multi-Lakes and Miown families (see BEAU BRUMMEL branch).

Mignon sired two early Phil-Mar champions, including Ch. Phil-Mar Lady Be Good, the dam of Ch. Perci-Bee's First Impression (15 Chs.) from which so many top producers descend.

In addition to Mignon, the combination of High Test and Highlight produced two nonchampion Meldon bitches of note: Meldon's Mar Mose and Marie. The broadest impact came through Mar Mose. Her granddaughter Ch. Benrook Bona (by DISPLAY) has a family of her own, based on her nine Handful champions. The Mar Mose son Ch. Meldon's Sea Biscuit is behind Barclay Square's foundation bitch, Trayhom Truly Fair, CD. Most importantly, Mar Mose's daughter Meldon's Memories, bred back to DISPLAY, produced Ch. Meldon's Ruffian, who has a branch of his own. Meldon's Marie produced Benrook Vogue (by DISPLAY), foundation for the Elflands.

Florence Bradburn's Elfland kennel was well established in Southern California when DISPLAY emerged on the scene. Miss Bradburn bred several champions during the forties based on her original foundation bitch, Vanessa Anfiger, bred by Anne Eskrigge. In the summer of 1952 Florence met Ben Burwell, a highly regarded professional handler who had come to California to show some dogs from the East Coast. According to Florence:

Ben put me in touch with Mac Silver, the manager of Benrook Kennel, who sent me Benrook Vogue and the beautiful Benrook Jewel II (Ch. Benrook Buckaroo-Benrook Brilliance). Ben was out here at the time of Jewel's first show, and he handled her to a five-point win from the puppy class. I finished her championship very easily myself.

**Ch. Frevohly's Best
Bon-Bon, UD**

Both Benrook bitches sent to Elfland carried lines to High Test, and eventually were meshed to form the Elfland family, which was active for nearly five decades. The quality of the Elfland breeding program reached its zenith with the advent of Ch. Samos of Elfland who was Best in Show (entry of 1,850 dogs) at the Santa Anna Kennel Club in 1964.

Although lines to the DISPLAY son Ch. Dorem High Test can be found in current show stock throughout the country, it was in California that this branch came forward with the greatest impact.

The Elfland family developed by Florence Bradburn was the first to bring High Test blood to the West. The success of this branch was greatly enhanced by the efforts of Ruth Ziegler's Allaruths. In the early 1950s, Mrs. Ziegler acquired Doman Mehitabel, CDX from Frederick von Huly, a breeder of some years both in the East and West. Blinken of Mandeville was selected as the sire for the first litter raised by Ruth. He was a litter brother to the top winning bitch of that period, Ch. Forest Nod of Mandeville, the first bitch to achieve two Bests in Show. Blinken and Nod were sired by High Test, and out of a High Test granddaughter. The Blinken-Mehitabel breeding produced Ch. Frevohly's Best Bon Bon, UD, the breed's first Champion - Utility Dog. Bon-Bon was described by Ruth as a bitch with both beauty and brains:

When she was six months old her obedience training began. Schatzie was a bright, quick learner and never resented discipline, but she was enamored of the world and all its interests and it was difficult to maintain her attention. When it was time to enter her in competition, a problem developed. I showed her three times in Novice and three times she gave a brilliant performance—and flunked. After being left on the Recall, she could not wait to be called but would bound down the ring to me before she ever heard "Schatzie come." And so we failed to qualify although we were going for 199 and 198 scores. A change of handlers seemed indicated, so June Williams took over and together they gained the CD degree.

In the meantime, Schatzie also began her show career. At 11 months she was Best of Winners and Best Opposite Sex at the Golden Gate K.C. in January 1955 and finished by going Best of Breed at Del Monte in May. She was handled at all times by Ric Chashoudian, who also finished all five of Schatzie's champion kids as well as several grandchildren.

Over the years Schatzie was bred to four different dogs of rather different type. I found it interesting to experiment with bloodlines and outcrossed her on three occasions. But in every case, she has produced what I call "Schatzie puppies." They are exceptionally strong in bone, coat, head and substance.

Bon-Bon was the first western-bred bitch to produce five champions. It was her breeding to Ch. Marwyck Pitt-Penn Pirate (44 Chs.) that proved most significant. From it came Allaruth's Jolly Anne (3 Chs.), plus Chs. Allaruth's Jorgette and Joshua. The latter, as the sire of Ch. Allaruth's Jericho (ex Cookie v. Elfland), has brought this family forward to the present.

Jericho was shown extensively in the early 1960s and was twice Best of Breed at the Northern California Specialty. He sired seven champions, all from line breedings. When bred back to the Bon-Bon daughter Ch. Allaruth's Miss Dinah Mite, he produced Ch. Allaruth's Jasmine, the dam of the corner-stone sire, Ch. Landmark's Masterpiece (32 Chs.).

The Jericho daughter Ch. Allaruth's Jemima, out of Fran Cazier's foundation bitch, Minchette Maier (6 Chs.), became the foundation for Dr. Jeanette Schulz's Janhofs, giving her two champions, including Ch. Janhof's Bon-Bon of Adford, who numbers among her four champion get Ch. Orbit's Lift Off, CDX, foundation for Carol Parker's very successful Skyline family.

Three decades and several generations later, Mrs. Ziegler topped Bon-Bon's record with the homebred bitch, Ch. Allaruth's Zephyr Too, who gave her six champions, five by Ch. Sole Baye's T.J. Esquire (25 Chs.), including Yvonne Phelps's Ch. Allaruth's Charles V Sole Baye, a top winner with fifteen Specialty Bests, three of which were A.M.S.C. Nationals. He is doing equally well as a sire, with over a dozen champions to date.

The Allaruth, Orbit and Skyline families are treated more fully in the chapter on the Diplomat branch.

The CH. MELDON'S MERIT branch

Ch. Meldon's Merit sired nine champions, five sons and four daughters. The current lines of descent from this branch were brought forward primarily through the Merit sons Ch. Handful's Me Too of Marienhof (see DIPLOMAT branch) and Ch. Kenhoff's I'm It.

The tail-male line of top producers from Merit extends only three generations, beginning with his son Ch. Kenhoff's I'm It (8 Chs.) and ending with the I'm It grandson Ch. Glenshaw's Gadget (7 Chs.).

In the early 1950s, activities in the northern Pennsylvania and Ohio areas hosted by members of the Penn-Ohio club played a major role in the

Minchette Maier

**Ch. Allaruth's
Zephyr Too**

71

Ch. Kenhoff's I'm It

breed's advancement. Mrs. Evashwick's Marwyck family based on Ch. Sorceress of Ledahof provided a number of breeders with foundation stock. Much of the remainder came from Grace and Herb Kaltoff's already well-developed Kenhoff family.

Built from lines to T.M.G., and brought forward by their Ch. Gracon Canis of Kenhoff (5 Chs.), the Kenhoffs were in good stead when DISPLAY emerged. The Tribute-Canis daughter Kenhoff's Handsome Annie, bred to DISPLAY produced the sisters Chs. Kenhoff's Katy Did Too and That's Me. Annie's sister Belinda of Kenhoff, bred to Merit, produced I'm It. Their sons and daughters, blended with the Tribute branch, formed the foundation for the Glenshaw Schnauzers bred by Chris and Robert Snowdon.

I was a frequent visitor to the Spruce Knoll farm in Pennsylvania as a youngster, Chris and Bob playing a major role in my development. When in 1959 it came time to plan the first issue of *Schnauzer Shorts,* the cover dog was their Ch. Glenshaw's Gadget. The Snowdons had initially achieved great success in Cocker Spaniels with a breeding program begun in 1934. Many Glenshaw homebreds earned Specialty, Group and Best in Show awards, and several were leaving a lasting imprint on the breed. Backed by the practical knowledge gained in those early years, the Snowdons were to enjoy immediate success with their first Miniature Schnauzer. Chris remembers it well:

The first youngster to come to our home was a five-month-old puppy who later became Ch. Kenhoff's I'm It. He was the winner of the American Miniature Schnauzer Club trophy for having won the most Group placements in 1953. That year he was Best of Breed at Morris & Essex in the east and Harbor Cities in the west, as well as the Chicago International. When bred to Ch. Kenhoff's Katy Did Too, owned by Norman Austin, he produced Chs. Salt 'n Pepper Sampler and Salesman, as well as Salt 'n Pepper Scintillation, the latter purchased by Richard Matheny. She produced four champions for him, including his record-setting Ch. Fancy Free Fancy Package, the first of the breed to win over 100 Bests of Breed.

I was extremely fortunate to make the acquaintance of Audrey Meldon while she owned DISPLAY and his two sons, Tribute and High Test (oh, that gorgeous, long, exaggerated head). I used to visit her, sit in her kennel and just watch all the many offspring of these dogs. I would ask who sired this one and that one—and always got an answer. I finally came to the conclusion that the way

Ch. Glenshaw's Top O' The Mark in 1962 winning the Terrier Group under Maxwell Riddle, handled by breeder-owner Chris Snowdon.

MAD RIVER VALLEY
KENNEL CLUB
MAR.10,1963
FIRST IN
TERRIER GROUP
JUDGE-MR.MAXWELL
RIDDLE

to do this was to line-breed closely to DISPLAY through his best producing sons —*Tribute, High Test and Diplomat. It seemed to me that in most instances DISPLAY potency came through his sons, while that of Tribute was most evident in the bitches. So that is what we did, and for 23 years never went out of this line.*

There would be eighteen Glenshaw champions, culminating in the Group and Specialty winning Ch. Glenshaw's Top O' The Mark, who carries seven lines to DISPLAY. Mark was the breed's number one dog in 1962, the year the Knight System ratings were initiated. Glenshaw was disbanded a few years later. The Snowdons can presently be found enjoying life with a few dogs in the hills of Arkansas.

The CH. BENROOK BEAU BRUMMELL branch

The DISPLAY son Am. and Can. Ch. Benrook Beau Brummell, sired 13 American champions, based principally on the Canadian connection provided by Ethel and William Gottschalk in Ontario. They purchased Beau Brummell in 1951, and he was Best of Breed at the first Specialty offered by the newly formed Miniature Schnauzer Club of Canada.

The tail-male line of top producers from the Beau Brummell branch extends five generations, ending with Ch. Travelmor's Witchcraft (5 Chs.). The Beau Brummell grandson Ch. Cosburn's Esquire (12 Chs.) would be instrumental in bringing the tail-male line forward.

Ch. Cosburn's Esquire

Esquire was a leading winner in the 1950s, beginning his show career as Winners Dog at the AMSC Specialty in February 1954, and finishing in six shows with five majors (RWD at Westminster). He won his twenty-sixth Best of Breed in November 1958, doing most of his winning while owned by Priscilla Deaver.

The story of Esquire and that of William and Olive Moore's Travelmor Kennel go hand in hand. It began in 1957, and as the Moores tell it:

Wish we could say that we knew Esquire from the beginning, but that beginning, like so many others, came in the form of Ollie's Christmas gift to Bill—Yankee's Dark Drama, known to us as Melody, and our top bitch.

The dominant person behind all of what quickly followed was Ed Boehm, who sold us Melody. Edward Marshall Boehm, widely known as the world's most famed bird sculptor, was also a top dog breeder and judge. He could "put down" a Schnauzer as well as any handler. Because of him, and with his help, we learned a great deal about the breed in a comparatively short time.

"It was together at Tom Gately's kennel that we first met Esquire. Ed felt, probed, posed and moved him—and was obviously impressed. He decided to buy him, and offered us a half interest. Tom showed Esquire for us all in November 1958, and at his last three shows, was pitted against one of the country's best known winners, Ch. Phil-Mar Lugar. We are proud to say that Esquire won two out of three, retiring from the ring in this final burst of glory at nearly six years of age.

The Moores became the sole owners of Esquire in 1960, also acquiring much of the late Edward Boehm's breeding stock when his kennel was dispersed. All the early Travelmor champions, owner conditioned and handled, were based on their blend of Tribute bitches to the Beau Brummell branch through Esquire.

Do-it-yourselfers, the Moores took great pride in one dog in particular, achieving an outstanding record with Ch. Travelmor's Witchcraft, who had three lines to Esquire. He was one of those rare individuals that retained a superior double coat, reminiscent of the early Marienhof dogs. The Moores with judicious care were able to show him over a three-year span, never once being completely stripped. In all he won 64 Bests of Breed and 25 Group placements. Among

Olive Moore with Ch. Travelmor's Witchcraft and Bill Moore with a son, Ch. Travelmor's Rango.

several Specialty Bests was the AMSC at Montgomery County under the famed all-rounder Percy Roberts.

Witchcraft sired five champions, plus the good producer, Travelmor's Tattle Tale (3 Chs.). Most importantly, his son Ch. Travelmor's Fantazio, exported to England (see BRITISH chapter), sired Eng. Ch. Buffel's All American Boy of Deansgate, one of England's top producing sire (9 Chs.).

An important addition to the family was made on March 16, 1971, when Jennifer Allen came to manage Travelmor. The Moores had advertised for a kennel maid in *Dog World*, and it was Jenny, then nineteen years of age, who answered their needs. A decade later, Jenny became their adopted daughter.

For the last two decades, Jenny has managed the breeding and showing at Travelmor, continuing the tradition of showing only what they breed, and breeding only what they show. This family has housed a series of top producing bitches, and from them have managed to finish at least one champion each year.

Ch. Travelmor's Turned On with Jennifer Moore

Jenny is much in demand as a judge, and has officiated at Specialty shows both here and abroad.

The Moores took a different tack in the mid-1970s, adding first-class members of the Delegate and Ruffian branches to their family. These included the Jump Up son Ch. Sky Rocket's Travel More (9 Chs.) and a Peter Gunn daughter, Ch. Reflections Lively Image. She gave them seven champions, including the good producing bitch Ch. Travelmor's Turned On (3 Chs.). Their offspring have brought this family forward to the present.

Ch. Benrook Beau Brummell exerted much of his influence in the state of Michigan. More than half of his champion get came from the Multi-Lakes Kennel near Detroit. Most important of these was his son, Ch. Budhof's Stylist of Multi-Lakes, out of the linebred DISPLAY daughter Dorem My Play. This line was brought forward by the Stylist son Miown Erich Von Brach (4 Chs.).

Harry and Patsy Laughter, along with their very talented children, bred, conditioned and handled over twenty champions bearing their Miown prefix. The star was clearly Ch. Miown Exotic Poppy. Her tragic death as a yearling left quite a void. I saw Poppy on her second coat, as a puppy champion at the 1969 AMSC Specialty in New York. Even at that age she was displaying talents that quickly made her one of the breed's all-time top winning bitches.

A champion at eight months, handled by Kathy Laughter, then a teenager, Poppy went to professional handler Joanne Trubee for a 1969 campaign that netted her two Bests in Show, thirteen Group placements and her second Michigan Specialty Best. That year has to go down in the record books as one of

**Ch. Miown Exotic Poppy
with Kathy Laughter**

the best ever. In addition to Poppy's pair of Bests, 1969 saw Ch. Mankit's Alex of Dunbar win five Bests in Show, Ch. Abingdon Authority four, and Ch. Mankit's To The Moon two.

Five generations of Miown champions were made up through the mid-1970s, and several current Michigan-based breeders carry Miown breeding in their foundation stock.

The Beau Brummell branch has its greatest effect through another Cosburn export, Can. Ch. Cosburn's Deborah, founding matron at Brittanhof in Illinois. Mr. and Mrs. Charles Brittan purchased Deborah in 1951, finishing five champions from her three litters by Ch. Applause of Abingdon, CD (7 Chs.).

Offspring from these breedings produced an immediate spread. A daughter, Ch. Fricka von Brittanhof, produced five champions at Helen and Harry Wiedenbeck's Helarry Kennel in Illinois. Fricka was one of the first

**Ch. Dansel
Dutch Treat**

bitches to go to Ruffian. Their son, Ch. Helarry's Dynamite, headed Jinx Gunville's Merry Makers Kennel, and as the grandsire of Ch. Merry Makers Dyna-Mite (15 Chs.) brings forward this aspect of the Beau Brummell branch.

The Applause-Deborah son Ch. Johannes von Brittanhof provided a strong base for the Dansel and Alpine families. Johannes was owned by Donald Doessel and is behind nine homebred Dansel champions, eight of them bitches.

This family was brought forward by Seme and Louis Auslander, also Illinois-based. Their purchase of Ch. Dansel Dutch Treat in 1965 began a breeding program that produced fourteen Alpine champions, including the Best in Show-winning bitch, Ch. Alpine Baby Ruth. The Auslanders chose to breed into the Tribute branch and came up with the top producing brace, Ch. Alpine Cyrus The Great (8 Chs.), and his son Ch. Alpine Great Scott (7 Chs.). Two Alpine bitches were well placed and have brought their bloodlines to the present. Ch. Alpine Double Dutch went to Dorothy and Edward Harvey in New Jersey, giving them four champions, including a top producing son, Ch. Deeanee Dutch Demon (6 Chs.). Several more generations of Deeanee homebreds would follow. Alpine Ultra Violet went to Shirley and Robert Rains in California, giving them four champions, including the Best in Show winner, Ch. Rainbou's Tornado.

By the early 1960s another top producing Brittanhof bitch emerged in the double Deborah great-granddaughter Typhoon von Brittanhof. Never bred to the same dog twice, Typhoon produced a champion in every litter save one, and that contained a dog with twelve points. Among her five champions was the Best in Show winner Ch. Rojo's Buster von Brittanhof.

Typhoon has an extraordinary line of champion descendants, numbering in the hundreds. These champions come mainly through her daughters, Ch. Thumbelina von Brittanhof and the sisters Regatta and Ch. Salty von Brittanhof. Thumbelina stayed in Illinois with Hope and Charles Meland and, linebred within the Tribute branch, gave them four Melandorf champions. Salty also stayed in Illinois to found the Iles Kennel of Mr. and Mrs. Jerauld Iles. They chose to outcross her, selecting Ch. Helarry's Harmony (21 Chs.) from the Ruffian branch. This combination produced Ch. Harga's Covington (3 Chs.) and the bitches Ch. Iles Heidi and Ch. Tasse Kuchen.

Two Salty granddaughters have had a major influence on current top winning and producing lines. One of these, Ch. Harga's Terri (by Covington), served as foundation matron for Carl and Carol Beiles's Carolane Kennel in New York, giving them seven champions, including the good producing bitch, Ch. Carolane's Fantasia (3 Chs.).

The other Salty granddaughter, Heather's Windy Weather (ex Kuchen), exerted her influence in the West, as foundation for Judy and Donald Smith's Jadee Kennel (see RUFFIAN chapter).

**Typhoon
von Brittanhof**

Ch. Marcheim Poppin' Fresh

Perhaps Typhoon's greatest impact came through her tightly line-bred granddaughter, Ch. Miranda von Brittanhof (ex Regatta). Purchased as a puppy by Mr. and Mrs. Charles Congdon, Miranda founded the Marcheim Kennel in 1967, along with Ch. Alpine Patent Pending, both of which they finished. All eight Marcheim champions trace to them. Linebred within the Tribute branch, Miranda produced the multiple Group and Specialty winner, Ch. Marcheim Poppin' Fresh (26 Chs.). At Marcheim, he sired Ch. Marcheim Helzapoppin (ex Patent Pending), the sire of seven champions, but his best effort came in the form of record-setting Ch. Hughcrest Hugh Hefner.

Hugh Hefner's youthful career was managed by Judy and Chris Hughes of Hughcrest Kennel in Illinois. He finished at eleven months of age with a Group First. In six weeks of showing as a champion in 1972, he won two more Groups and a pair of Specialty Bests. Purchased in the spring of 1973 by Kelly Hoskins, he was turned over to Clay Coady who professionally managed his career thereafter. He finished 1973 as the number two Schnauzer (Knight System).

Hugh Hefner was far and away the number one Schnauzer for the next two years, and in 1974 established several new "one-year" records: the most Specialty wins (7), the most Breed wins (56), the most Group placements (36) and the most Knight points (1,354). In a career that spanned five years, Hugh Hefner was for a time the leading Specialty winner (14), Breed winner (131), Group winner (29), Group placer (92) and holder of Knight points accumulated (3,413). His record of five Bests in Show is surpassed by only three others: Ch. Hi-Charge of Hansenhaus (10), Ch. Abingdon Authority (9) and Ch. Mankit's Alex of Dunbar (7); his Specialty record, only by Ch. Das Feder's Drivin' Miss Daisy (20), Ch. Sibehil's Dark Shadows (18), Ch. Blythewood National Acclaim (17) and Ch. Penlan Peter Gunn (15).

Hugh Hefner sired 15 champions, including Ch. Hughcrest Harvey Wallbanger (8 Chs.), a double Poppin' Fresh grandson. Harvey is the grandsire of Ch. Wan-El Wildfire (5 Chs.), owned by Anne Lockney. Two more generations of top sires were developed at Ruedesheim, beginning with the Wildfire son, Ch. Ruedesheim's Bonus (24 Chs.) and his sons Ch. Ruedesheim's Capitalist (8 Chs.) and Ch. Ruedesheim's Advantage v. Belgar (8 Chs.).

The most important family being developed from Poppin' Fresh comes through his daughter, Jana PD, the dam of seven Regency champions, all sired by Ch. Skyline's Blue Spruce (55 Chs.). The Regency successes are given further attention in the chapter on Ch. Meldon's Ruffian.

Ch. Hughcrest Hugh Hefner winning Best of Breed at the South Florida Specialty in January 1973 under Olive Moore, handled by Clay Coady.

We have attempted in this chapter to examine the four branches from DISPLAY that have not progressed in tail-male but have female lines still active. Although virtually all current show stock carry lines to Ch. Gengler's Drum Major, Ch. Dorem High Test, Ch. Meldon's Merit and/or Ch. Cosburn's Beau Brummell, they have been meshed with tail-male lines from the four stronger branches—those of Tribute, the brothers Delegate and Diplomat, and most emphatically, Ruffian.

7
The
Dorem Tribute
Branch

**Ch. Dorem
Tribute**

CH. DOREM TRIBUTE, whelped July 2, 1946, was far and away the leader among DISPLAY's nine top producing sons. His record of 41 champion get is just one short of the number achieved by his illustrious sire.

Tribute was sold to Audrey Meldon as a three-month old puppy and made an auspicious ring debut just four months later, going Best of Winners at the AMSC Specialty in New York. He was Reserve the next day at Westminster, where DISPLAY won the breed, and was Winners or better in five of the next seven shows, twice going Reserve to Ch. Dorem Delegate. Tribute's first appearance as a champion was exactly one year after his debut, defeated again at the AMSC Specialty and Westminster by DISPLAY. Then he took four straight breed wins, going on to two Group Second, and was not shown again by Mrs. Meldon.

How he returned to Dorem is explained by Dorothy Williams:

After repeated efforts, I finally persuaded Mrs. Meldon to sell Tribute. Nicholas Daks and I bought him in December 1949, and I bought him outright a year later. He took Best of Breed every time shown by me except at the AMSC Specialty 1950, where he went Best Opposite Sex to my Ch. Dorem Inspiration, and at Westminster and the 1952 Specialty where he never made the grade.

Ch. Dorem Favorite   **Ch. Benrook Buckaroo**

I consider his top win to be the Best of Breed award gained at the AMSC Specialty in February 1951, at almost five years of age.

Tribute had only sired four champions when he came back to Dorem. Mrs. Meldon had pushed DISPLAY and High Test in preference to him. However, for us he sired 75 litters and had 37 more champions before his retirement at age 12. He died on July 17, 1959.

Whereas the breed since the 1950s is 99 percent DISPLAY, it is also 98 percent Tribute. There are few, if any, American champions of the last four decades that do not carry hundreds of lines to Tribute. The Tribute branch claims sixty-four top producing sires tracing to him in direct tail-male line. In our examination of each of the other branches from DISPLAY, the name of Tribute will appear almost as a constant, and his influence is inestimable.

Tribute sired three top producing sons: Ch. Meldon's Seabiscuit (5 Chs.), Ch. Benrook Buckaroo (17 Chs.), and most importantly, Ch. Dorem Favorite (16 Chs.). The line from Seabiscuit extends only through his daughter, Ch. Minquas Athena, while there are six generations of top sires descending from Buckaroo and thirteen from Favorite.

The CH. BENROOK BUCKAROO line

Ch. Benrook Buckaroo had enjoyed considerable success as a young show dog before being purchased by John and Claire Specht to head their Jonaire Kennel in Mt. Pocono, Pennsylvania. Buckaroo sired 17 champions, ten for Jonaire, and half of these out of their foundation bitch, Ch. Winsome High Style, including Ch. Jonaire Pocono High Life, the sire of Ch. Jonaire Pocono Rock 'N Roll (11 Chs.). Buckaroo had left four champions at Benrook, and it is from these breedings that the tail-male and female lines progressed. Ch. Benrook Jewel II went to California to give a new start for the Elflands. Ch. Benrook Randy went to Maryann Vann to head her Belvedere Kennel in Illinois.

**64 Sires of 5 or more A.K.C. Champions
trace in direct tail-male lines to**

CH. DOREM TRIBUTE

*Sires that are in *italic* produced fewer than 5 Champions, *Ch. Mankit's Eager* (4)
and *Ch. Valharra's Trademark* (4) missing the mark by one.

A1 Ch. Meldon's Seabiscuit (5)

A2 Ch. Benrook Buckaroo (17)

    B1 *Ch. Joniare Pocono High Life**

        C1 Ch. Jonaire Pocono Rock 'N Roll (11)

    B2 Ch. Benrook Randy (10)

        C2 Ch. Melmar's Random Rain (5)

            D1 Ch. Melmar's Jack Frost (18)

                E1 Ch. Adford's Bob White (6)

                E2 Ch. Orbit's A-OK of Adford (5)

                    F1 Ch. Orbit's Time Traveler (5)

                        G1 Ch. Gandalf of Arador (5)

A3 Ch. Dorem Favorite (16)

    B3 Fanciful of Marienhof (10)

        C3 Ch. Yankee Pride Colonel Stump (15)

    B4 Ch. Dorem Original (13)

        C4 *Ch. Geelong Playboy**

            D2 Ch. Geelong Little Sargent (11)

    B5 Ch. Mankit's Adam (10)

        C5 Ch. Trayhom Tramp-A-Bout (7)

            D3 Mankit's Hector (6)

            D4 Ch. Winsomor Critique (5)

                E3 Ch. Fancway's Tom Terrific (6)

    B6 Ch. Perci-Bee's First Impression (15)

        C6 Ch. Phil-Mar Emmett (9)

        C7 Ch. Phil-Mar Thunderbolt (6)

        C8 Ch. Dorem Vanguard (6)

        C9 Ch. Phil-Mar Lugar (26)

            D5 Ch. Dorem Denominator (7)

            D6 Ch. Blythewood Main Gazebo (31)

                E4 Ch. Blythewood Chief Bosun (11)

                E5 Ch. Blythewood His Majesty (11)

                E6 Ch. Swinheim Salutation (6)

D7 *Ch. Mankit's Eager**

    E7 Ch. Mankit's Moonshot (5)

        F2 Ch. Mankit's Signal Go (21)

            G2 Ch. Barclay Square Brickbat (9)

            G3 Ch. Zomerhof's Ruffy Ringo (7)

            G4 Ch. Mankit's Bang Bang of Dunbar (7)

                H1 Ch. Shirley's Show Time (7)

            G5 Ch. Mankit's Dashing Dennis (8)

                H2 Ch. Mankit's To The Moon (11)

                H3 Ch. Mankit's Alex of Dunbar (5)

            G6 Ch. Mankit's Xerxes (21)

                H4 Ch. Alpine Cyrus The Great (9)

                  I1 Ch. Alpine Great Scott (7)

        F3 Ch. Mankit's Yo Ho (7)

            G7 Ch. Marcheim Poppin' Fresh (26)

                H5 Ch. Marcheim Helza Poppin (7)

                H6 Ch. Hughcrest Hugh Hefner (15)

                  I2 Ch. Hughcrest Harvey Wallbanger (8)

                    J1 *Ch. Hughcrest Blue Beard**

                        K1 Ch. Wan-El Wildfire (5)

                          L1 Ch. Ruedesheim's Bonus (24)

                            M1 Ch. Ruedesheim's Advantage

                            V Belgar (8)

                            M1 Ch. Ruedesheim's

                            Capitalist (8)

            G8 Ch. Moore's Max Derkleiner (7)

                H7 Ch. Valharra's Max Pax (7)

                  I3 Ch. Paxon's Magic Factor (5)

                    J2 *Valharra's Max Master **

                        K2 Ch. Paxon's Re-Play (7)

                  I4 *Ch. Jo-Mar's Bric A Brac**

                    J3 *Jo-Mar's Magic Marker [B/S]**

                        K3 Ch. Aljamar Hot Ice [B/S] (5)

              H8 *Ch. Valharra's Trademark**

                I5 Ch. Valharra's Extra (12)

                  J4 Ch. Valharra's Double Extra (12)

                    K4 Ch. Valharra's Jaxson (6)

                      L2 Ch. Faro of Arador (7)

                  J5 Ch. Valharra's Extra Allaruth (7)

                  K5 Ch. Skyline's Chindee Morgan (7)

                J6 Ch. Sunshine Sounder (11)

                  K6 Ch. J. R. Boomer of Hansenhaus (6)

**Ch. Benrook Randy
with Ben Burwell**

Ch. Melmar's Jack Frost

Randy was the leading winner in 1958, with a record of two Bests in Show, and over two dozen Group placements from 40 Bests of Breed. He sired ten champions, most importantly a trio out of the Ruffian daughter Ch. Melmar's Rain Song, bred in Seattle by Mel and Virginia Schultz. These included the Best in Show winner Ch. Melmar's Random Rain (5 Chs.), who in turn produced the influential sire, Ch. Melmar's Jack Frost (18 Chs.).

Jack Frost was owned by Adele and William Staniford (Adford). With two lines to Ruffian, he was a departure from the lines and families developing in Southern California, and served as an outcross for the tightly bred Diplomat bitches of Allaruth, Fancway and Orbit breeding. He also carried the black and silver gene and sired two champions of this then rare color variety, including the Group winner, Ch. Tiger Bo Von Riptide. Jack Frost produced two top producing sons and a top producing daughter.

The Jack Frost sons Ch. Adford's Bob White (6 Chs.) and Ch. Orbit's A-OK of Adford (5 Chs.) both appear in modern pedigrees, the latter principally through his son Ch. Orbit's Time Traveler (5 Chs.), and his son Ch. Gandalf of Arador (5 Chs.).

The Jack Frost daughter, Ch. Janhof's Bon-Bon of Adford, bred by Dr. Jeanette Schultz, has had the broadest impact on contemporary lines and families through her daughter (by Time Traveler) Ch. Orbit's Lift Off, CDX, foundation for all the Skyline top producers.

Ch. Dorem Favorite winning Best of Breed at the American Miniature Schnauzer Club Specialty, February 8, 1953, under Marie Slattery, handled by Stephen Shaw.

The CH. DOREM FAVORITE line

More than three-quarters of the top producing sires that descend from the Tribute branch came through his son (and maternal great-grandson) Ch. Dorem Favorite. He was obviously a "favorite" at Dorem, as Miss Williams describes:

Ch. Dorem Favorite and his sister Fashion are probably the most similar pair of champions we ever bred. They are both pure silver. The dog is very masculine, taking after his sire, Tribute, and the bitch very feminine, as was her dam, Dorem Flair. Both parents were silver, although Tribute darkened with age.

Favorite, like so many of his predecessors from Dorem, enjoyed instant success in the show ring. He earned four points and a Group Third at his first show at nine months. At his next show a month later, he was Best of Breed at the AMSC Specialty for five points. The next day at Westminster he was Reserve, but his sister Fashion was Winners Bitch. Favorite won the breed in his next three

Ch. Dorem Original   **Ch. Yankee Pride Colonel Stump**

outings, twice more gaining Group Thirds. Lightly shown in 1953, he added nine Bests of Breed out of thirteen times shown.

Favorite's first litter produced Ch. Dorem Original (13 Chs.), out of the DISPLAY daughter Ch. Dorem Choice Play. Original's career as a stud dog was sporadic, having been sold at the age of two years and reacquired in January 1958. According to Dorothy Williams's records he sired thirty-eight males and fifty females, from which emerged sixteen champions as well as sixteen others with champion descendants. Ch. Geelong Playboy came from his first litter and is behind ten Geelong champions bred by Randolph Higgins, including the top producing sire, Ch. Geelong Little Sargent (11 Chs.).

Original is best known for his outstanding daughters. Ch. Dorem Originality (ex Dorem Fame) is the dam of Ch. Dorem Denominator (7 Chs.) and Helarry's foundation bitch, Ch. Dorem Symphony II (4 Chs.). The Original daughter Ch. Allaruth's Miss Dinah Mite is the maternal granddam of Ch. Landmark's Masterpiece (32 Chs.). All the Winsomors and Barclay Squares carry lines to the Original daughter Ch. Gunlad Meg. At Bethel, Robert Moore's foundation bitch, Ch. Benrook Bethel, by DISPLAY out of a Tribute daughter, produced Ch. Bethel's Original Ember (5 Chs.) by Original. Three Ember daughters, all by Ch. Helarry's Harmony (21 Chs.) from the Ruffian branch, advanced the Bethel family, producing foundation stock for Shorlaine, Shadowmark and eventually Carolane.

Ch. Dorem Favorite was used by Mrs. Slattery early in his stud career, giving her Fanciful and Ch. Fashion of Marienhof. Fanciful, although well over the size limit, was purchased by Mr. and Mrs. Peter Babisch to head their Yankee Pride Kennel in Michigan. Fanciful sired ten champions, including Ch. Yankee Pride Colonel Stump. Whelped July 13, 1956, he was finished and then sold to Mrs. Joseph Sailer and turned over to professional handlers Tom and Kay Gately, with whom he lived out his entire life. Shown a total of ninety-five times over a period of six years and ten months, he earned 80 Bests of Breed, 13 Group Firsts,

30 additional placements, and three Bests in Show. His Specialty record is equally impressive, including three consecutive AMSC and Mount Vernon Specialty wins, the last from the veterans class, October 13, 1963. Add to this his three consecutive breed wins at Westminster, along with a Group Second and Third, and we have a most extraordinary record.

Colonel Stump lived past fifteen years, and left 15 champion get. Current lines to him can be found principally through the Dansel and Alpine families.

The strongest tail-male lines from Ch. Dorem Favorite were brought forward by a breeding program begun in the 1960s, based on DISPLAY's last and most important champion daughter, Ch. Gladding's Bie Bie (10 Chs.). Bred by Mary Seamans of New Hampshire, Bie Bie

Ch. Gladding's Bie Bie

was purchased as a puppy by Mr. and Mrs. Emanuel Miller of Indiana.

The Millers selected the Tribute son, Favorite, for Bie Bie's first breeding, and from it came their first four champions. The lone male, Ch. Mankit's Adam, was the first to finish, followed closely by Chs. Mankit's Ada, Alfreda and Augusta.

Rarely does a first homebred champion from an unestablished breeding program receive much recognition from the fancy. Adam was an exception and sired ten champions, including a pair for Blythewood and Winsomor. His most important son for several reasons was Ch. Trayhom Tramp-A-Bout (7 Chs.). The Mankit and Trayhom families, both human and canine, were as one throughout the 1960s. Wayne and Twylla Miller (Trayhom) were not only successful breeders, but as professional handlers, almost exclusively of Mankit stock, they brought both prefixes into national prominence.

Tramp-A-Bout was not the first Trayhom champion, but surely one of the best. He was given a grand reception at the AMSC Specialty in February 1961 as an eleven-months puppy, where judge William Kendrick carried him through to Best of Breed. Tramp completed his title with five Bests of Breed and a Group Firsts, and added two more Group wins on his first specials coat before his untimely death at just fifteen months of age.

His few litters were born at Trayhom, Mankit, or at Mildred and Howard Amato's Winsomor Kennel in Ohio. Tramp's blood flows prominently

Ch. Perci Bee's First Impression
Ch. Phil-Mar Lugar
Ch. Phil-Mar Lucy Lady
Ch. Mankit's Eager
Ch. Dorem Favorite
Ch. Mankit's Augusta
Ch. Gladding's Bie Bie
CH. MANKIT'S MOONSHOT
Ch. Handful's Pop Up
Ch. Trayhom Talleyrand
Handful's Snow Flurry
Ch. Mankit's Countess Talleyrand
CH. DOREM DISPLAY
Ch. Gladding's Bie Bie
Fritzi of Gregglee

in West Coast lines through his son Ch. Winsomor Critique (5 Chs.) and his son Ch. Fancway's Tom Terrific (6 Chs.). Most importantly, Tramp can be found in the pedigrees of two record-holding bitches. He is the paternal grandsire of the breed's top dam, Ch. Faerwynd of Arador (16 Chs.), and the paternal great-grandsire of the top winning bitch, Ch. Winsomor Miss Kitty. Shown thirty-two times as a champion, from January through October 1966, Miss Kitty's record stands at 29 Bests of Breed, including two Specialties, 15 Group Firsts and three Bests in Show. She remains one of only two bitches with three Bests in Show.

The three champion sisters of Ch. Mankit's Adam were like peas in a pod, their heads almost identical. Augusta, however, became far and away the most influential. Although Augusta's record of nine champion get fell one short of her dam's, she is behind twenty-two of the thirty-two champions bred at Mankit. Their choice of Ch. Phil-Mar Lugar (26 Chs.) as Augusta's first mate added more blood from the Tribute branch and worked well. Ch. Mankit's Eager was the result. Although falling one short of the five champions designating a top producer, Eager leaves an extensive tail-male line, not only of top producers but of top winners as well.

As the Millers began linebreeding on Bie Bie, the results were a succession of multiple

Ch. Mankit's Signal Go

Ch. Mankit's To The Moon winning Best in Show for the second consecutive year, at the Montgomery County Kennel Club All-Terrier classic in 1969 under John Marvin, handled by Wayne Miller.

Best in Show winners. Ch. Mankit's Signal Go (21 Chs.), by Ch. Mankit's Moonshot (5 Chs.), an Eager-Augusta son, was the trendsetter. Signal Go was a champion by ten months of age, and in a specials career that spanned five years (1964-68), earned three Bests in Show, eight Specialty Bests, 24 Group Firsts and 48 additional placements, always handled by Wayne Miller.

The Miller combination brought forth a sixth generation Mankit in 1968. The new youngster carried nine lines to Bie Bie, and an incredible 171 lines to DISPLAY. On the Montgomery County weekend that year, Mankit's To The Moon came to these events with one major and some single points. At the Devon Show he scored a five-pointer as Winners Dog, the breed going to his uncle Ch. Mankit's Xerxes (21 Chs.). At the AMSC Specialty, To The Moon cleared the breed and later was selected Best in Show by James Farrell. A year later he returned to win an unprecedented *second* Best in Show at Montgomery County.

To The Moon set several records before he and his handler, Wayne Miller, retired. This team accounted for twelve Specialty Bests, seven of these in 1969, the year in which he led the breed (Knight System) with the largest point total (877) to date, as well as earning two Bests in Show. These records are even more remarkable when one recalls that To The Moon was sharing the show circuit with kennel mate Ch. Mankit's Alex of Dunbar, who was himself a recordsetter, with seven Bests in Show, five in 1969.

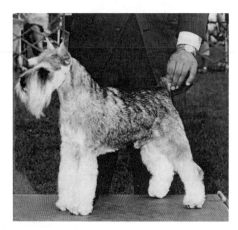

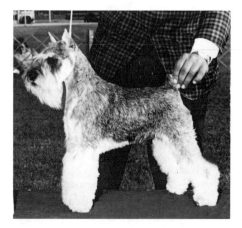

Ch. Mankit's Yo Ho   **Ch. Mankit's Xerxes**

With the retirement of their handlers and mentors in 1970, the Mankit breeding program tapered off, but not before thirty-two Mankit champions had been made up. The most important part of the Mankit influence is seen through the broad effects of their many outstanding stud dogs. Over thirty top producing sires trace from Ch. Mankit's Eager, representing more than half of those descending from the Tribute branch. Two Eager grandsons shared equally in this broad extension. Ch. Mankit's Signal Go (21 Chs.) claims five top producing sons, including Ch. Mankit's Dashing Dennis (8 Chs.), the sire of To The Moon (11 Chs.) and Alex (5 Chs.).

Signal Go's younger brother Ch. Mankit's Yo Ho (7 Chs.) claims fewer top producing sons, but has had a far greater impact on current lines and families, with eighteen additional top producing sires in succeeding generations. Four generations descend from the Yo Ho sons, Ch. Marcheim Poppin' Fresh (26 Chs.) and Ch. Moore's Max Derkleiner (7 Chs.), principally at Valharra but also in the backgrounds of the Hughcrest, Marcheim, Ruedesheim, Paxon, Arador and Hansenhaus families.

Shirley and Dick Willey were the first to bring Mankit bloodlines to the West Coast. They bred their first litter in 1968, sired by their first Miniature Schnauzer, Shirley's New Beau, CDX, and out of their second, Shirley's Sugar 'N' Spice, CD. In the next two decades, and over six generations later, the Willeys could claim over two dozen homebred champions and almost an equal number of obedience winners descending from their initial blend.

In January 1970, Ch. Mankit's Bang Bang of Dunbar was acquired as an unshown yearling by the Willeys and successfully incorporated into their family. He sired seven AKC and two Japanese champions, as well as four obedience winners, two of them also conformation champions. Bang's best producing son is their Ch. Shirley's Show Time (7 Chs.) out of Ch. Shirley's Show Off, CD (4 Chs.).

The tail-female aspect of the Mankit-Trayhom combination had as its principal torch bearer a bitch linebred within the Diplomat branch. Trayhom Truly Fair, CD, had produced a champion at Trayhom before being sold to Dale and William Miller to found their Barclay Square breeding program now well into its fourth decade.

Perhaps one thirty-year-old picture of nine frowzy little urchins all lined up in a row epitomizes what was and is the Barclay Square "line."

Dale Miller best describes how it was

Ch. Barclay Square Brickbat and Ch. Barclay Square Becky Sharp

---

Becky Sharp sits on the left —just a few months from completing her title and then on to produce nineteen puppies, twelve of whom finished readily and seven others who likely could have as well. She's our history maker, but not our trend setter. Some of those, unheralded, sitting with her, present a more accurate picture. It started with my love affair with Ch. Trayhom Tramp About. Arguably today's Schnauzers are sounder, better balanced and more pleasing to the eye, so Tramp has become, no doubt, glorified in my mind's eye over time. He came through with a vengeance in Becky's mother, Barclay Square Brick Silver, and it is she who I still see in my crew today. She had lots of help from Ch. Mankit's Yo Ho, whose dam was a littermate to Tramp's sire and Yo Ho's son, Ch. Marcheim Poppin' Fresh. In later years, among others unrelated, some of the Irrenhaus

---

A litter of nine by Ch. Mankit's Signal Go out of Barclay Square Brick Silver. The two puppies at the left became Ch. Barclay Square Becky Sharp and Ch. Barclay Square Brickbat.

dogs especially helped me to keep that same style I like — Chs. Irrenhaus Blue Print, Stand Out and Classic. As impressive as their records are, I thought them quite overlooked. Today I see those favorite old dogs exemplified most in the Rampage and Repitition dogs, many of whose pedigrees go back in similar directions.

Barclay Square has and always will be just a home with some very nice Schnauzers therein. Though without exception, every one of my bitches goes back to Becky Sharp. There is no Barclay Square "line", just a "look"— partly borrowed with my thanks to many breeders — which remains today. My passion for an obsession with the show ring has evolved into an every so often pastime. Thirty-five years of constant coat stripping I leave to those who still think it's fun!

Brick Silver produced three champions and four top producers. Ch. Barclay Square Brickbat, a brother to Becky Sharp, sired nine champions, eight of them bearing Barbara Vohsen's Archway prefix. Two nonchampion Brick Silver daughters also carried on, Barclay Square Bid To Fame producing four champions for Zomerhof, and Barclay Square Bold Type, three at home.

Becky proved to be the most influential of the Brick Silver offspring. Her first breeding to Ch. Mankit's Xerxes produced an all-champion litter of four, including the Best in Show winner Ch. Barclay Square Be Grand, owned by Jeannette and Allen Stark. Be Grand sired three champions, but more importantly is the sire of Ted and Betty Bierman's foundation bitch, Ballwin Bonnie Bedelia, dam of five Ballwin champions in Texas, and Grace Church's Cinder von Kirche, CDX, dam of three Kazels champions in Missouri.

The Xerxes-Becky Sharp combination was repeated three more times, resulting in twelve champions. It was Becky's last champion daughter, Bugle Ann, that brought the Barclay Square breeding program forward. Their bloodlines are well dispersed throughout the States, as well as in the Rosehill dogs of Canada. They have had a broad influence on continental bloodlines through seventh-generation Barclay Square littermates.

In the late 1970s, longtime Swedish breeders Benny and Ulla Blid (Maximin) imported Barclay Square Maximin Midas and Minx, out of the Bugle Ann daughter Ch. Barclay Square Bugle Call Rag and sired by Ch. Sky Rocket's Uproar (35 Chs.). Their influence is recorded in the chapter covering England and the Scandinavian countries.

The broadest extension of the Xerxes line is found in Anne Lockney's Ruedesheim family in Oklahoma, where Xerxes lived out his retirement years. Two bitches from this family, Ruedesheim's Runzel and Ruedesheim's Splendor (5 Chs.), both Xerxes granddaughters, served as foundation for over four dozen Ruedesheim champions, eight with International titles.

Mrs. Lockney chose the Delegate and Diplomat branches for her particular blend. From the Delegate side she bred Splendor to Ch. Penlan Peter's Son (25 Chs.). Three champions emerged, including the good producing bitch Ch. Ruedesheim's Cameo (5 Chs.) and the influential sire Ch. Ruedesheim's Entrepreneur (16 Chs.), who claims four top producing sons: Ch. Ruedesheim's

Ch. Ruedesheim's Entrepreneur

Momentummm (11 Chs.), Ch. Ruedesheim's Landmark (7 Chs.), Ch. Ruedesheim's Encore of Wil-O-Be (5 Chs.), and Ch. Aachen Sling Shot (6 Chs.). Yet another top winner and producer, Ch. Tomei Super Star (30 Chs.), is out of Ch. Ruedesheim's Party Girl, a Splendor granddaughter.

Runzel, carrying two lines to Xerxes, was bred into the Diplomat branch, producing Ch. Ruedesheim's Free Spirit by Ch. Landmark's Masterpiece (32 Chs.). Spirit, in turn, produced Landmark and Momentummm.

Ch. Ruedesheim's Momentummm was clearly one of Ann's favorites. Brought out as a puppy in 1980, handled by Priscilla Wells, he completed his

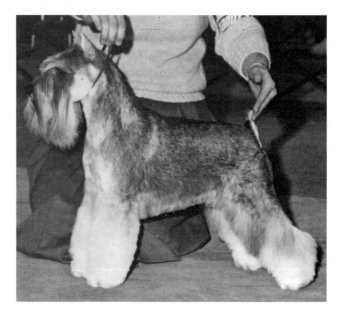

Ch. Ruedesheim's Momentummm

**Ch. Bark's
My Fair Lady**

championship in just six outings, including a Best of Breed from the classes at the Heart of America Specialty. He started his Specials career on the Florida circuit in January 1981, handled by Claudia Seaberg, and ended the year as the number two Schnauzer, with thirty-one Breed wins, including three more Specialty Bests.

That he would be instrumental in bringing the Ruedesheim family forward is best illustrated by the fact that he gave Ann the good producing bitch, Ch. Ruedesheim's Creme De La Creme (3 Chs.), that, when bred to Ch. Rampage's Waco Kid (24 Chs.), produced Ch. Bark's My Fair Lady, one of the breed's all-time top dams with eleven champions, all by Ch. Ruedesheim's Bonus (24 Chs.).

Bonus seemed to be the summation of the Ruedesheim breeding program, carrying half a dozen lines to Ch. Mankit's Xerxes through Ruedesheim homebreds. Bonus has further distinquished himself as the sire of five top producers, two sons — Ch. Ruedesheim's Advantage V Belgar (8 Chs.) and Ch. Ruedesheim's Capitalist (8 Chs.), and three daughters: Ch. Ruedesheim's I'm Scrumptous, Ch. Ruedesheim's I'm Stunning and Int. Am. Mex. Ch. Ruedesheim's Front Page. Scrumptous claims a top producing son Ch. Ruedesheim's Fortune Seeker II (5 Chs.) among her six champions. Page served as foundation for the Dynasty Schnauzers of Mildred and Duncan Shultz of Colorado, giving them four champions, including Ch. Dynasty's Title Page, Best of Breed at the 1992 A.M.S.C. Specialty at Montgomery County — from the classes! Stunning saw her first three finish in 1996.

My Fair Lady may best be remembered as the dam of the first bitch to ever achieve Top Schnauzer, which Ch. Ruedesheim's Precocious accomplished in 1989, handled by Carol Garmaker to a record of 54 Breed wins, including a Specialty. She also earned an all-breed Best in Show, four Group Firsts

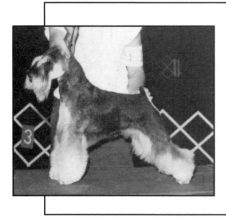

Ch. Hughcrest Harvey Wallbanger
Ch. Hughcrest Blue Beard
Ponosa Step Lightly
Ch. Wan-El's Wildfire
Ch. Mankit's Xerxes
Ch. Ruedesheim's Miss Mitzi
Pretty Pansy II
CH. RUEDESHEIM'S BONUS
Ch. Ruedesheim's Momentummm
Ch. Ruedesheim's Energizer
Ch. Repitition's Bonnie Belle
Andy And Tracy's Heidelberg (B/S)
Ch. Ruedesheim's Entrepeneur
Pepperoni Pizza
Mysterious Tuffi

and 28 additional placements — the best one-year record for a bitch to that date.

The Ruedesheim family has had an influence on all the color varieties, particularly through the host of black and silver descendants of Bonus. That the Ruedesheim dogs have found their way to virtually all sections of the country only adds to the impact this family has had on the breed. And, there are blacks, too, mainly through the Shegar breeding program of Gary and Sheila Prather of Kentucky. They began with the Bonus daughter Ruedesheim's Endowment SG, a Cameo granddaughter, giving them six champions, including Ch. Shegar's Bo-daious Ta-Ta, the top winning black bitch in both 1992 and '93. An Endowment granddaughter gave Shegar the leading black bitch for '94 in Ch. Shegar's Class Action.

Ch. Ruedesheim's I'm Precocious winning Best in Show at the Greater Emporia Kennel Club in May 1989 under Lorraine Masley, handled by Carol Garmaker.

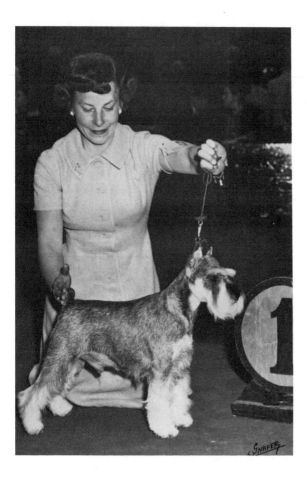

**Ch. Perci-Bee's
First Impression
with Marguerite
Wolfe.**

Returning to Tribute's most influential son, Ch. Dorem Favorite, we find that more than half of the top producing sires descending from Tribute carry lines to the Favorite son Ch. Perci-Bee's First Impression (15 Chs.). His handler, Marguerite Wolfe (Phil-Mar), remembered him with enthusiasm:

Perci-Bee was a small dog that did a lot of winning. He was bred and owned by Claire Shelley of Huntington, New York. Claire bought Ch. Phil-Mar Lady Be Good from me and bred her to Ch. Dorem Favorite, a gorgeous exaggerated dog. They produced Perci-Bee, at 131/4 inches, one of the greatest small terriers I have ever seen. He was perfectly balanced, with a long neck and beautiful head and expression. A showing fool, he actually asked for all his wins. He did not have the most desirable front. Because of his depth of chest and huge ribbing, his front legs were not closely placed. But could he move! He outshowed every terrier in the ring.

Of further note is the enviable show record that Perci-Bee made in his relatively short career in the ring. His record includes 53 Bests of Breed and 26 Group placements. He led the breed in 1956, won four Specialties in a day which saw many fine champions being shown, and was a Westminster breed winner.

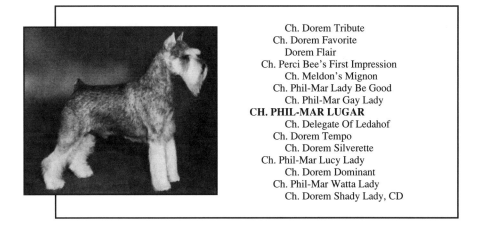

Ch. Dorem Tribute
Ch. Dorem Favorite
Dorem Flair
Ch. Perci Bee's First Impression
Ch. Meldon's Mignon
Ch. Phil-Mar Lady Be Good
Ch. Phil-Mar Gay Lady
CH. PHIL-MAR LUGAR
Ch. Delegate Of Ledahof
Ch. Dorem Tempo
Ch. Dorem Silverette
Ch. Phil-Mar Lucy Lady
Ch. Dorem Dominant
Ch. Phil-Mar Watta Lady
Ch. Dorem Shady Lady, CD

His early death at six years of age cut short the full measure of a remarkable and valuable sire.

Although Perci-Bee left four top producing sons, the lines from Ch. Dorem Vanguard (6 Chs.), Ch. Phil-Mar Emmett (9 Chs.) and Ch. Phil-Mar Thunderbolt (6 Chs.) have not progressed. Perci-Bee's son Ch. Phil-Mar Lugar (26 Chs.), however, has brought the line forward.

The CH. PHIL-MAR LUGAR line

Ch. Phil-Mar Lugar was unquestionably Phil-Mar's most successful homebred and his quality was well rewarded. The breed's leading winner in 1959-60, Lugar won an all-breed Best each year and retired with a record of 70 Bests of Breed, including two Specialties. In Group competition he was placed forty times, including a dozen Group Firsts. He was viewed positively by an ever-widening group of fanciers and used extensively. An impressive list of over forty top sires trace in direct tail-male lines to Lugar, the large majority through his son Ch. Mankit's Eager, that we have already discussed. The other line resulted from the six champions produced for Blythewood, including the outstanding sire Ch. Blythewood Main Gazebo (31 Chs.).

Joan Huber of the Blythewood Kennel in Pennsylvania, became involved with the Tribute branch early on in a breeding program which began in the early 1950s and has produced nearly 200 champions. It was yet another instance in which one good bitch started it all. Mrs. Huber recalled it as follows:

My first homebred, Ch. Blythewood Merry Melody was one of a litter of seven whelped on March 22, 1956, out of Minquas Blythe Spirit, CD and by Ch. Delfin Janus. She was my choice in the litter from the time she was born. Melody did well in the show ring, and her lovely, hard, steel-colored coat with her white furnishings and whiskers made her a crowd pleaser. Despite my novice, incompetent handling, she finished with three majors in stiff eastern competition. When I think back on those early shows now, I can count hundreds

**Ch. Blythewood
Merry Melody**

of mistakes I made in handling and grooming. I guess everyone's first show dog which is owner-handled suffers the same way. However, you can never again have the good feeling that comes with finishing your first dog.

Melody founded an extraordinary family, bred exclusively within the Tribute branch, first with three champion daughters by Favorite; three more, along with a son, by Lugar; and her eighth champion, a daughter, by Perci-Bee. Ch. Blythewood Sweet Talk (Favorite-Melody) was chosen to bring this family forward, and did so with remarkable success, producing seven champions, including Gazebo, who leaves three top producing sons: Ch. Blythewood Chief Bosun (11 Chs.), Ch. Blythewood His Majesty (11 Chs.) and Ch. Swinheim Salutation (6 Chs.).

Top dogs and top wins have been a tradition at Blythewood, starting with Ch. Blythewood Merry Maker (Favorite-Melody), one of the few bitches to win an AMSC Specialty, and Ch. Blythewood Chief Bosun (11 Chs.), the number one Schnauzer (Knight System) in 1966, after setting a record as a puppy, finishing at seven months of age, shown only seven times.

**Ch. Blythewood
Main Gazebo
with Joan Huber**

Joan has been a trendsetter in grooming and presentation, and there has always been a "Blythewood style," based on a clean, sharp look. When asked about her secrets, she replied:

There really are no deep secrets, as such. Knowing your breed inside and out is a must. This knowledge is supposed to allow you to decide what visual appearance the breed should have in every detail of conformation. Once you have a mental picture of what the breed should look like, trimming is done to achieve the ideal. I'm a perfectionist! I devote a lot of time to "detail," starting with the health and conditioning of the animal.

It is attention to detail that is of ultimate importance. A top groomer must have an eye for line and form, but the majority of breeders can achieve remarkable results if enough attention is given to basics, like the proper initial stripping, where attention is given to each animal's individual skeletal and muscular structure. I work hard toward clearly defining lines. I do not like a fuzzy look, with brows running into stop and side-lines. I like a "stylized" sharp look, neat in every detail.

101

A crusader on several levels, Joan had her way concerning one of the most important problems faced by Miniature Schnauzer breeders to this day. Her story bears repeating:

A college education aimed at a teaching career found me highly motivated in the area of biology in general, and genetics in particular. However, it was not until 1961 and my marriage to Bob Huber that my interest was specifically directed to "modes of inheritance" of genetic problems. Being married to a veterinarian who was an associate of Dr. Lionel Rubin, one of the top canine ophthalmologists in the country, brought me in direct contact with up-to-date theories concerning inherited defects. Bob and I initiated a test-breeding program with Dr. Rubin's help, and came to accept the hypothesis concerning the mode of inheritance of congenital juvenile cataracts (CJC). We found it followed a very definite pattern and was a simple autosomal recessive gene. We made blind-to-blind breedings and got all blind; we bred carrier-to-carrier and got the simple Mendelian percentages. For over a year, we sold no puppies with papers for breeding or show, because all were the results of test breeding.

As an "active" member of the AMSC board, I made a presentation on this medical problem. The results were "horrendous!" Word soon flashed across the nation, and back, that "all Blythewood dogs are blind!" But I got what I wanted. The board did agree to appoint a committee to look into health problems. A small beginning, but "a beginning."

Her efforts, along with those of many others, have reaped rewards beyond measure. The problem of CJC is in a position to be completely eradicated, as long as tested animals continue to dominate in current breeding programs.

As one of our leading professional handlers for over thirty years, Joan Huber has piloted several dogs to the number one spot — her own Ch. Blythewood Chief Bosun in 1966, Ch. Mutiny Uproar in 1970, and Homer and Isabelle Graf's Best in Show-winning Ch. Sky Rocket's Bound To Win in 1973. The number one spot for 1986 and '87 was also piloted by Joan, establishing all kinds of new records in the process. That Ch. Sibehil's Dark Shadows was black made his record all the more remarkable.

Joan's breeding program took a new tack when in 1973 she purchased Valharra Prize of Blythewood. As Joan tells it:

My mother and I lost my father on December 18, 1972. At this time their only dog, Ch. Blythewood Pageantry, was getting up in years, so I was looking for a new dog to comfort my mother and Page. I had long admired the beautiful dogs being bred by Dr. Harry and Enid Quick. One dog that was particularly magnificent was Ch. Valharra's Dionysos, and one of his most outstanding sons was Harry's favorite house dog, Ch. Valharra's Studley Dudley.

I found out from the Quicks that the breeding which produced Studley had been repeated, and that there were three females. They allowed me to visit their kennel and have pick of those bitches. Her official name became Valharra Prize of Blythewood, and what a prize she proved to be. Not only was she a

**Ch. Blythewood
National Acclaim
with Joan Huber**

fabulous friend and companion for my mother, but also became one of the top producing bitches of all time. Sym was a strong bitch of excellent bone and substance, about 13 3/4 inches at the shoulder, and had gobs of white furnishings and a good jacket. She was never shown but remained mother's constant companion for nearly 16 years.

Mother loves to raise puppies for me, and whelped all of Sym's litters. The first four tight linebreedings produced some good pups, but nothing spectacular. In October 1977, when Sym was five years of age, mother brought her to the kennel for breeding. Over the years, she had seen so many excellent pups by Ch. Blythewood National Anthem, and suggested using him, even though the pedigree was not tight. They did complement each other structurally, and that first litter was incredible.

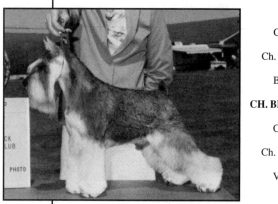

Ch. Cobby Land Rising Son
Ch. Eclipse Shadow of the Son (B/S)
Cobby Land T.M. Georgie Girl
Ch. Blythewood My Best Shot
Ch. Sky Rocket's Uproar
Blythewood Glorious Sky
Blythewood Glory Bound
CH. BLYTHEWOOD SHOOTING SPARKS
Ch. Sky Rocket's Bound To Win
Ch. Blythewood National Anthem
Blythewood Symphony
Ch. Blythewood She's A Fox
Ch. Valharra's Dionysos
Valharra Prize of Blythewood
Valharra's Valid Victory

From that litter of five, two dogs and two bitches were shown and finished. The star was clearly Ch. Blythewood National Acclaim (32 Chs.). He began his show career at ten months of age by being shown at two of the shows on the Montgomery Country weekend, winning 5 points at Devon, then going on to win Best in Sweepstakes under Carol Parker (Skyline) and Best of Breed under Anne Clark, over one of the largest entries in AMSC history. The next year he embarked on his specials career, and was always a dog to be reckoned with. He broke the breed record at that time for winning Specialties, seventeen in all, and was Best in Show in March 1979, defeating an entry of 2,271 dogs at the Kennel Club of Northern New Jersey.

Because of this fabulous litter, Valharra Prize of Blythewood was bred four more times to Anthem, and every time produced some top ones. There would be eleven champions in all, including Am. and Can. Ch. Blythewood National Newsman, Canada's all-time top sire.

Acclaim would enjoy considerable success as a producer, with a top producing son, Ch. Jilmar's Allstar (19 Chs.), and several daughters. Perhaps the most interesting among the latter is the Acclaim daughter Ch. Blythewood Stand Up And Cheer, who produced five champions from breedings to Acclaim's brother, Newsman. The same pattern of success was followed with Wade, Brian and Patricia Bogart's Acclaim daughter, Ch. Sumerwynd's Standing Ovation (5 Chs.), who produced Ch. Sumerwynd's Still Sizzlin (6 Chs.) when bred to Newsman.

Joan has had the pleasure of showing three Blythewoods to Best in Show: Ch. Blythewood His Majesty, Ch. Blythewood National Acclaim and Ch. Blythewood Shooting Sparks, the latter her most successful homebred sire, with 53 champion get, including the good producing sires, Ch. Blythewood Ewok Von Der Stars (15 Chs.), who carries three lines to Anthem, and Ch. Blythewood Storm Damage (5 Chs.).

Blythewood has been a breeding kennel for over four decades and is a constant supplier of first-class foundation stock throughout the world.

Henrietta Tare in New Jersey has bred over two dozen champions based on one bitch— Blythewood Shady Lady. She produced the first five Tare champions, four by Ch. Blythewood Ricochet of LaMay (22 Chs.). Foremost among them was Ch. Tare Misty Morning, serving as foundation for Barbara Mazgiel's Contempras, giving her four champions. This family continues forward through Misty's son, Ch. Contempra Foolish Pleasure (7 Chs.), and daughter, Ch. Contempra Belle Starr.

**Ch. Markworth Lovers Lane
with Joan Huber**

The latter, owned by Martin Marks of New York, gave him the good producer Markworth Contempra Collage (4 Chs.), dam of Best in Show-winning Ch. Markworth Lovers Lane. Martin's first Miniature Schnauzer became Ch. Geelong Little Mister in 1970. Eighteen champions later came the recordsetting Lovers Lane. In 1985, shown on three coats, she won 44 Bests of Breed, including two Specialties, tabulating more Knight points in one year than any bitch to that date. Her record also included a Best in Show, four Group Firsts, and 22 additional placements. Thereafter, Markworth breeding focused totally on the Ruffian branch. Lane, a Target daughter, gave him two champions in her only litter, bred to her half brother Ch. Sathgate Breakaway (26 Chs.). All Markworth champions since descend from her son Ch. Markworth Lovers Legacy.

Three other Tare bitches tracing to Shady Lady have become top producers: Tare Bruiser Barbie (3 Chs.), Ch. Tare Twenty-Four Karat (3 Chs.) and Tare-Royalcourt Happy Hooker (3 Chs.), the latter as foundation for the on-going breeding program of Gloria Lewis's Royalcourts, first in New Jersey and currently in Florida.

Homer and Isabel Graf (Reflections) round out the group in New Jersey who have based breeding programs on Blythewood stock. Ch. Blythewood Maid Marion (3 Chs.), a daughter of Ch. Mankit's Adam, was their foundation bitch, and two top producing bitches have since emerged. Ch. Reflections Refreshin' Image (3 Chs.) numbers among her get Ch. Reflections Lively Image (7 Chs.),

**Ch. St. Roque's U Take My Breath Away
with Bill Burns**

who brought new life into the Travelmors.

Blythewood lines were brought forward in the West by Jean Heath (Black Watch), with Blythewood Morning Star (6 Chs.), and by Earl and Marietta Hungerford (Hanalea). Three generations later, Hanalea's Pele's Pride (4 Chs.) would provide Jay and Janet Balch (Island) with a fine beginning. Dan Durigan (Fairwynd) started his breeding program with a Pride granddaughter, Island Summer Wind, and finished her third champion in 1995.

Ch. Blythewood Honey Bun (Perci-Bee-Melody) served as foundation for the Bon-Ell family developed in California by Jack and Dori Prosen. Honey Bun is best remembered as the great-granddam of Ch. Landmark's Masterpiece (32 Chs.).

A double Anthem grandson from Blythewood went to the already established breeding partnership of Stephe Marquart and Bill Burns (St. Roque) in California. Stephe started in obedience in 1970, and gained two CDX and one UD title on her first three Miniature Schnauzers. They finished Ch. Blythewood Acclaim T'St. Roque in 1982, and when bred to his granddaughter, St. Roque's Penny Lover, got their best winning and producing bitch to date, Ch. St. Roque's U Take My Breath Away, whose fourth champion finished in 1995.

Perhaps the most prolific family based on Blythewood lines was developed in Pennsylvania by John Constantine (Adamis). His foundation bitch was the Acclaim daughter Blythewood Wild 'N

Ch. Adamis First Edition

**Ch. Adamis Cocked And Loaded
with John Constantine**

Wicked, giving him a top producer in her first litter, bred to Ch. Irrenhaus Stamp of Approval (9 Chs.). Staying with Irrenhaus studs from the Ruffian branch, Ch. Adamis First Edition (4 Chs.) includes among her get another generation of top producers in Ch. Adamis Class Act, dam of three champions, plus the good producer, Adamis Femme Fatale (3 Chs.). Ch. Adamis First Class, a sister to Class Act, gave John his best producing bitch, Adamis Fahrvergnugen, dam of seven champions. One of these, Ch. Adamis Cocked And Loaded, needed only eight shows to finish, while still a puppy, always breeder-owner handled. He had a great first year at stud, before being exported to Taiwan. He produced nine champions in 1995, including Ch. Adamis Annie Oakley, a Best in Show winner, owner-handled by Carla Nickerson (NickNack), who purchased her as a puppy. Over two dozen Adamis champions have been made up in less than a decade.

Blythewood lines have had a dramatic effect on activities north of the border, most importantly in British Columbia at Annfield, and in Ontario at Cherrylane. Theirs and other efforts are chronicled in the chapter on Canadian progress.

8
The
Ch. Diplomat of Ledahof
Branch

**Ch. Diplomat
of Ledahof**

SECOND RANKED among DISPLAY's top producing sons, Ch. Diplomat of Ledahof was the sire of 29 champions, the last of them whelped in 1956. Diplomat was undoubtedly a "favorite son" at Ledahof, where he enjoyed over fourteen years as companion to his breeder, Leda Martin, and her daughter Joan Dalton. He was the culmination of a breeding program that was launched in the late 1920s and highlighted by the "D Litter," containing Chs. Diplomat, Delegate, Destiny and Debutante of Ledahof.

Diplomat served notice as a prepotent sire early on, when linebred to Mrs. Evashwick's great foundation bitch, Ch. Sorceress of Ledahof (12 Chs.). The initial breeding produced four champion sons, one of which died at the age of two, while the others became top producers: Ch. Marwyck Scenery Road (9 Chs.), Ch. Marwyck Brush Cliff (7 Chs.) and Ch. Marwyck Penn Hurst (5 Chs.). Contemporary lines to this breeding trace principally through the Brush Cliff daughter, Doman Mehitabel, CDX, who is behind all the Allaruth dogs.

Lines to Scenery Road and his top producing son, Ch. Abingdon's Applause, CD (6 Chs.) can be found in current show stock carrying Brittanhof and Helarry breeding.

Bred back to Diplomat, Sorceress produced the S.D. Comet, Cupid, Blitzen trio of champions, with Ch. Marwyck S.D. Comet by far the most important. As the dam of Ch. Marwyck Pitt-Penn Pirate (44 Chs.), her tail-male influence is considerable.

Mrs. Slattery (Marienhof) also used Diplomat early on in his stud career, getting his top producing namesake, Ch. Diplomat of Marienhof (11 Chs.), from which came in successive generations virtually all the Handful champions bred by Gene Simmonds. Miss Simmonds has neatly condensed the "Handful Story" as follows:

In 1951 my last two house pets and stud dogs had passed away, Ch. Hosea of Marienhof, the last uncropped champion, age 17, and Am. Can. Ch. Handful of Marienhof, age 16. I had two new puppy males who became Ch. Handful's Me Too of Marienhof and Ch. Diplomat of Marienhof, but I needed a bitch to start Handful again.

Ch. Marwyck S.D. Comet

After a talk with Shirley Angus of Benrook, I was to obtain the choice of two bitches, Benrook Bellona and Benrook Bona, from a litter of six by CH. DOREM DISPLAY out of Ch. Meldon's Manana, whelped April 16, 1950. The pair, along with the male pups, were to be exhibited at the Specialty in New York and Westminster, where I was to make my selection. Seeing all six in a playpen, one quick look separated the two bitches from their four brothers, and an even

Ch. Diplomat of Marienhof surrounded by his first two champion daughters Ch. Handful's Ruddy Duck and Ch. Handful's Teal.

40 Sires of 5 or more A.K.C. Champions
trace in direct tail-male lines to
CH. DIPLOMAT OF LEDAHOF

*Sires that are in *italic* produced fewer than 5 Champions, *Ch. Mutiny Master Spy* (4), *Ch. Glory's Eager Beaver* (4) and *Ch. Blythewood Winsome Lad* (4) missing the mark by one.

A1 Ch. Marwyck Scenery Road (9)
    B1 Ch. Applause of Abingdon, CD (6)
A2 Ch. Marwyck Brush Cliff (7)
A3 Ch. Marwyck Penn Hurst (5)
A4 Ch. Diplomat of Marienhof (11)
    B2 Ch. Handful's Bantam (10)
    B3 *Ch. Handful's Blue-Winged Teal**
        C1 Ch. Handful's Pop Up (8)
A5 Ch. Asset of Ledahof (10)
    B4 Ch. Marwyck Pitt-Penn Pirate (44)
        C2 Ch. Fancway's Pirate Jr. of LaMay (25)
            D1 Ch. Caradin Fancy That (9)
            D2 Ch. Blythewood Ricochet of LaMay (22)
                E1 Ch. Boomerang of Marienhof (10)
                    F1 Ch. Allaruth's Daniel (8)
                        G1 Ch. Valharra's Dionysos (28)
                            H1 Ch. Valharra's Big Sir (5)
                            H2 *Ch. Valharra's Studley Dudley**
                                I1 *Ch. Zomerhof's Archipelago**
                                    J1 Ch. Zomerhof's Limited Edition (20)
                    F2 *Allaruth's Hang-Up**
                        G2 Ch. Allaruth's Mama's Boy (5)
                        H3 Ch. Country Squire Soot N Cinder (5)
        C3 *Ch. Allaruth's Joshua**
            D3 Ch. Allaruth's Jericho (7)

A6 Ch. Delfin Janus (34)
  B5 Ch. Windy Hill Defiance (12)
  B6 Ch. Mutiny I'm Grumpy Too (17)
    C4 *Ch. Mutiny Master Spy**
      D4 Ch. Landmark's Masterpiece (32)
        E2 Ch. Skibo's Fancy Clancy (14)
          F3 Ch. Far Hills Midnight Angel (5)
          F4 *Ch. Glory's Eager Beaver**
            G3 Ch. Sercatep's Strut N Proud [B/S] (14)
              H4 Ch. Sycamore Sojourner [B/S] (9)
                I2 Ch. Sercatep's Nite Flite [B/S] (8)
          F5 *Ch. B'Adams Ragtime Cowboy Joe**
            G4 *B'Adams Buckeye Buckeroo**
              H5 Ch. Jacqueminot Joint Venture, CD (5)
        E3 Ch. Lanmark's Playboy (10)
          F6 Ch. Playboy's Block Buster (22)
            G5 Ch. Hi-Charge of Hansenhaus (11)
            G6 Ch. Baws Strait Shot of Hansenhaus (5)
          F7 Ch. Playboy's Special Edition (7)
        E4 *Ch. Blythewood Winsome Lad**
          F8 *Ch. Cobby Land Rising Son**
            G7 Ch. Eclipse Shadow Of The Son [B/S] (5)
              H6 Ch. Sycamore Solar Eclipse [B/S] (9)
              H7 *Ch. Blythewood My Best Shot**
                I3 Ch. Blythewood Shooting Sparks (53)
                J2 Ch. Blythewood Ewok Von Der Stars (15)
        E5 *Ch. Walters' Irish Coffee**
          F9 *Walters' Dapper Dan**
            G8 Ch. Walters' Tradewinds (5)

Ch. Sercatep's Nite Flite   **Ch. Blythewood Ewok Von Der Stars**

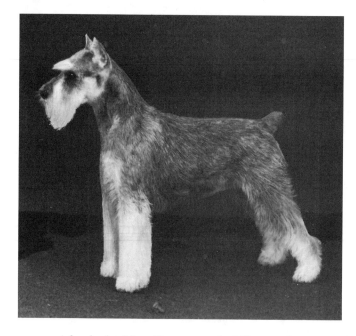

**Ch. Benrook
Bona**

quicker look told me Bona was mine! She was far more Schnauzery, lower and cobbier than her sister, with a quality head, beautiful neck and lay-back of shoulder, a good spring of rib and enough loin to allow perfect movement, front and rear. Yes, I definitely wanted Bona.

Due to illness and emergencies, Bona was forced to wait until May to come to Handful. She loved to show and finished easily. It was not possible to start breeding her until May 1952. Since she was always guarded by Me Too and Diplomat, neither dared to breed her. Finally, we took all three into the vets, tried both, and with no luck, drove them back to Handful, threw all three over the garden fence, and by the time we went through the house, Bona and Me Too were tied, while Diplomat sat on the terrace looking very sad and lonely.

The first litter contained two males, never shown or bred, and four bitches. All four bitches were shown, and Chs. Handful's Ruddy Duck and Teal finished. The other two, nearly finished, were bred and produced champions.

**Ch. Handful's
Bantam**

Top wins, top pups for the next year or so finally made it necessary to thin out a bit. The first to go were Ch. Handful's Bantam and Ch. Handful's Wren, to California, and sister, Ch. Handful's Quail, to Florida, starting those regions on their way. The long-standing Handful policy began at this point. When a new region wanted a Handful Schnauzer, it meant that they must take the best we had to be their house pet, their show dog and their start in producing the best possible in their area.

The magic that was Handful occurred in the 1950s, with twenty-five homebred champions emerging in short order. Several families were developed from sons and daughters of the Diplomat-Bona cross. Their best producing son, Ch. Handful's Bantam (10 Chs.), exerted his influence on the West Coast, primarily as the maternal grandsire of Ch. Windy Hill Defiance (12 Chs.). The most significant of the Diplomat-Bona offspring turned out to be the nonchampion sisters, Handful's Snow Flurry and Snow Flake. Both went to the Midwest, Snow Flurry to found Trayhom and Snow Flake for Ursafell.

Snow Flake, linebred within the Diplomat branch, produced Ursafell Niblet. Inbred to her sire, Ursafell Sandpiper, Niblet produced Miss Little Guys, the matriarchal head of a tail-male line of current top producers second to none. Through her only champion son, Ch. Sky Rocket's First Stage (8 Chs.), has emerged no fewer than four dozen more top producers (see RUFFIAN branch).

Snow Flurry, as the foundation for Twylla and Wayne Miller's Trayhom Kennel, produced three champion sons, each an outstanding winner and producer. Twice bred into the Diplomat branch, she produced Ch. Trayhom Talleyrand (by Ch. Handful's Pop Up) and Ch. Trayhom Tatters (by Pirate). Her most important breeding, into the Tribute branch, produced Ch. Trayhom Tramp-A-Bout.

The most profound influence Diplomat would have on the breed was through his sons, Ch. Asset of Ledahof (10 Chs.) and Ch. Delfin Janus (34 Chs.). Asset, out of the Diplomat daughter Annabelle of Ledahof (3 Chs.), enjoyed considerable success as a show dog in the early 1950s under the ownership of Dorothy and Allen Hauck of Ohio, winning several Groups. He proved quite an asset as a sire. Among his ten champion get was the leading sire of the 1960s and 1970s, the great Pirate, from which trace in tail-male line eleven more top-producing sires.

Ch. Asset of Ledahof

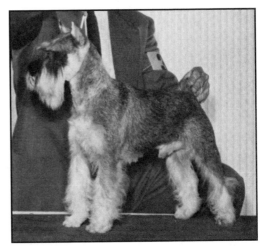

CH. DOREM DISPLAY
Ch. Diplomat of Ledahof
Ch. Enchantress
Ch. Asset of Ledahof
Ch. Diplomat of Ledahof
Annabelle of Ledahof
Stardust of Ledahof
CH. MARWYCK PITT-PENN PIRATE
CH. DOREM DISPLAY
Ch. Diplomat of Ledahof
Ch. Enchantress
Ch. Marwyck S.D. Comet
Ledahof Sentry
Ch. Sorceress of Ledahof
Ch. Enchantress

The CH. MARWYCK PITT-PENN PIRATE line

The linebreeding wisdom instilled by her mentor Leda Martin was brought to fruition in 1954 by Marion Evashwick. On February 15th that year was born the record-setting cornerstone sire, Am. Can. and Mex. Ch. Marwyck Pitt-Penn Pirate (44 Chs.). His breeding offers a lesson in successful mixing and matching based on a single individual—Ch. Enchantress (8 Chs.). Pirate is intensely line-bred to the Enchantress son Diplomat, who was not only his double grandsire, but one of his paternal great-grandsires. A fourth line to Enchantress in this extremely tight pedigree comes through Pirate's maternal granddam, the Enchantress daughter Sorceress.

Pirate was started on his show career by Mrs. Evashwick, achieving his first big win at the tender age of seven months—Best of Breed from the puppy class at the Michigan Specialty. He finished at eleven months with four majors, after which he was sold to Dr. Rod King. Eventually Jean and Glenn Fancy (Fancway) of California acquired half ownership of Pirate, showing him throughout the West, as well as in Mexico and Canada, earning both additional titles. His show career spanned five years, during which he won 75 Bests of Breed, his last at six years of age. In addition, he earned 38 Group placements, ten of them firsts, and was Best in Show at the Sequoia Kennel Club's first all-breed show.

At some point Pirate became solely owned by the Fancys and lived the last eight years of his life as their cherished house pet and the ardent companion to their two young sons and baby daughter. I was introduced to Pirate in their home in 1962. At eight years of age he was still in his prime, looking very competitive. He was obviously intelligent and possessed extraordinary dignity and serenity, but was not without this breed's typical sense of humor. As to type, Pirate was racy in outline, well up on leg, but without exaggeration. He had a neat head with no suggestion of coarseness, small eyes and well-set ears. Only moderately angulated at both ends, his movement, coming and going, was good.

Ch. Fancway's Pirate Jr. of La May

Given every advantage, Pirate in short order became the leading producer throughout the early 1960s. By 1966 he had passed the longtime record established by DISPLAY, and before his death, September 23, 1965, had produced 44 champions, plus others that gained titles in Canada and Mexico.

It was very late in Pirate's stud career when he produced his most important son. Aptly named, Am. Can. and Mex. Ch. Fancway's Pirate Jr. of LaMay became his forty-second champion as well as his top winning and producing offspring. Bred by Virginia LaMay of Reno, Nevada, Pirate Jr. went to the Fancys as a four-month-old puppy and immediately began to follow the pattern established by his sire. Pirate Jr. scored his first important win at seven months at the Chicago Specialty in April 1965, winning the Sweepstakes under Helen Wiedenbeck (Helarry) and going Reserve to the ultimate Best of Breed winner in the regular classes under Marguerite Wolff (Phil-Mar). The next day he won his first five points. With all but one win from puppy class, his title quest included six Bests of Breed and five Group placements.

Pirate Jr. enjoyed continued success as a yearling, returning to the Chicago Specialty in 1966 to go Best of Breed under Leda Martin (Ledahof), and added another Specialty Best in Denver under yet another breed pioneer, Gene Simmonds (Handful). He continued to win well for the next two years, topping the AMSC Regional Specialty in 1967 and the Southern California Specialty in 1968. Pirate Jr. also went north and south of the borders to gain titles in Canada and Mexico. He was eventually sold to Jane and Charles Post (Postillion) for whom he sired three champions, including their Best in Show winner, Ch. Postillion's Riviera Pirate.

The Fancys described Pirate Jr. in these words:

Beautifully balanced Schnauzer type, with a hard coat and very short back. He moves to perfection and shows like a terrier should. Perhaps his best feature is his well-angulated rear, producing that strong driving movement so essential in the breed. He is truly a great dog in a small package, being only 12 3/4 inches tall.

Although he may not have achieved in numbers the record of his famous sire, Pirate Jr. left an indelible mark of his own with four top producers, two sons and two daughters, including the breed's all-time top dam, Ch. Faerwynd of Arador (16 Chs.).

Ch. Blythewood Ricochet of La May

Virginia LaMay, who bred Pirate Jr., also bred his first champion and best producing son, Ch. Blythewood Ricochet of LaMay. Sold as a puppy to Joan Huber (Blythewood), Ricochet finished in just seven days on the 1967 Florida circuit, earning two five-point majors, one of these with Best of Breed. Shown sparingly as a yearling champion, his wins included the New York Specialty, and he returned to Florida the next year to dominate the circuit, including Best of Breed at the South Florida Specialty.

Bred primarily to eastern bitches, Ricochet sired 22 champions, including eight at Blythewood. Among his get are three top producers — a son, Ch. Boomerang of Marienhof (10 Chs.), owned by Ruth Ziegler (Allaruth), and two daughters. The Ricochet daughter Tare-Royalcourt Happy Hooker (3 Chs.) served

Ch. Jilmar's Allstar

as foundation for Gloria Lewis (Royalcourt) now in Florida. The Ricochet daughter Ch. Tare Misty Morning served as foundation for Barbara Mazgiel (Contempra), giving her four champions, including the good producing son, Ch. Contempra Foolish Pleasure (7 Chs.).

Lisa Grames, formerly of Florida and now in Massachusetts, has based her Jilmar breeding program on the Diplomat Branch, starting with a Dionysos daughter, Gough's Silver Shining Star. Her only litter was sired by Ricochet, getting Lisa's first homebred champion from him, as well as Jilmar's Star Image. Bred to Ch. Moore's Max Derkleiner, Image produced two bitches, both retained, and the dams of Jilmar's next generation of champions. Ch. Jilmar's Stardust produced two champions, while her sister Jilmar's Starlet produced four, including two top producing sons. Most noteworthy is Starlet's son Ch. Jilmar's Allstar (19 Chs.), by Ch. Blythewood National Acclaim (32 Chs.). He became the youngest male to achieve an AKC title, finishing on the day he turned seven months. In 1981 he was number five Knight System, with 23 BOB and two Group Firsts. The Allstar son Ch. Jilmar's Night Moves (7 Chs.) carries forward this line of top producers.The other good producing Starlet son was Ch. Jilmar's Pulsar (9 Chs.), who sired Ch. Jilmar's Barbarella, dam of three champions in one litter, including Night Moves. Jilmar has averaged a champion each year since 1975, most owner-handled.

Ch. Jilmar's Night Moves with Lisa Grames

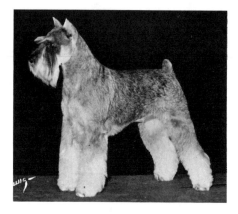

Ch. Fancway's Vampira

In addition to a strong tail-male line of top producers based on Ch. Marwyck Pitt-Penn Pirate, several important families were founded on Jean and Glenn Fancy's limited breeding program throughout the 1960s. Seldom housing more than three or four adults, through judicious placement of homebreds and occasional stud puppies, over three dozen Fancway champions were produced, all tightly linebred to Pirate.

The most significant litter bred by the Fancys was whelped in May 1964 and carried five lines to Pirate. From it came the top producing sisters Ch. Fancway's Vampira (6 Chs.) and Ch. Fancway's Voodoo Doll (3 Chs.), the former foundation for Margaret Haley's Aradors and the latter for Carole Hansen's Hansenhaus Kennel, both in the Los Angeles area.

The importance of starting with a good bitch is clearly illustrated in both cases. Mrs. Haley waited three years to get Vampira, and Mrs. Hansen secured Voodoo Doll as a proven producer.

Like so many successful breeders, Mrs. Haley's first experience with Miniature Schnauzers was an oversized "pet shop" male. What he lacked in type he made up for in brains, earning two obedience degrees and serving as Margaret's introduction to the Southern California Club.

Mrs. Haley writes about what followed:

I decided I wanted to get a puppy bitch and try to do the whole "show bit" myself. As luck would have it, it was Jean Fancy that I contacted, and she said if I would stick with her, she would see that I got a good one. It took almost three years to get Vampira. Jean eventually had two litters and let me have my pick of the bitches. I brought Vampira home when she was nine weeks old. Jean kept Voodoo Doll.

Vampira was a good-sized bitch—13 1/2 inches, well balanced, good body, solid

Ch. Faerwynd of Arador

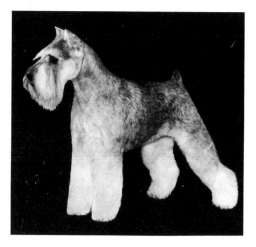

topline, beautiful shoulders and front, lovely, dark, hard coat, and effortless movement. She needed a stronger rear, more eyefill, smaller eye and more furnishings.

Vampira was entirely owner-conditioned and shown and became the first bitch to win a California Terrier Group. Her six champion offspring were a result of tight linebreeding within the Diplomat branch and include a top producing son, Ch. Gandalf of Arador (5 Chs.), by Ch. Orbit's Time Traveler (5 Chs.). Mrs. Haley explained her choice of studs:

Ch. Gandalf of Arador

I linebred her, trying to keep what I liked of Pirate, while trying to improve her faults. Pirate Jr. added bone, hindquarters and furnishings, Boomerang gave me beautiful head and eye, Time Traveler ideal outline and super temperament.

Had Vampira produced only one litter, her importance would have been assured, as the Pirate Jr. daughter Ch. Faerwynd of Arador claims the title as the breed's all-time top producing dam. Faerwynd produced two litters at Arador resulting in six champions, and then she was acquired by Enid Quick in Illinois, founding her Valharra family.

Mrs. Quick used her Ch. Allaruth's Daniel (8 Chs.) for Faerwynd's first Valharra litter and hit the jackpot! Ch. Valharra's Dionysos was a standout puppy, the first to top both AMSC Sweepstakes, first at Montgomery County and then in New York. Dionysos enjoyed two full years of showing, handled professionally by Robert Condon. His record included a Best in Show, six

Ch. Laddin of Arador
(Gandalf - Faerwynd)
with Margaret Haley

**Ch. Valharra's Dionysos
with Robert Condon**

Specialty Bests, eight Group Firsts and 23 additional placements.

His accomplishments as a sire are equally noteworthy with 28 champions, the large majority bred at Valharra. Although Dionysos did leave one top producing son, Ch. Valharra's Big Sir (5 Chs.), it was through Big Sir's halfbrother Ch. Valharra's Studley Dudley, and his son Ch. Zomerhof's Archipelago, that this tail-male line traces ten generations to the present in the form of Ch. Zomerhof's Limited Edition (20 Chs.).

The line of descent from Dionysos is brought forward several generations, principally through daughters. His best producing daughter, Valharra Prize of Blythewood, is the dam of eleven Blythewood champions bred by Joan Huber. Valharra's Victoria, by Dionysos out of a Daniel daughter, is the dam of six Paxon champions bred by Aileen and Richard Santo of New York. Paxon, using Valharra stock, has bred over a dozen champions, including two top producing Victoria sons, Ch. Paxon's Re-Play (7 Chs.) and Ch. Paxon's Magic Factor (5 Chs.). For Valharra, Dionysos sired Ch. Valharra's Dubarry, who gave Enid three champions sired by three different Valharra studs.

After a second Daniel litter, which produced two more champions, Enid decided on outcross breedings for Faerwynd, using her Ch. Moore's Max Derkleiner (7 Chs.) twice and Ch. Penlan Paperboy (44 Chs.) once. From the first Max litter, three finished and another had thirteen points—all were males. The first to finish was Ch. Valharra's Max Factor, winning three Sweepstakes and a Group as a puppy. His untimely death as a yearling was a great blow. His brother Ch. Valharra's Max Pax followed through with equally impressive wins, including Best in Sweepstakes at AMSC Montgomery County as well as at the Chicago Specialty. He finished with three five-pointers, two earned at AMSC and Southern California Specialties. Max Pax also was short-lived but did sire seven champions, including Magic Factor.

Faerwynd's litter by Paperboy also had three male champions, most notably Ch. Valharra's Prize of Penlan (8 Chs.). Her final litter, by Max, produced a single bitch puppy, Ch. Valharra's Melba Moore, CD (3 Chs.).

Although the breeding program at Valharra has tapered off, over forty

Ch. Valharra's Extra is Best of Breed at the 1977 Chicago Specialty under Richard Hensel, handled by Robert Condon.

champions were produced in less than a decade. Perhaps their crowning achievement was Best in Show and multiple Specialty winning Ch. Valharra's Extra, an outstanding dog on all counts. Extra is the sire of 12 champions, including three top producing sons: Ch. Valharra's Double Extra (12 Chs.), Ch. Sunshine Sounder (11 Chs.) and Ch. Valharra's Extra Allaruth (7 Chs.), the latter, number one (tie) Miniature Schnauzer of 1982 (Knight System). Each of

Ch. Valharra's Extra Allaruth

**Ch. Playboy's Talk of the Town
with Carole Hansen**

the Extra sons has carried this top producing heritage another generation.

At the February 1985 Southern California Specialty, Ch. Valharra's Double Extra came from the veterans class to win Best of Breed at seven years of age. Like his sire, he is full of virtues, and his condition was a credit to owners Violet and Robert Baws. Double Extra has a top producing daughter in Ch. Skyline's Everlasting (5 Chs.), but it is through the Double Extra son, Ch. Valharra's Jaxson (6 Chs.), that we find the longest extension of the Arador-Valharra family in the littermates Ch. Fannon of Arador and Ch. Faro of Arador (7 Chs.). They carry lines to Vampira in all quarters of their pedigree, three descending from Faerwynd.

Vampira's litter sister Ch. Fancway's Voodoo Doll had already produced Ch. Caradin Fancy That (9 Chs.) before she was acquired by Carole Hansen in 1969. She took a slightly different path in her choice of studs for Voodoo Doll, going into the Ch. Delfin Janus line from the Diplomat branch, using her Masterpiece son, Ch. Lanmark's Playboy (10 Chs.), who had done some top-class winning including Specialty Bests. This breeding gave her the two good producing bitches Ch. Playboy's Talk of the Town (3 Chs.) and Ch. Playboy's Shady Lady.

The most successful sires at Hansenhaus carry no lines to Voodoo Doll. Playboy and his two top producing sons, Ch. Playboy's Block Buster (22 Chs.) and Ch. Playboy's Special Edition (7 Chs.), were selected as the outcrosses for her descendants. They will be considered further, as a part of the Janus line.

Ch. Lanmark's Playboy

Playboy is behind virtually all the Hansenhaus Schnauzers, half of his champion get being their top producers. The most notable, Ch. Love-A-Lot of Hansenhaus (6 Chs.), carries three lines to Playboy and is the dam of the good producer Ch. Hi 'N' Mighty of Hansenhaus (6 Chs.), foundation sire for Bonnie Warrell's Belgar family in Southern California. Bonnie also purchased the Hi 'N' Mighty daughter Ch. Belgar's Hi Heaven of Hansenhaus, from which several generations of Belgar champions have emerged.

Block Buster gave Carole Ch. Glory Be of Hansenhaus, dam of five champions, including a good producing son, Ch. JR Boomer of Hansenhaus (5 Chs.). Boomer enjoyed extraordinary success as a show dog, earning eleven Specialty Bests

**Ch. Playboy's Block Buster
with Ric Chashoudian**

over a four year period. He had the distinction of winning Best of Breed at the AMSC's first midwest Specialty in 1986, and he did it at five years of age. Boomer, as the sire of Ch. Tejas New Years Eve, brought this family to Texas, giving Connally and Bolivia Powell (Tejas) four champions. Block Buster also sired Carole's Ch. Hundred Proof of Hansenhaus, out of a Boomer

**Ch. JR Boomer
of Hansenhaus**

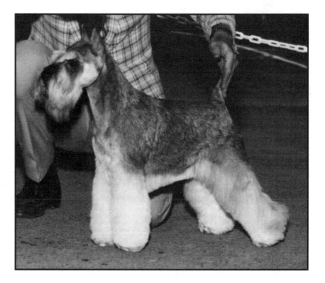

daughter, and he helped bring this family forward as the sire of her most recent top producer, Ch. Touch of Class Hansenhaus, dam of four champions to date. During the last 25 years, Hansenhaus has finished over fifty champions, thirty-two of them homebred.

Hansenhaus has always been a cooperative effort. Voodoo Doll's two champion daughters have champion descendants bearing several prefixes. You will find Shady Lady behind champions currently being bred by Belgar and St. Roque. Talk of the Town is behind champions being bred by Belgar, B-Majer, Kelvercrest and Hi-Crest.

Many Hawaiian-bred champions carry lines to Talk of the Town principally through her son Ch. Hi-Charge of Hansenhaus (11 Chs.), co-owned with Arnold Hirahara (Hi-Crest). Hi-Charge, with ten Bests in Show, is the record holder in this department and was among Hawaii's top winning dogs of all breeds, before being exported in 1985 to Australia, where he lived out his retirement years with Marelyn Woodhouse (Schonhardt).

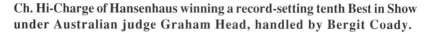

Ch. Hi-Charge of Hansenhaus winning a record-setting tenth Best in Show under Australian judge Graham Head, handled by Bergit Coady.

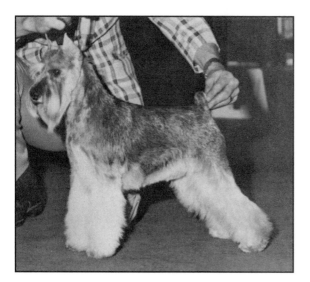

**Ch. B-Majer Bolero
v. Kelvercrest**

Hi Charge left his mark on the mainland through his daughter, Ch. B-Majer Bolero v. Kelvercrest, dam of five champions shared by Peggie Blakley (B-Majer) and Vera Potiker (Kelvercrest). Bolero is one of four champions out of B-Majer Mazurka, a Block Buster daughter. Four of Bolero's champions were sired by Ch. Regency's Right On Target (78 Chs.) and include a good producing son, Ch. B-Majer King Of Swing (6 Chs.), who, in turn, gave the Blakleys Ch. B-Majer Nocturne (4 Chs.), dam of the black sire Ch. B-Majer Harlem Nocturne (5 Chs.).

B-Majer got its start in 1971 with Blakley's Eda-Than, who never showed in a point class but did win several veteran classes, the last at over seventeen years of age. Currently into a sixth generation, B-Majer has bred thirty-six champions and bought and finished six more. In recent years, they have turned much time and attention to breed rescue,

**Ch. B-Majer King of Swing
with Peggie Blakley**

**Ch. Skibo's Just Call Me
Angel
with Shirley Reynolds**

and as Peggie puts it: *a very emotionally rewarding undertaking which expands by leaps and bounds as time goes by, peaking in 1994 with 123 being placed in happy homes.*

Yet another Fancway bitch would serve as foundation for a breeding program in Texas. Fancway's Carefree was purchased by Margaret Smith of Dallas and produced three champions bearing her Skibo prefix. Carefree is intensely linebred to Diplomat, carrying four lines to Pirate. She is a granddaughter of two of the West's leading sires, Pirate Jr. and Masterpiece.

Carefree went to live with Shirley and Dale Reynolds in 1973, at three years of age. Shirley whelped her second and third litters, retaining Ch. Skibo's Just Call Me Angel (7 Chs.) from the second and Am. and Can. Ch. Skibo's Fancy Clancy (14 Chs.) from the third. This pair formed the foundation for the Reynolds' Far Hills breeding program, now into the fifth generation, having produced over forty champions based on the Clancy-Angel combination.

**Ch. Skibo's
Fancy Clancy**

Some exciting wins came their way, beginning with Clancy, a Best in Show winner both here and in Canada, where he was the number one Miniature Schnauzer in 1977. His son Ch. Far Hills Midnight Angel (5 Chs.) earned over 50 Bests of Breed and over three dozen Group placements, including five Group Firsts. Another Clancy son, Ch. Glory's Eager Beaver (4 Chs.), produced one of the breed's leading black and silver sires, Ch. Sercatep's Strut N Proud (14 Chs.), from which two more generations of top producing B/S sires descend.

The Clancy-Angel grand-daughter Ch. Far Hills Flamin' Fandango (3 Chs.) was the top bitch in the breed for 1981, with 25 Bests of Breed, 37 Best Opposite Sex awards and 11 Group placements, including two Group Firsts. These wins were accomplished breeder-owner conditioned and handled by Mrs. Reynolds. Fandango's daughter Ch. Far Hills Go Getter (3 Chs.) brought this

**Ch. Far Hills Flamin' Fandango
with Shirley Reynolds**

family forward, primarily through her son Ch. Far Hills Big Bucks (6 Chs.).The last ten Far Hills champions finished in the 1990s came from Big Bucks daughters and include yet another top producing bitch, Ch. Far Hills Instant Recall (3 Chs.).

A linebred Angel daughter, Ch. Far Hills Twinklin' Angel, gave new life to the well-established Mai-Laurs, being bred in Maryland by Laurese Byrd Katen. There are four generations of Mai-Laur champions descending from Twinklin' Angel.

Shirley sums up her quarter century with the breed:

At Far Hills we strive to achieve the total dog — companion and show dog — one that is comfortable at home with the family as well as in the show ring. At home my dogs lounge on the furniture and run through the grass and trees. They also adjust beautifully to the rigorous routine of the shows. I have always strived for a good, solid foundation, taking into consideration the individual dog as well as the pedigree. It seems to be the only way that I can produce with consistency in both type and temperament. After twenty-five years I still get excited when I see a pretty pup, and I await with anticipation the excitement of the competition and the satisfaction of the recognition of Far Hills's presence in the show ring.

Dorem Cockade
CH. DOREM DISPLAY
Ch. Dorem Searchlight
Ch. Diplomat of Ledahof
Dorem Spotlight
Ch. Enchantress
Ch. Dorem Liberty
CH. DELFIN JANUS
Ch. Sandman of Sharvogue
Ch. Tweed Packet of Wilkern
Ch. Debutante of Ledahof
Ch. Minquas Merry Elf
Ch. Meldon's Merit
Minquas Melita
Minquas Vivacious

The CH. DELFIN JANUS line

Ch. Delfin Janus (34 Chs.) is far and away the top producing Diplomat son. He was the jewel in the Delfin crown, and his impact on the breed was profound. Whelped July 6, 1952, Janus was bred by Mae Dickenson, out of her Ch. Minquas Merry Elf, a triple great-granddaughter of DISPLAY.

Janus was a champion at nine months of age. Shown nine times, he was Winners Dog or better at six shows, going on to earn five Bests of Breed and two Group placements. He continued his career as a yearling champion adding more Breed wins and Group placements, failing, however, to win a Group.

Janus lived for over sixteen years as Mrs. Dickenson's companion, producing twelve of her twenty homebred Delfin champions. Six of these were out of Delfin's other foundation bitch, Ch. Minquas Athena, and include Ch. Delfin Victoria. Bred back to her sire, Victoria produced three champions and produced three more by other sires. The last Delfin champion finished in 1966.

As one of the youngest sires of the early 1950s that carried several lines to DISPLAY, Janus was broadly used by eastern breeders. In addition to champions produced at Delfin, others came from Blythewood, Mai-Laur, Melmar, Minquas, Mutiny, Rik-Rak, Travelmor and Windy Hill.

An extraordinary family of international champion-obedience titlists was developed by Nancy Ackerman (Rik-Rak), beginning with the Janus daughter Ch. Brenhof Katrinka, CD. She became the first champion Miniature Schnauzer to earn CD degrees here and in Canada. Her daughter, Am. and Can. Ch. Rik-Rak Rebel's Banner, CD, also owns a "first," earning bench and obedience titles in both countries. Banner continued this unusual line by producing Ch. Rik-Rak Regina, CD, dam of two champions. Another first came to Rik-Rak when the Janus daughter Ch. Delfin Echo produced Am. Can. and Mex. Ch. Rik-Rak Ramie, the first of the breed with titles in three countries.

**Ch. Mutiny
I'm Grumpy Too**

The major families based on Janus were developed by Mrs. Huber at Blythewood, the Prosens at Bon-Ell, the La Bountys at Mutiny and the Goulds at Windy Hill. The Janus daughter Ch. Blythewood Merry Melody (8 Chs.) is behind a host of top winning and producing Blythewood champions (see TRIBUTE chapter), while the Janus sons Ch. Delfin Paion and Ch. Mutiny I'm Grumpy Too exerted an equally profound influence in the West.

Barbara and Robert LaBounty came to California in the early 1960s, bringing Paion and Ch. Minquas Alicia with them. Combined, they produced Ch. Mutiny Coquette who went to Thelma Gould's Windy Hill Kennel in San Francisco.

Coquette is the dam of three Windy Hill champions, including Ch. Windy Hill Wishing Star. Bred back to Janus, Wishing Star produced her own "star" in the top producing sire Ch. Windy Hill Defiance (12 Chs.). There would be over two dozen Windy Hill champions produced over the next two decades.

A dozen more Mutiny champions emerged during the 1960s, high-lighted by Ch. Mutiny Pandemonium who established a record in 1967, topping the largest entry for a Miniature Schnauzer bitch to that date with her Best in Show in California, from the classes at thirteen months of age, handled by Barbara. Pandemonium was an inbred daughter of Mutiny's kingpin stud, Ch. Mutiny I'm Grumpy Too (17 Chs.).

Grumpy was clearly the heir apparent in the Janus line, and Jack and Dori Prosen were among the first to recognize this. Their Bon-Ell breeding program based on the Janus granddaughter Ch. Blythewood Honey Bun, stayed within the Janus line to produce most of their dozen or so Bon-Ell champions but first brought in the Tribute branch by breeding Honey Bun to Ch. Melmar's Jack Frost. Bon-Ell Bit O'Honey (4 Chs.) from this breeding produced two top producing bitches when bred to Grumpy: Ch. Bon-Ell Mighty Fine (3 Chs.) and

Ch. Delfin Janus
Ch. Mutiny I'm Grumpy Too
Ch. Minquas Alicia
Ch. Mutiny Master Spy
Ch. Delfin Apollo
Bon-Ell Ulla
Ch. Blythewood Honey Bun
CH. LANDMARK'S MASTERPIECE
Ch. Allaruth's Joshua
Ch. Allaruth's Jericho
Cooki v Elfland
Ch. Allaruth's Jasmine
Ch. Dorem Original
Ch. Allaruth's Miss Dinah Mite
Ch. Frevohly's Best Bon-Bon, UD

Ch. Bon-Ell Sand Storm (3 Chs.). Bit O'Honey, bred to Ch. Landmark's Masterpiece, produced Ch. Bon-Ell Dust Storm, the dam of Ch. Bon-Ell Moonglow (4 Chs.).

The Prosens can claim much of the credit for progress being made in England. They sent over the inbred Grumpy son Eng. Ch. Risepark Bon-Ell Taurus (5 Chs.) to Peter Newman with remarkable long-term results. The Bon-Ell breeding program here has its greatest spread through Bon-Ell Ulla, the dam of Gloria Weidlein's Ch. Mutiny Master Spy.

Although Master Spy falls one short of the mark designating a top producer, his son Ch. Landmark's Masterpiece (32 Chs.), also owned by Mrs. Weidlein, has a dynasty of his own, leaving over a dozen top producers to date in direct tail-male line.

The CH. LANDMARK'S MASTERPIECE line

Masterpiece caused quite a sensation on his first show weekend in July 1966, scoring Best of Breed at Santa Barbara at age six months and one day. Shown in the classes by Ric Chashoudian, he was then piloted to Group Second (to the BIS-winning Scottie) by Barbara LaBounty. His record thereafter was a fitting tribute to his quality.

Mrs. LaBounty (now Rhinehart) relates her personal feelings about Masterpiece:

He was truly different—like a whole step forward for the breed in several respects. "Lump" had very heavy bone that ran clear into his feet—tight feet with thick pads. He had a foreface we'd only read about in the standard— length with real eye fill, and a mouth full of strong, large teeth, square across the end.

Conformation-wise he was the dog I'd always dreamed of. Prior to Lump, while Gloria and I were traveling to shows, we'd spend many long hours in the car discussing structure.

I remember trying to describe my ideal—a short topline with long underline. It's a horsey term, but applies equally to dogs. It means that both the neck and tail come off the top of the dog, while a well-laid shoulder and correspondingly angled rear quarters stand the legs over a lot of ground. It means a short back (not short body) with room underneath to reach and really cover ground like a working dog. I thought this ideal was only a wishful dream until little Lump arrived and began to grow. Then there it was!

I said he was a whole step forward for the breed, but in one respect he brought the past with him. He had a coat of iron. His was truly a terrier jacket. He had adequate furnishings, but a real old-fashioned coat. And what a value this turned out to be in his producing years.

Ch. Landmark's Masterpiece with Ric Chasoudian

Masterpiece finished by going Best of Winners at the Montgomery County AMSC Specialty, again handled by Barbara. As a champion, handled by Ric, he earned over thirty Bests of Breed, including two at Westminster. Perhaps his best win was Best of Breed at the February 1967 AMSC Specialty, topping seventy-four entries, including ten champions under Marguerite Wolfe (Phil-Mar). Masterpiece was shown one last time as a veteran, winning Best of Breed at the Southern California Specialty in 1972.

Masterpiece was a much admired dog, and by his owner Mrs. Weidlein, much loved:

If he were a person, you would definitely call him a gentleman. Happy, healthy, well adjusted, he could take care of any situation that arose—a perfect companion, and a perfect house dog.

Ch. Landmark's Masterpiece at eleven years of age

**Ch. Playboy's
Block Buster**

Masterpiece's top producing son was Ch. Skibo's Fancy Clancy (14 Chs.), and through his grandson the B/S Ch. Sercatep's Strut N Proud (14 Chs.) he has had a strong impact on black and silvers throughout the world. The strongest tail-male line from Masterpiece comes through his son Ch. Lanmark's Playboy (10 Chs.) and broadens considerably through the Playboy sons Chs. Playboy's Block Buster (22 Chs.) and Special Edition (7 Chs.).

Block Buster served notice as a seven-month-old puppy when he topped forty-nine class entries as Best of Winners at the Northern California Specialty in September 1972, owner-handled by Carole Hansen. He went east in February and was Best of Winners at Westminster. In his debut as a yearling champion Buster was Best of Breed at the AMSC Specialty in California, handled by Ric Chashoudian, and went from success to success. He was number three (Knight System) in 1974 and his total record includes two Specialty Bests, 35 other Bests of Breed, and 21 Group placements including three Group Firsts.

As a sire, Buster proved equally outstanding, producing almost all of his champions for local Southern California breeders. He sired six Rainbou champions, three at Baws, including Ch. Baws Strait Shot v. Hansenhaus (5 Chs.), and left four at Hansenhaus, including Strait Shot's sister Ch. Glory Be of Hansenhaus (5 Chs.). Buster's best-producing son and daughter had the broadest influence on Hawaiian breeding. Ch. Hi-Charge of Hansenhaus (11 Chs.) and Ch. Sugar Ruff Scruff (6 Chs.) are behind many island champions.

**Ch. Glory Be of Hansenhaus
with Carole Hansen**

**Ch. Walters' Tradewinds
with Sheryl Stump**

Dolores Walters used Masterpiece as a cornerstone for her breeding program which enjoyed success in all color varieties. Best known for her blacks (see BLACK chapter), it is a salt and pepper double Masterpiece great-grandson, Ch. Walters' Tradewinds (5 Chs.), that carries the tail-male line of top producers to the present. Tradewinds, located in the Pacific Northwest, left champion descendants at Abiqua, Linalee and Mi-Sher. Tradewinds has a top producing daughter in Ch. Linalee's EZ Love'n of Mi Sher (3 Chs.).

Masterpiece had a broad influence on all color varieties, particularly in the black and silvers derived from his salt and pepper son Ch. Blythewood Winsome Lad. The B/S Ch. Eclipse Shadow of the Son (5 Chs.) is doubly bred on Winsome Lad, and brings in other lines from Janus through the Defiance daughter, Ch. Sparks Maidel of Defiance. Shadow is the sire of the good B/S sire Ch. Sycamore Solar Eclipse (9 Chs.). More black and silver champions descend from the Lad son Ch. Tammashann's Town Strutter. The Masterpiece son, Ch. Aljamar P.M. Lightning Bug, is the sire of Aljamar Fanny May (4 Chs.), foundation for another strong black and silver family (see BLACK AND SILVER chapter).

Winsome Lad gains particular significance four generations later, as Blythewood's most successful sire, Ch. Blythewood Shooting Sparks (53 Chs.), and his son, Ch. Blythewood Ewok Von Der Stars (15 Chs.), are in direct tail-male line from Lad.

The Masterpiece son Ch. Starfire Criterion Landmark only sired a few litters before he was sold to the Continent, where his impact is extraordinary. His influence here comes from a single litter out of Jean and Glenn Fancy's Specialty-winning Ch. Walters' Country Girl. Two good producers emerged, including Fancway's Carefree, who started the Far Hills.

The male from this breeding, Fancway's Daktari, only sired two litters, but is a principal factor in the Sole Baye breeding program begun in 1962. Yvonne Phelps, starting with a "pet" bitch, registered as Hilda V, was fortunate to meet up with Gloria Weidlein early on. Gloria was to be her friend and mentor, guiding "Billie" through the early years. She took her Masterpiece daughter and first champion, Ch. Sisterce of Sole Baye, to Daktari and got Ch. Manta of Sole Baye, dam of Billie's first top producer, Ch. Sole Baye's Miss Musket (7 Chs.).

Billie remembers her:

Miss Musket was a good all-around bitch and beautifully coated. Her last wins were actually in a thirty-

**Ch. Sole Baye's Miss Musket
with Yvonne Phelps**

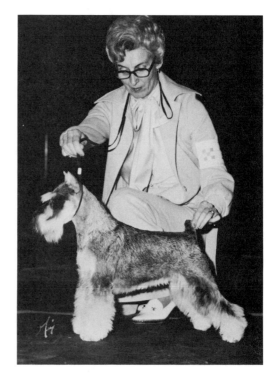

134

**Ch. Sole Baye's
John Henry**

six-week coat. It never grew longer, just thicker. I handled her all the way up to her final major, and Maripi Wooldridge finished her for me. It was decided she would be bred to Ch. Sunshine Sounder, owned by Kathy Dumble. This produced an exciting litter of six pups. Two were sold as pets that would have been easy finishers. I must interject at this point, it becomes very necessary to sell some pups to help finance the careers of those retained.

The other four were outstanding, and finished easily and quickly. The first to finish was Ch. Sole Baye's Mira Femme, with back-to-back Specialty majors. Owned by the Watanabes, she went to Japan and gave an excellent accounting of herself there. Second was Ch. Sole Baye's Sound-Off, winning a five-pointer at Devon prior to leaving for his new home in Brazil with Jose Machline. He compiled a fantastic record of Group and Best in Show wins. The third, Ch. Maizelle of Sole Baye, went to Linda Ramsey, serving as foundation for Yasmar. Fourth was to become my own Ch. Sole Baye's Sundowner, who enjoyed multiple Specialty wins and a host of Group placements, ending in the Top Five during the time he was specialed.

The breeding of Miss Musket to Sounder was so successful that I repeated it twice more, but with mixed results. Her fourth and final breeding was to Ch. Tomei Super Star, then owned by Dr. & Mrs. Beiles. Two of the three pups made it to the ring — Ch. Sole Baye's John Henry and Ch. Sole Baye's Tamure — and what treasures they were to become for me.

John Henry became the key male in the Sole Baye breeding program, and might have had a far greater impact had he not been exported to Spain, where he became a Best in Show winning International Champion, and did much to advance the breed throughout Europe. He had already produced Sole Baye's most successful producer — Am. and Can. Ch. Sole Baye's T.J. Esquire, the West's leading winner in 1986. T.J. won his sixth Specialty Best at six years of age at the 1990 Southern California Specialty. Five years later at the Great Western weekend in 1995, T.J. made a final appearance, looking absolutely fit,

Ch. Sole Baye's T. J. Esquire

to win the Veterans Stakes at the AMSC Specialty. By this time he was the sire of 26 champions, including a pair of Sandcastle blacks, plus six that earned titles in other countries. His most important son, Am. and Can. Ch. Allaruth's Charles v. Sole Baye, bred by Ruth Ziegler (Allaruth) and owned by Billie, was, like T.J., shown throughout his career by Maripi Wooldridge, enjoying even greater success in the show ring. His three-year career earned him fifteen Specialty Bests, including three AMSC wins, and he was the number two Schnauzer during this period. Charles is the sire of 14 champions to date, six out of the T.J. daughter Ch. Sole Baye's Winning Colours, a granddaughter of Ch. Sole Baye's Tamure (4 Chs.). The T.J.-Tamure son, Ch. Sole Baye's Sonny Boy, became a very influential sire in Japan, already with over a dozen champions.

Not to be forgotten is Linda Ramsey's Miss Musket daughter, Maizelle, dam of Yasmar's Hot Toddy, who gave her three champions, including the B/S Ch. Yasmar's Kiss Me Kate, who served as foundation for Brian Matisin and Michael Hilgenberg (Desert Song), giving them three champions — all black and silver. Hot Toddy is also the dam of Specialty-winning Ch. Yasmar's Tiffany Starfire, foundation for the Sunfire Schnauzers owned by Don and Marian Roberts and their daughter Cherryl Lyons. Tiffany was the first and only bitch to gain a Top Twenty breed ranking for four consecutive years, and is the dam and grandam of champions. The number of Yasmar homebred champions since 1980 tallied twenty when Ch. Yasmar's Lindsay Charise finished in 1996. She carries two lines to Maizelle.

Ch. Allaruth's Charles v. Sole Baye

Sole Baye to Yasmar to Desert Song and Sunfire — this is how families progress. In 1994, the Sole Baye breeding program was to record champion number thirty-two, fulfilling Billie's wish of averaging a champion every year. In addition, Sole Baye champions have been made up in Canada, Australia, Japan and Brazil, and AKC champions have been sent to Japan, Spain and Argentina where they have acquitted themselves admirably, both as winners and producers.

Returning to Masterpiece, we find that there were several top producing daughters from which strong families developed. Palmyra's Peridot (6 Chs.) is the dam of Ch. Blythewood Palmyra I'm Amy (3 Chs.) and Ch. Reflections Winning Image. Image, in turn, is the dam of Ch. Reflections Refreshin' Image (3 Chs.), who produced Ch. Reflections Lively Image, the dam of seven Travelmor champions, including a pair that have left an extraordinary mark in England.

A Masterpiece daughter, Ch. Ruedesheim's Free Spirit (3 Chs.), gave Ruedesheim a pair of top producer sons: Ch. Ruedesheim's Landmark (7 Chs.) as well as Ch. Ruedesheim's Momentummm (11 Chs.), and they are behind a host of champions bred at Ruedesheim.

**Ch. Yasmar's Tiffany Starfire
with Clay Coady**

A dozen Fotinakes champions stem from the Masterpiece daughter Fotinakes Heide (3 Chs.), and another daughter, Ch. Shirley's String of Pearls, produced three champions for Shirley Willey.

Masterpiece appears in the pedigrees of many dozens of champions as the maternal grandsire of Ch. Allaruth's Daniel (8 Chs.), who is doubly bred within the Diplomat branch, being by the Pirate great-grandson, Ch. Boomerang of Marienhof. It is through the Daniel son Ch. Valharra's Dionysos (28 Chs.) that the longest extension of the Diplomat branch exists.

The Diplomat branch from DISPLAY continues to be a strong force in current lines and families. It is clear that two distinct lines have developed, one through Pirate and the other through Masterpiece. Many successful winners and producers have resulted from a blend of these two lines, while others have come from outcrosses to the other branches—Tribute, Delegate and particularly Ruffian.

9
The
Ch. Delegate of Ledahof
Branch

**Ch. Delegate
of Ledahof**

CH. DELEGATE OF LEDAHOF, as one of DISPLAY's early champions, might have enjoyed a far more impressive stud career had he been as widely publicized and as centrally located as his litter brother, Ch. Diplomat of Ledahof. Delegate's five champions seem to compare poorly with the twenty-nine champions produced by his more broadly used brother. However, among the five was Ch. Dorem Tempo, who so impressed the mistress of Phil-Mar that Mrs. Wolff bred DISPLAY's sister, Ch. Dorem Shady Lady, as well as a Shady daughter and granddaughter to him. Tempo produced a champion in each litter, including three Best in Show winners.

Like his sire, Tempo was lightly used at stud, producing six champions from only nine breedings. Virtually all modern descendants from the Delegate branch trace through Tempo's son, Ch. Phil-Mar Gay Knight, although an unfinished son, Belvedere's Andy, sired a top producer in Ch. Belvedere's Gay Boy (5 Chs.). There are current lines that trace to Gay Boy, principally through the Zomerhof family.

The Delegate son, Ch. Rannoch's Rampion, sired Eng. Ch. Rannoch Dune Randolph of Appeline, who was exported to England and left many champion descendants.

The main tail-male line of descent from the Delegate branch comes through the Tempo son Gay Knight. Five of his nine champion get came out of the Phil-Mar Kennel. The Gay Knight son Ch. Haldeen's Allegro, not of Phil-Mar breeding, figures prominently in many current lines and families, as he appears twice in the pedigree of the influential sire, Ch. Sky Rocket's Uproar (35 Chs.) from the Ruffian branch.

**Ch. Dorem Tempo
with Stephen Shaw**

By far the most important of the Gay Knight offspring was Ch. Phil-Mar Dark Knight, who brought with him three lines to Tribute. Well received by eastern breeders, Dark Knight sired 18 champions. His blood flows currently and most prominently in the Midwest, however, through the efforts of Mr. and Mrs. Landis Hirstein, whose Penlan breeding program through 1996 has produced over 150 champions.

The Delegate branch *is* Penlan, with forty-two top producing sires tracing in direct tail-male lines to their Dark Knight son, Ch. Penlan Paragon. Penlan, like so many successful ventures, was based on good advice:

Invest in the best bitch you can find.

This advice was followed by Penny and Lanny thirty-five years ago, and the bitch was Helarry's Lolly.

Of Lolly, Penny once wrote:

Words cannot express the joy Lolly has brought us, nor the gratitude we feel towards her breeder, Helen Wiedenbeck of Helarry Kennel. Lolly's show career, although productive, was cut short because of the expected arrival of our first daughter, but to watch her children and grandchildren carry on her royal heritage in the ring and in the whelping box is more than we ever hoped for. The foundation was cast and we were fortunate to build upon it.

47 Sires of 5 or more A.K.C. Champions
trace in direct tail-male lines to
CH. DELEGATE OF LEDAHOF

*Sires that are in *italic* produced fewer than 5 Champions.*

A1 Ch. Dorem Tempo (6)
  B1 *Belvedere Andy**
    C1 Ch. Belvedere Gay Boy (5)
  B2 Ch. Phil-Mar Gay Knight (9)
    C2 Ch. Phil-Mar Dark Knight (18)
      D1 Ch. Penlan Paragon (11)
        E1 Ch. Penlan Paragon's Pride (30)
          F1 Ch. Penlan Paperboy (44)
            G1 Ch. Richlene's Big Time (16)
              H1 Ch. Falling Timbers Country Boy (10)
                I1 Ch. Richlene's Grand Slam (7)
                  J1 Ch. Richlene's Square Deal (15)
              H2 Ch. Richlene's Marathon II (12)
                I2 Ch. Richlene's Escapade (7)
            G2 Ch. Charmar Copy Cat (24)
              H3 Ch. Maroch Master Charge (13)
              H4 Ch. Tel-Mo's Top Cat (10)
            G3 Ch. Valharra's Prize Of Penlan (8)
              H5 Ch. Jilmar's Pulsar (9)
                I3 Ch. Gailwind's Scandal Sheet (6)
            G4 Ch. Deeanee Dutch Demon (6)

Ch. Richlene's Escapade   **Ch. Maroch Master Charge**

Ch. Classic Midnight Cowboy   **Ch. Dimensions Over The Road**

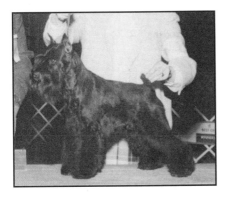

**Ch. Penlan
Paragon**

Lolly, whelped January 28, 1961, was tightly linebred within the Tribute and Ruffian branches, carrying five lines to the former and two to the latter; in addition, she carries one line to High Test. Initially Lolly was bred back closely into the Tribute-Ruffian side of her pedigree, giving the Hirsteins their first champions, as well as their principal producing bitch, Penlan Cadet Too. Never shown, as she was over fourteen inches, Cadet was retained none the less, and as Penny once said, *"Her exaggerated quality has paid off in the whelping box."*

Cadet produced a champion in every litter, and each was a Best of Breed winner from the classes and/or a Specialty-point winner. She seemed to produce consistent quality whether inbred to her own sons or loosely linebred. Penny wrote the following about Cadet:

We attribute Cadet's success as a producer to two things; her line-bred pedigree based on top producing dogs and bitches, and the exaggeration of Cadet herself. Being genetically clean, with a tightlybred pedigree and exaggeration in every physical aspect, she proved to be dominant in her offspring, with only subtle influences from her mates. Each was selected for specific reasons, such as the desire for a wider-moving rear and a shorter back. The resulting offspring are the proof of her success.

The first few Penlan champions were shown professionally by Richard and Joanne Trubee. They handled Ch. Penlan Proud Knight, Penlan's first Specialty winner, and showed the littermates, Chs. Penlan Paragon and Paramour. Paragon, whelped May 11, 1977, was Penlan's first Group winner.

In an effort to backtrack a bit, to not only get a closer line to DISPLAY,

Penlan Cadet Too
pictured on opposite page

but also lines to his sister, Shady, the Hirsteins selected Ch. Phil-Mar Dark Knight for Cadet's third breeding. Paragon was the result, and became Penlan's cornerstone sire, giving them 11 champions, all out of Penlan bitches, including a trio of champions when bred back to his dam. One of these, Ch. Penlan Paragon's Pride, was definitely a "keeper," and Penny's description of Pride explains why:

As an individual Pride stands 13 5/8 inches tall, with an elegant clean head, tremendous reach of neck, and a short, compact body. His topline is firm, tail set high and he has well-angulated, wide-moving hindquarters.

Pride, like his sire, finished with a Group First from the classes as a puppy. He was the first Penlan stud to receive the attention of other breeders, and sired 30 champions, including three top producing sons. The Pride son Ch. Penlan Paperboy was the obvious heir apparent, and became the sire of 44 champions.

I first saw Paperboy at the New York AMSC Specialty in February 1972. Shown as a 6-9 months puppy, he was Best in Sweepstakes under Patsy Laughter (Miown) and Best of Winners under the famed all-rounder, Alva Rosenberg. Compact and stylish, he excelled in all areas and outmoved the competition with ease.

Ch. Penlan Paragon's Pride with Landis Hirstein

Ch. Penlan Paperboy

The Hirsteins decided to go back to the Ruffian branch for Cadet's next breeding, to Ch. Helarry's Dark Victory. Only one pup emerged, but a real flyer and a significant producer. The singleton was Ch. Penlan Prelude To Victory, finished as a puppy with two five-pointers, including the 1969 AMSC Specialty at Montgomery County, where Robert Moore (Bethel) awarded her WB, BW and BOS. Prelude produced four champions, including Ch. Penlan Proud Of Me (by Pride), the dam of the outstanding winner and sire Ch. Penlan Peter Gunn (73 Chs.).

The pedigree of Peter Gunn shows the only infusion of "outside"

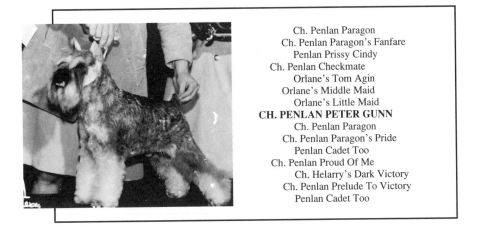

Ch. Penlan Paragon
Ch. Penlan Paragon's Fanfare
Penlan Prissy Cindy
Ch. Penlan Checkmate
Orlane's Tom Agin
Orlane's Middle Maid
Orlane's Little Maid
CH. PENLAN PETER GUNN
Ch. Penlan Paragon
Ch. Penlan Paragon's Pride
Penlan Cadet Too
Ch. Penlan Proud Of Me
Ch. Helarry's Dark Victory
Ch. Penlan Prelude To Victory
Penlan Cadet Too

blood brought into the Penlan family, through Checkmate's dam, Orlane's Middle Maid. Ch. Penlan Checkmate came to Penlan in 1971 as payment for stud service and eventually was sold to Jean and Charles Kriegbaum in Pennsylvania. Checkmate sired 34 champions, including four top producing sons. With the addition of Checkmate was added a strong concentration from the Tribute branch, with over a dozen crosses to the Tribute son Ch. Dorem Favorite (15 Chs.). Checkmate carried additional lines to Diplomat, Merit and Ruffian, so that all the important branches are incorporated in the background of Peter Gunn.

Ch. Penlan Checkmate

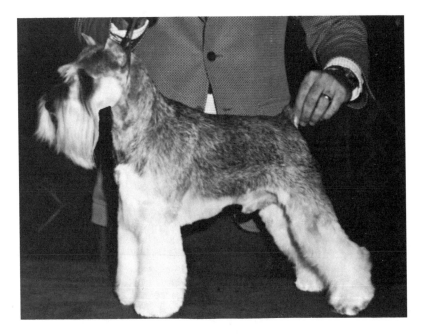

Ch. Penlan Peter Gunn going Best of Winners at the AMSC Specialty in February 1975 under Anne Rogers Clark, handled by his breeder Landis Hirstein.

Lanny and Penny brought Peter Gunn to the New York AMSC Specialty in 1975 as a yearling, along with a homebred puppy bitch, (Ch.) Penlan Pin-Up of Wolffcraft, they had sold to James Wolff and Paul Reycraft (Wolffcraft) of Indiana. Peter Gunn went Best of Winners at the Specialty, repeating the next day at Westminster, while Pin-Up won the Sweepstakes under Marguerite Wolff (Phil-Mar). Both finished quickly, Peter Gunn undefeated in the classes.

Sold as a fifteen-month-old champion, Peter Gunn began a spectacular specials career, managed professionally by Claudia Seaberg, with complete support given him by his owners Carol and Dr. Carl Beiles (Carolane). In 1977, Peter Gunn topped all systems with a pair of Bests in Show, eight Group Firsts and six Specialty Bests, the same year in which sixteen of his get completed their titles! This was the first of several breed "records" set, as he also led the breed in Specialty wins (15) until these records were surpassed. Before his retirement, he had won over 100 Bests of Breed and 60 Group placements, over two dozen of them firsts. As the sire of 73 champion get, including four top producing sons, he is considered one of the breed "greats". He produced multiple champion litters from thirteen different bitches, and he can be found in the pedigrees of over five hundred champions, including more than sixty blacks.

Ch. Penlan Peter's Son going Best of Breed at the Gateway Specialty in September 1976 under Edward Jenner, handled by his breeder Landis Hirstein.

Although his effect on the breed went well beyond his home territory, for Carolane alone, he sired twenty-two champions between 1975 and 1988, and is behind dozens more that have come from their ongoing breeding program. The most recent to achieve top producing status is Ch. Carolane's Celebration (3 Chs.), and she is out of double granddaughter of Peter Gunn. The Beiles had also ventured into breeding blacks, and have in Ch. Carolane's Midnight Magician, a fourth generation of homebred black champions, all descending from Peter Gunn. A multiple Group and Specialty winner, Magician was Best of Breed at Westminster in 1994 and was among the top ten in 1993 and '94.

The Hirsteins dominated the top spots in the various rating systems through much of the 1970s. They had become well established as professional handlers but continued to support their own breeding whenever possible.

In 1973, Ch. Penlan Paperboy missed being number one (Knight System) by fifteen points. Three years later, the number three and number four rankings were held by the Penlan duo Ch. Penlan Peter's Son (25 Chs.) and his sire, Peter Gunn, both AMSC Specialty winners. In 1977, this pair was joined in the top ten by yet another Penlan—Ch. Penlan Pistol Packer (7 Chs.). The Hirsteins piloted the Paperboy son Ch. Cyngar's Ultimatum, bred and owned by Cynthia Garton, to number one in 1978, and two years later another of their

Ch. Penlan Pride's Promise

charges, Ch. Bardon Bounty Hunter (10 Chs.), bred and owned by Barbara Snobel, was number one. He is by Checkmate out of a Peter's Son daughter. Number two that year was Ch. Penlan Pride's Promise (8 Chs.), the last champion produced by Pride, while in the classes, another Penlan was setting his own pace.

Ch. Penlan Pacesetter was purchased as a puppy by Gene Simmonds (Handful) and went out to California with the Hirsteins in June 1980 for the 100th Anniversary Specialty of the American Miniature Schnauzer Club (AMSC), going Best in Sweepstakes under Cynthia Garton (Cyngar). The next year he led his nearest competitor in the Knight System ratings by over 350 points. He was an AMSC Specialty winner and became Penlan's third Best in Show winner. Pacesetter, in his later years, enjoyed retirement in Kentucky with David Hallock (Whim-Cin).

Penlan's fourth Best in Show winner followed in 1982. Ch. Penlan Promissory (27 Chs.), sired by my personal Penlan "favorite," Pride's Promise, represents all that is Penlan, and was well rewarded as a show dog. He earned four Bests in Show (two from the classes) and six Specialty Bests and eventually became Penlan's fourth generation of top-producing sires.

Ch. Penlan Promissory with his breeder-owners Mr. & Mrs. Landis Hirstein

Ch. Penlan Portside is Best of Winners and BOS over Specials at the 1994 AMSC Spring Specialty under Ric Chashoudian, handled by his breeder-owner Landis Hirstein; Vera Potiker presenting trophy.

On the Florida circuit in 1995, Ch. Penlan Portside became Penlan's fifth Best in Show winner. He served notice as a puppy, going Best of Winners and Best Opposite Sex over eight male Specials at the A.M.S.C. Spring Specialty in Chicago, and finished on the Montgomery County weekend, scoring Best of Winners over sixty-seven class entries at Hatboro.

Penlan since its inception has bred more top producers than any other kennel, before or since. Eleven sires of five or more champions, and sixteen dams of three or more champions carry the Penlan prefix, and all descend from Helarry's Lolly. More important, perhaps, is that the Hirsteins have shared their wealth of experience and have provided foundation stock for new breeders throughout the Midwest and East.

In the Midwest, Patricia and Richard Roozen founded their Ardicia breeding program on Ch. Penlan Paramour (Dark Knight-Cadet), giving her owners three champions, including Ch. Ardicia's Autumn Venture, dam of three more Ardicia champions.

Bernice Vrablik (Valencia) in Illinois has bred over a dozen champions, having based her entire breeding efforts on Penlan stock. She hit the jackpot with Ch. Valencia's Lindeza Lucinda, a Peter's Son daughter that produced five champions from breedings to Promissory.

The Hirsteins were chosen as mentors by Barbara and Donald Snobel, and kept them right on the mark beginning with Ch. Penlan Persistance, by Paperboy. She gave them Ch. Bardon Liberated Lady Byrd, who in turn produced Ch. Bardon Borne A Starr. Clearly the "star" of the Bardon breeding

**Ch. Penlan
Persnickety**

Ch. Penlan Polarity is Best of Breed at the 1988 Heart of America Specialty under breeder-judge Paul Thomann, handled by his breeder-owner Landis Hirstein; Jack Wilson presenting trophy.

Ch. Penlan Polarize is Best of Breed at the 1989 Des Moines Specialty under breeder-judge Shirley Rains, handled by his breeder-owner Landis Hirstein.

Ch. Penlan
Pawnbroker

**Ch. Bardon
Bounty Hunter
with Landis Hirstein**

program, among her six champion get is Ch. Bardon Bounty Hunter, winner of twelve Specialties and the sire of ten champions.

In the East, Joseph Williams began his Charmar breeding program with Penlan Prim 'N Proper (by Pride), giving him three champions. Prim 'N Proper, bred to Checkmate, produced Ch. Charmar Checkerberry, dam of Ch. Charmar Copy Cat (by Paperboy), sire of 24 champions. Eight were out of Lynda Lucast's Peter Gunn daughter, Carolane's Annie Get Your Gun (10 Chs.), including a Best in Show and AMSC Specialty winning son, Ch. Tel-Mo's Top Cat (10 Chs.).

**Ch. Tel-Mo's Top Cat
is Best in Show
at the Leavenworth
Kennel Club in 1982
under Al Treen,
handled by Kurt
Garmaker.**

**Ch. Penlan Perfect Choice
with Richard Smith**

The Tel-Mo Kennel in Minnesota was founded in 1960 by Leslie Maudsley and is presently being maintained by her daughter Lynda Lucast. Originally founded on Blythewood and Mutiny stock from the Ch. Delfin Janus line, a new tack was taken with the purchase of Annie.

The greatest extension of the Penlan family can be found in Fort Wayne, Indiana. Since 1966, Richard and Arlene Smith (Richlene) have built a firm foundation based on a pair of Penlan Cadet Too daughters. Ch. Penlan Perfect Choice was aptly named, giving the Smiths four champions, including a pair of top producing bitches.

Ch. Penlan Paragon's Exceptional turned out to be truly exceptional, giving the Smiths four champions, plus nearly four dozen more in the next four generations. Her best producing son, Ch. Richlene's Big Time (16 Chs.), brings the tail-male line from Delegate another generation, through his top producing son Ch. Falling Timbers Country Boy (10 Chs.), out of Ch. Richlene's Sugar Baby (3 Chs.), foundation matron at Joy Hathaway's Falling Timbers Kennel. Country Boy, from his Florida base, had a considerable impact on Liebestraum, Shorlaine, Da-Lin and Datura families. The top producing tail-male line extends two more generations from Country Boy, through his son Ch. Richlene's Grand Slam (7 Chs.), and his son Ch. Richlene's Square Deal, an active sire with 15 champions to date.

**Ch. Penlan Paragon's
Exceptional**

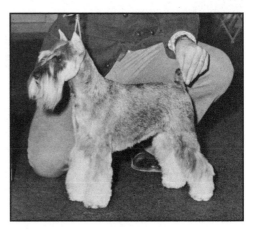

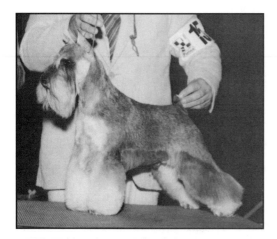

**Ch. Richlene's
Square Deal**

The tail-female line from Exceptional is brought forward by two daughters: Ch. Richlene's Holiday Surprise (3 Chs.), by Peter Gunn, and Richlene's Tweetie Pop (4 Chs.), by Checkmate. Surprise, bred into the Ruffian line, is the dam of Ch. Richlene Round-Up (10 Chs.), and also gave Evelyn Hole (Homestead) her start with Richlene's Fiesta, dam of three champions.

The Tweetie Pop daughter, Ch. Richlene's Hearts And Lace, carries this strong family several generations further as the dam of five champions, including Richlene's top winner in the early '80s, Sweepstakes, multiple Group and six-time Specialty winning Ch. Richlene's Marathon II (12 Chs.), by Big Time. Hearts And Lace also gave them the good producing bitch, Ch. Richlene's Single Serving (3 Chs.), by Pride's Promise.

Carol Beagle (Blackwitch), whose black and silver family was already well established, was fortunate to purchase as a puppy, Ch. Richlene's Cheese N Crackers, out of Single Serving, giving her five salt and pepper champions, sired by either Richlene or black and silver Blackwitch studs.

An Exceptional granddaughter, Ch. Richlene's Royal Dainty, served as foundation for Cheryl Coffman's salt and pepper breeding program, already well established in blacks. A daughter, Jacqueminot January, bred to a Royal Dainty grandson, Ch. Jacqueminot Joint Venture, CD (5 Chs.), gave her Ch. Jacqueminot Jordache, the dam of six champions.

**Ch. Richlene's
Round-Up**

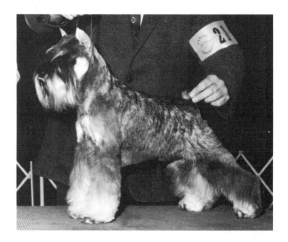

**Ch. Richlene's
Top Billing
with Sandra Nagengast**

Exceptional is represented by yet another top producer, her grandson Ch. Richlene's Top Billing. He was not the first Richlene to go to Sandra and Daniel Nagengast (Angler) in Connecticut. Like the Hirsteins and the Smiths, the Nagengasts were "do it yourselfers" and finished two other Richlenes before Top Billing was purchased as a six-month-old pup, in partnership with Barbara Hall (Wyndwood). After a speedy title quest, handled by Sandra, he provided them with the thrill of winning Best of Breed at AMSC Montgomery County, at just fourteen months of age. Top Billing is the sire of 14 champions, and his good producing grandson, Ch. Wyndwood Sport About (7 Chs.) carries two lines to him. The Angler-Wyndwood partnership also went to Richlene for their Tweetie Pop daughter, Ch. Richlene's Angler's Keepsake, which produced three Angler champions, including Ch. Angler's Puttin' On The Ritz (5 Chs.).

One of the Ritz champions, Ch. Angler's Art Deco, was purchased as a puppy by Edward and Patricia Roozen (Deco) of New Jersey and was the number one bitch, all systems, in 1988, before providing them three champions.

Although George and Joan Downs founded their Downwind breeding program on the last champion to carry the Helarry prefix, Ch. Helarry's Downwind Pride, finished in 1976, they are another prime example of those who have extended the Penlan/Richlene line. They have bred ten champions since 1990, including Ch. Downwind Cleopatra, a daughter of Square Deal, who gave them four champions in a single litter by Marathon II.

There are many other current breeders who are indebted to the Hirsteins and the Smiths for their foundation stock, and many more will have progressed by using Penlan and Richlene studs. Although their successes have been charted within the Delegate branch from DISPLAY, one must consider that they owe as much, even more, to the Ruffian branch, as is emphasized in that chapter.

10
The
Ch. Meldon's Ruffian
Branch

**Ch. Meldon's
Ruffian**

C‍H. MELDON'S RUFFIAN, whelped December 23, 1950, heads a branch from DISPLAY noted not only for its Best in Show winners but also for a line of top producing sires that covers a broader spectrum currently than any other branch from DISPLAY.

Ruffian was sold as a young puppy by Mrs. Meldon, and through a set of circumstances found his way to the kennel of professional handlers Larry and Alice Downey in Illinois. They were able to buy him for their clients, Mr. and Mrs. George Hendrickson, although he remained with the Downeys until his death November 2, 1965.

Ruffian's show career began as a puppy, but his big winning came as a yearling in February 1952, taking two Groups and a Best in Show from the classes to finish. Ruffian was not campaigned extensively by current norms. Alice Downey explains why:

By today's standards Ruffian would not hold up for coat and furnishings. He wasn't shown extensively because of his soft coat, but fortunately his descendants did not have the problem. He was outstanding for head and eye, had an excellent neck and front, and was extremely sound. Above all else, he was elegant and showy, as were so many of his descendants.

Ruffian's record bears noting, as he placed in the Group twenty-seven out of the twenty-nine times he won Best of Breed, and became the breed's second multiple BIS winner. His record, following in the footsteps of his

Ch. Meldon's Ruffian, at thirteen months of age, with Larry Downey

illustrious sire, was the basis for a string of BIS-winning descendants second to none.

Ruffian sired 26 champions, half of them for Harry and Helen Wiedenbeck's Helarry Kennel, and most of them handled by the Downeys. The Helarry breeding program began shortly after Ruffian came on the scene. Their top producing bitch Helarry's Delsey (6 Chs.) carries a line to Ruffian, as well

85 Sires of 5 or more A.K.C. Champions trace in direct tail-male lines to

CH. MELDON'S RUFFIAN

*Sires that are in *italic* produced fewer than 5 Champions.

A1 Ch. Helarry's Ruff Stuff (7)
A2 *Ch. Helarry's Dynamite**
   B1 Ch. Amigo of Merry Makers (5)
A3 Ch. Helarry's Dark Victory (35)
   B2 Ch. Helarry's Harmony (21)
   B3 Ch. Abingdon Authority (7)
A4 Ch. Helarry's Danny Boy (7)
   B4 Ch. Helarry's Colonel Dan (22)
      C1 *Iles Colonel Smokey**
         D1 Ch. Merwood's Applejack (5)
            E1 Ch. Richlene's Round-Up (10)
               F1 Ch. Richlene's Top Billing (14)
                  G1 *Ch. Wyndwood Top Sider**
                     H1 Ch. Wyndwood Sport About (7)
A5 *Ch. C-Ton's Bon Fire**
   B5 *Ch. Jay Dee's Sky Rocket**
      C2 Ch. Sky Rocket's First Stage (8)
         D2 Ch. Sky Rocket's Uproar (35)
            E2 Ch. Bandsman's Skyrocket In Flite (6)
            E3 Ch. Sky Rocket's Victory Bound (5)
            E4 Ch. Shorlaine Dynamic Flash (20)
               F2 Ch. R-Bo's Victory Flash (30)
               F3 Ch. Shorlaine Stanley Dangerfeld (10)
               G2 Ch. Liebestraum's Despirato (6)

Ch. Wyndwood Sport About   **Ch. Liebestraum's Despirato**

E5 Ch. Jadee's Jump Up (40)
   F4 Ch. Sky Rocket's Travel More (9)
   F5 Ch. Repitition's Upcharge (5)
      G3 Ch. Repitition's Best Beau (6)
         H2 Ch. Repitition's Rebel Warrior (17)
            I1 Ch. Repitition's Darth Vader [B/S] (6)
E6 Ch. Sky Rocket's Bound To Win (25)
   F6 Ch. Postillion's Buccaneer (8)
   F7 Ch. Contempra Foolish Pleasure (7)
   F8 Ch. Blythewoood National Anthem (25)
      G4 Ch. Blythewood National Acclaim (32)
         H3 Ch. Jilmar's Allstar (19)
            I2 Ch. Bandsman's Free For All (8)
      G5 Ch. Blythewood National Newsman (7)
         H4 Ch. Sumerwynd Still Sizzlin (6)
            I3 Ch. Sumerwynd Bandsman Upbeat (5)
               J1 *Jerry O's Bandsman**
                  K1 Ch. Sumerwynd Bandsman Showoff (12)
      G6 Ch. Far Hills Big Bucks (6)
      G7 *Ch. Blythewood National Accord**
         H6 Ch. Gailwind's Village Gossip (6)
D3 Ch. Sky Rocket's Upswing (15)
   E7 Ch. Jadee's Hush Up (11)
      F9 Ch. Jerry O's Secret Agent (9)
         G8 *Ch. Regency's Double Agent**
         H7 Ch. Regency's Born To Boogie (9)

Ch. Repitition's Dark Vader

Ch. Regency's Born To Boogie

Jerry O's Target Practice, CDX   **Ch. Irrenhaus Classic**

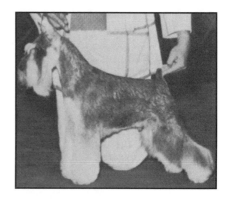

G12 Ch. Rampage's Kat Burglar (6)
  H18 Ch. Rampage's Waco Kid [B/S] (24)
    I11 Ch. Jerry O's Rain Check [B/S] (14)
      J6 Ch. Bandsman's Newsprint [B/S] (26)
        K3 Ch. Bandsman Special Assignment (7)
        K4 Ch. Beucinder's Blackheath Brio [B/S] (5)
      J7 Ch. Carlyn's Check My Label (7)
    I12 Ch. Repitition's Mirror Man, CD [B/S] (8)
    I13 *Ch. Rampage's Kid Moody**
      J8 Ch. Rampage's Express Mail (33)
        K5 Ch. Rampage's Representative (45)
          L1 Ch. Regency's Absolut (8)
          L2 Ch. Repitition's New Beginnings (6)
          L3 Ch. Ruedesheim's
              Fortune Seeker II (5)
        K6 Ch. Adamis State-Of-The-Art (7)
  H19 *Ch. Meadoway's Pickpocket**
    I14 Ch. Meadoway Yankee Doodle Dandy (B/S) (10)
      J9 Ch. Meadoway Yankee Pedlar (6)
G13 *Ch. Rampage's Bold Print**
  H20 *Lee Jax Saint Nicholas [B/S]**
    I15 *Ch. Lee Jax Yeoman Of The Guard [B/S]**
      J10 Ch. Meadoway's Southpaw [B/S] (5)
        K7 *Ch. Repitition's PB Personality [B/S]**
          L4 Ch. Repitition's
              Black 'N White [B/S] (10)

Ch. Carlyn's Check My Label   **Ch. Repitition's Black 'N White**

 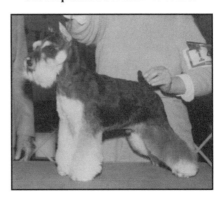

as two to Tribute and two more directly to DISPLAY. Her first breeding was to Ruffian and produced a bonanza in the Best in Show brothers, Ch. Helarry's Chester and Ch. Helarry's Dark Victory (35 Chs.). Repeat breedings produced four more champions, including the top producing sons, Ch. Helarry's Danny Boy (7 Chs.) and Ch. Helarry's Ruff Stuff (7 Chs.).

No Miniature Schnauzer before or since has enjoyed a more spectacular beginning than that experienced by Ch. Helarry's Dark Victory. Whelped November 19, 1958, he was purchased through the Downeys by Joseph Obsfeldt, but like Ruffian, he lived out his entire fifteen years with Alice and Larry. Dark Victory was shown for the first time on the January Florida circuit in 1960 and completed his championship by winning three consecutive Bests in Show. Yet another BIS came his way in November 1961.

The BIS legacy continued as Dark Victory sired three multiple BIS winners: Ch. Victoria of Mary-O (2 BIS), Ch. Helarry's Harmony (5 BIS) and Ch. Abingdon's Authority (9 BIS).

Authority, bred by Mona Meiners (Abingdon), carries three lines to Delsey, being a Dark Victory son out of a Danny Boy daughter, whose dam is by Chester—a tight line of BIS champions, indeed. Authority was campaigned by the Downeys under the sponsorship of the Hendricksons. He not only surpassed the Best in Show record of DISPLAY but went on to almost double it, gaining his ninth Best in 1969. His record of twenty-six Group Firsts was also tops in the breed to that date.

Authority sired seven champions, including a trio of littermates bred by Grace Church (Kazels). One of these, Ch. Kazels Favorite, was the number one Schnauzer, all systems, in 1972, handled by Clay Coady to a one-year record of four Bests in Show, 13 Group Firsts and 16 other placements from 37 Bests of Breed. In addition, Favorite won four Specialties that year, including two AMSC wins. Owner-handled thereafter, he won another BIS and went on to earn a total of 135 Bests of Breed. The fact that he won BOBs in each of his eight years of showing continues to be a breed record.

Dark Victory's BIS heritage was also carried a generation further by his top producing son Ch. Helarry's Harmony (21 Chs.). Purchased as a nine-

Ch. Abingdon's Authority

month-old puppy by Bette and Edward Bracy, professional handlers in Tennessee, Harmony had all the advantages. The Bracys were breed specialists and knew he was a good one. His show career began at fourteen months of age, and he never looked back. Harmony earned 39 Bests of Breed and 17 Group Firsts. Almost one-third of the time he topped the Group he went on to BIS—five times in all, equally the record of DISPLAY.

Bette described Harmony:

A Schnauzer of great substance, with a short, hard back, soundness at both ends, and an exceptional front. These qualities, along with his tremendous terrier spirit, make for a great deal of Schnauzer in this 13 1/2-inch frame.

Being the fourth generation of BIS winners in his tail-male line, it was inevitable that Harmony would continue this heritage. He is the sire of two BIS winners, Ch. Franzels Quicksilver and Ch. Blue Devil Sharpshooter, both earning their top wins from the classes.

Harmony is best known for his producing daughters. Robert Moore (Bethel) used him

Ch. Helarry's Harmony with Edward Bracy

**Ch. Shorlaine
Dynamic Flash**

to great advantage, getting the good producers Ch. Bethel's Lacie and Ch. Bethel's Lulu. Lacie, bred to Dark Victory, produced Rita Lawson's foundation bitch, Ch. Shadowmark's Casey of Ayoub's, dam of four champions by the Ruffian grandson Ch. Helarry's Colonel Dan. There would be a dozen more Shadowmark champions, all bred within the Helarry line.

Ch. Bethel's Lulu was also bred to Colonel Dan and produced Ch. Bethel's News Flash, foundation for Lori Bush's Shorlaine Kennel in Florida. Her crowning achievement came in the form of the BIS and Specialty-winning News Flash son, Ch. Shorlaine Dynamic Flash, sired by yet another BIS winner, Ch. Sky Rocket's Uproar. Dynamic Flash continued this heritage as the sire of 20 champions, including BIS-winning Ch. R-Bo's Victory Flash.

Victory Flash, bred and owned by Mary Ann Ellis (R-Bo) of Georgia, climaxed a breeding program begun in 1962. He enjoyed an outstanding show career, professionally handled by Claudia Seaberg. During a four-year campaign he won over 90 BOBs and over 50 Group placements, including a dozen Firsts. Victory Flash had his best year as number one Schnauzer (Knight System) in 1979, also winning several Specialties including the AMSC Montgomery County. He is the sire of 30 champions, including a daughter, Ch. R-Bo's Devil Flash (4 Chs.), who continues this family through a top producing son, Ch. R-Bo's Devil's Advocate (9 Chs.), owned by Paula Steele, DVM (PostScript).

Dynamic Flash had considerable impact on breeding programs in the South, particularly Florida. His paternal granddaughter Rising Sun Dazzling Display served as foundation for C. R. and Betty Woodard's Datura Kennel, giving them six champions, including Ch. Datura's Nightin-Gale (3 Chs.), when bred back to Dynamic Flash. She, in turn, gave Datura their best producing bitch to date, Ch. Datura's Star Lifter (7 Chs.) by Ch. Tomei Super Star (30 Chs.). In 1995, the Woodards celebrated their twenty-fifth homebred champion.

**Ch. R-Bo's
Victory Flash
with Claudia Seaberg**

**Ch. R-Bo's
Devil Flash**

**Ch. Harga's
Terri**

Another Dynamic Flash daughter, Sunnymark's Sugar Brandy, founded Linda Conner's Da-Lin's Kennel in Alabama. She gave her seven champions, including a pair by Dynamic Flash's best producing son, Ch. Shorlaine Stanley Dangerfeld (10 Chs.).

Ch. Bethel's News Flash had a further impact on the breed through Dynamic Flash's sister, Shorlaine Jeanie Jump Up, dam of the top producing bitch, Carolane's Heaven Sent (9 Chs.). Linebred to Carolane's "super sire", Ch. Penlan Peter Gunn (73 Chs.), Heaven Sent produced eight of her champion get. A nonchampion from one of these breedings produced Carolane's Annie Get Your Gun, dam of ten Tel-Mo champions, and further generations are winning today (see DELEGATE branch).

Yet another family would result when the Lacie-Lulu sister, Bethel's Karla, owned by the Bracys, was bred to the Harmony son Ch. Harga's Covington. From this breeding, Carol and Dr. Carl Beiles (Carolane) purchased Ch. Harga's Terri as a puppy in 1967, and she became their first top producer. Terri can be found behind more than 100 Carolane champions bred during the last three decades. Bred exclusively to studs from the Delegate branch, Terri produced seven champions, all but one of which have champion descendants. Her three champion daughters by Ch. Penlan Paragon's Pride (30 Chs.) were all noteworthy. Ch. Carolane's Fantasy was the top winning bitch in 1974 and the dam of two champions; Ch. Carolane's Fantasia gave them three champions; Ch. Carolane's Fancy Free is the dam of two

Ch. Carolane's Fantasy

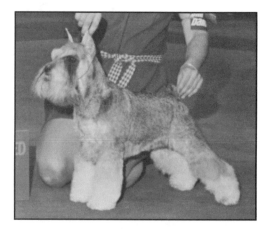

**Ch. Helarry's
Colonel Dan**

champions, including a good producing son, Ch. Carolane's Fancy That (7 Chs.).

Another family has developed from a Shorlaine-Carolane-Penlan blend. Dr. Karl Barth (Karlshof) in Tennessee purchased Ch. Shorlaine Sheik of Carolane, a Peter Gunn son out of a Heaven Sent daughter, to blend with a breeding program already in progress. Sheik sired his Ch. Karlshof Kopakobana, who, in turn, gave him Ch. Karlshof Kornukopia, sired by Ch. Penlan Promissory (27 Chs.). Kornukopia is the dam of five Karlshof champions to date, including Ch. Karlshof Handful of Whim-Cin, the top winning male in 1994. Owned by David Hallock (Whim-Cin), and handled by Lanny Hirstein, his two-year career netted him over 60 BOBs and 30 Group placements, plus several Specialty wins.

It is interesting to note here that Peter Gunn is out of a Dark Victory granddaughter, Ch. Penlan Proud of Me. Her dam, Ch. Penlan Prelude to Victory, is out of Penlan's foundation bitch, Penlan Cadet Too. This makes Peter Gunn intensely linebred to Ruffian, although he appears in the tail-male line from the Delegate branch.

Of the four top producing Ruffian-Delsey sons, Ch. Helarry's Danny Boy proved most effective in bringing this line forward. Danny Boy had to take a back seat as a show dog in favor of his brothers, Dark Victory and Chester. He did, however, win four Specialties, most importantly the Chicago Specialty in 1961, topping fifty-three entries under Dorothy Williams (Dorem).

The Danny Boy son Ch. Helarry's Colonel Dan is intensely linebred to Delsey, being out of her double granddaughter, Delsey's Sweet Heidi. Colonel Dan is the sire of 22 champions and is best known as the producer of first-rate bitches. Foremost among them is Ch. Wynmore Summer Song, bred by Josephine Moore (Wynmore). Purchased as a puppy by professional handler Claudia Seaberg, Summer Song was allowed an extraordinary career in the show ring, and was number one bitch for two consecutive years. After one coat as a

**Ch. Merry Makers Dyna Mite
with Jinx Gunville**

champion in 1970 which netted her eleven BOBs and ten Group placements, Summer Song really took off the next year, winning two Bests in Show, a Specialty Best and 21 Group placements, including nine Firsts, out of 26 Bests of Breed.

The Colonel Dan daughters bred at Bethel and Shorlaine did much to bring this family forward. A litter sired for Penlan, however, would prove to be the most influential.

The Penlan family, already chronicled in the Delegate chapter, has its roots deeply within the Ruffian branch. Lanny and Penny Hirstein's foundation bitch, Helarry's Lolly, is out of a Ruffian-Delsey daughter and was bred to a Ruffian-Delsey son to produce their Penlan Cadet Too (10 Chs.). The three principal Helarry studs have their broadest impact through the Penlan breeding program.

Although the Ruffian son Ch. Helarry's Dynamite failed to make the mark as a top producer, he leaves a legacy through a son, Ch. Amigo of Merry Makers (5 Chs.), and a grandson, Ch. Merry Makers Dyna Mite (15 Chs.). The Merry Makers were established four decades ago by Mabel (Jinx) Gunville in Illinois. Here is where Dyna Mite spent his autumn years as a cherished house pet. His death occurred the same week in which his namesake was born. Appropriately named, "Topper" was dynamite in the show ring with a record of three Bests in Show and a dozen Group Firsts, frequently owner-handled, but more often by Robert and Madeline Condon.

The Condons, in addition to their roll as professional handlers, also did a bit of breeding. Their Amigo daughter, Ch. Madeline's Sweet Charity, is the dam of three champions, including Ch. Madeline's Sweet Cyn, by Dark Victory. She, in turn, is the dam of Cyngar's Eliza Doolittle (3 Chs.), by Pride, the dam of the BIS-winning bitch, Ch. Cyngar's Light Up (3 Chs.).

These top producing bitches are deeply entrenched in the Ruffian branch, Sweet Charity being out of Pickwick's G.W. Dark Angel (3 Chs.), a Ruffian granddaughter and double great-granddaughter. Angel is one of several producing bitches to emerge from the longtime breeding program at Pickwick Kennel in Michigan, established in the mid-1950s by Ursula Buys and brought forward by her son Bruce Derrickson.

If any Ruffian litter should be singled out as most significant it would have to be the one produced by the Tribute daughter, Miss Belvedere. C-Ton's Abigail, from this breeding, gains a strong hold on breed progress as the dam of Helarry's Delsey. Abigail's brother, Ch. C-Ton's Bon Fire, begins a tail-male line of top producers of extraordinary importance. Ch. Jay Dee's Sky Rocket, by Bon Fire out of a Ruffian daughter, brings the line forward as the sire of BIS-and multiple-Group-winning Ch. Sky Rocket's First Stage (8 Chs.).

Few successful breeding programs begin with the purchase of a male. Such was the case with Judie and Frank Ferguson (Sky Rocket). First Stage came to live with the Fergusons after a successful show career. Essentially a pet, he was little used at stud. He did, however, produce eight champions, the most important from a breeding to a local "pet" bitch. Mrs. Ferguson describes the events that followed:

**Ch. Sky Rocket's Upstart
with Judie Ferguson**

This bitch (Tessie Tigerlily) was quite nice and could have done well in the show ring, but she was just a family pet. The bitch had a litter of four (2 dogs, 2 bitches). Due to whelping problems the litter was delivered by section and had to be hand raised.

When the puppies were six to eight weeks old the owner was anxious to sell. We had not seen the litter but assumed they would be quite nice since the mother and her pedigree were sound. Between the William Hoehns and ourselves we sent two buyers to the breeders The buyers were helped and advised about how to pick the best puppy. When the litter was eleven weeks old the breeder called again, now desperate to sell her remaining two puppies before ear cropping. Sight unseen, we bought the remaining puppies, a dog and a bitch, at pet price.

The two rejects—the two puppies no one wanted to buy—were Ch. Sky Rocket's Uproar and Ch. Sky Rocket's Upstart. "Uppity" was the dam of one Best in Show winner and "Bounder" the sire of three. Through their sons and daughters this winning heritage is being continued. Both were the producers of top-ranked winners and producers, but above all else, both were wonderful family pets. Pretty good for two puppies the breed couldn't sell.

The CH. SKY ROCKET'S UPROAR line

Whelped February 6, 1968, Ch. Sky Rocket's Uproar was an extraordinary individual and enjoyed an extraordinary show career. Finished as a yearling, always conditioned and handled by the Fergusons, he was well received his first year as a Special. He ranked number four in 1970 with a record of 21 Bests of Breed including two at Specialties. The next year was his, earning the largest number of Knight points (970) to that date, and leading all systems. His record that year included a Best in Show and 18 Group placements, seven of them Firsts. Uproar also topped five more Specialties, including the AMSC at Montgomery County over a field of 117 under Gene Simmonds (Handful).

Uproar's success as a sire was immediate and dramatic. The trend began with his best producing son, Ch. Sky Rocket's Bound To Win (25 Chs.), owned by Isabelle and Homer Graf (Reflections). Joan Huber helped to find this one, and piloted him throughout his career. He was "Bound To Win," and did!

Ch. Sky Rocket's Uproar winning Best of Breed at the 1971 AMSC Specialty at a rain-soaked Montgomery County under breeder-judge Gene Simmonds, handled by Judie Ferguson; Emanuel Miller presenting trophy.

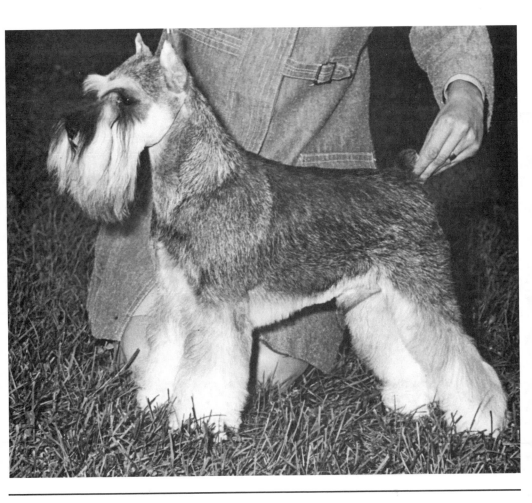

Ch. C-Ton's Bonfire
Ch. Jay Dee's Sky Rocket
Oh By Jingo

Ch. Meldon's Ruffian
Miss Belvedere
Ch. Meldon's Ruffian
Phil-Mar's Glory Lady

Ch. Sky Rocket's First Stage
    Ursafell Sandpiper
Miss Little Guys
    Ursafell Niblet

Talisman of Ledahof
Ursafell Forest Filligree
Ursafell Sandpiper
Handful's Snowflake

CH. SKY ROCKET'S UPROAR
    Ch. Bramble of Quality Hill
    Ch. Wid's Von Kipper, CDX
    Mildot's Whiskers Allegresse, CDX

Ch. Gengler's Drum Major
Ch. Dream Girl Of Silver Oaks
Ch. Haldeen's Allegro
Haldeen's Miss Whiskers, CD

Tessie Tigerlily
    Ch. Haldeen's Allegro
Martin's Countess Von Heidi
    Malmer's Miss Tammy

Ch. Phil-Mar Gay Knight
Dorem Music
Ch. Trayhom Talleyrand
Marbert's Tune Topper

Ch. Sky Rocket's Bound To Win is Best in Sweepstakes at the February 1973 AMSC Specialty under breeder-judge Sue Baines, handled by Joan Huber.

Starting as a 6-9 months puppy in the fall of 1972, he won the Sweepstakes at the New York Specialty, won his classes and was Reserve at the AMSC Montgomery County, and capped it the following week with a Best of Breed at the Mount Vernon Specialty. He was brought out again at the February AMSC, where Sue Baines (Irrenhaus) had her work cut out as the entry of forty-two Sweepstakes puppies included some of the best. The 9-12 puppy dog class of eight saw first go to Bound To Win, second to Ch. Jadee's Jump Up (40 Chs.) and third to Ch. Playboy's Block Buster (22 Chs.). All would be breed leaders and

Ch. Sky Rocket's Bound To Win

**Ch. Sumerwynd's
Still Sizzlin
with Wade Bogart**

top sires. Bound To Win won the Sweepstakes and in 1973 went on to beat by just a few points two of the best — Ch. Hughcrest Hugh Hefner (15 Chs.) and Ch. Penlan Paperboy (44 Chs.) — as number one Miniature Schnauzer (Knight System). His record that year included a Best in Show, six Group Firsts and four Specialty Bests, including the AMSC Montgomery County, and his second win at Mount Vernon. He did just as well in 1974, repeating at Montgomery County and winning a third consecutive Mount Vernon Best.

Bound To Win did more than just win, claiming three top-producing sons and four daughters among his 25 champion get. Joan Huber managed the careers of most of his offspring, beginning with her own father-son brace of top producers, Ch. Blythewood National Anthem (25 Chs.) and Ch. Blythewood National Acclaim (32 Chs.). Joan also handled Ch. Postillion's Buccaneer (8 Chs.), Ch. Contempra Foolish Pleasure (7 Chs.) and the bitch Ch. Wademar Aagin (4 Chs.).

In addition to Acclaim, Anthem leaves two other top producing sons, Ch. Far Hills Big Bucks (6 Chs.) and Am. and Can. Ch. Blythewood National Newsman (7 Chs.), a brother to Acclaim, who went north of the border to become Canada's all-time top sire.

Bound to Win can claim a large part of the credit for the successes of the Sumerwynd breeding program founded by the brothers Wade and Brian Bogart, along with Brian's wife Patricia. Their foundation bitch, Ch. Sumerwynd's Standing Ovation, is a daughter of Acclaim, out of the Bound To Win daughter Ch. Blythewood What's New Nikia. Ovation gave them five champions, most notably a son, Am. and Can. Ch. Sumerwynd Still Sizzlin (6 Chs.), when linebred

**Ch. Giminhof
Ruffle 'N
Flourishes**

to Newsman. The Sizzlin son, Ch. Sumerwynd Bandsman Upbeat (5 Chs.) resulted from a very successful period developed with the combination of Sumerwynd with Carole Weinberger's Bandsman family. The Ovation daughter, Sumerwynd's Society Page, by the B/S Ch. Bandsman's Newsprint (26 Chs.), gave them four champions, three by their the good producing sire, Ch. Sumerwynd Bandsman Showoff (12 Chs.). The Bogart family can now claim over 30 homebred champions.

Acclaim is also the sire of the good producing Ch. Blythewood Rocket Man (3 Chs.), owned by Karen and Gary Clausing (Giminhof) in Kansas. Rocket Man will be remembered as the sire of two top producing daughters: Ch. Giminhof Ruffle 'N Flourishes (7 Chs.) and Rocket's Ups Shanna (6 Chs.).

Ruffle, out of a black Giminhof bitch, is the foundation for Susan Atherton's Sathgate Kennel, now in California. Six of her champions are from two litters sired by Ch. Regency's Right On Target (78 Chs.) and include BIS-winning Ch. Sathgate Breakaway (25 Chs.) who was honored as Best of Breed

Ch. Sathgate Celestial and Ch. Sathgate Champagne winning Best Brace in Show at the 1985 Montgomery County Kennel Club under Henry Stoecker, handled by Susan Atherton.

at AMSC Montgomery County in 1985. His younger sisters, Ch. Sathgate Celestial and Ch. Sathgate Champagne (4 Chs.), won Best Brace in Show that year. Breakaway returned to Montgomery County three years later to win the AMSC Specialty from the Veteran Class. This is a family in which top producing bitches abound. Besides Champagne, who produced Ch. Sathgate Fascination, dam of a litter of three champions by Breakaway, there is Champagne's sister, Ch. Sathgate Barnburner (4 Chs.), and her granddaughter, by Breakaway, Ch. Sathgate Knickers (5 Chs.). Always owner conditioned and handled, the

Ch. Sathgate Breakaway

175

**Ch. Irrenhaus Flights of Fancy
with Sue Baines**

twenty-eight homebred Sathgates champions have enjoyed many successes at Specialties.

Shanna is owned by professional handlers Priscilla and Clarence Wells, in Oklahoma. Their Aachen Kennel houses mostly clients' dogs, but they try to raise a litter or two when time and space permits. Shanna has a top producing son, Ch. Aachen Sling Shot (6 Chs.)

The partnership of Sue Baines and Jacquelyn Hicks (Irrenhaus) was among the first to capitalize on the Bound To Win qualities. He gave them a trio of champion bitches out of their Ch. Winagin Showstopper that included Ch. Irrenhaus Fancy Finish (5 Chs.). Linebreeding Fancy Finish to Ch. Skyline's Blue Spruce (55 Chs.) gave them two showstoppers in Ch. Irrenhaus Blueprint (19 Chs.) and Ch. Irrenhaus Flights of Fancy (8 Chs.).

Flights of Fancy and Blueprint were shown alternately in 1978 and both accumulated outstanding records. Flights of Fancy was the number one bitch that year, winning 23 Bests of Breed including a Specialty, going on to earn two GroupFirsts and nine additional placements. Blueprint almost duplicated her record with 21 Bests of Breed, one at a Specialty, plus 14 Group placements including two Firsts.

**Ch. Irrenhaus
Blueprint**

**Ch. Irrenhaus
Survivor**

Both were even more impressive as producers. Flights of Fancy established a new record as the dam of six champions from a single litter, linebred to the Blueprint son Ch. Imperial Stamp O'Kharasahl (8 Chs.). Ch. Irrenhaus Stand Out was clearly the stand out among the sextuplets and became a BIS winner. Stand Out sired 21 champions, most notably the number one Schnauzer, all systems 1984, Ch. Irrenhaus Survivor (16 Chs.), out of the Blueprint daughter Ch. Irrenhaus Bluet (3 Chs.). Survivor would sire the last important stud dog that came from Irrenhaus before their breeding program ceased. Well-named Ch. Irrenhaus Classic (6 Chs.) did much to advance activities at Barclay Square, Adamis and Gough's, including a multiple BIS and AMSC Specialty-winning son, Ch. Gough's Class Act O'Pickwick, co-owned by Bruce Derrickson (Pickwick) and Alice Gough. His five Bests in Show during 1995 tied a breed record. Needless to say, he was the year's number one Schnauzer — all systems.

**Ch. Gough's Class Act O'Pickwick
with Bill McFadden**

Ch. Maroch's Star Attraction

John and Joan Gulbin (Maroch) of Staten Island, New York, went to Bound To Win early on, getting Ch. Maroch's Standing Ovation. Linebred back to Uproar, she gave them their top producer, Ch. Maroch's Star Attraction, dam of six champions, including the good producing son Ch. Maroch Master Charge (13 Chs.). The wealth was spread through Star Attraction's daughter, Ch. Maroch Cobby Cuddler, dam of Ch. Maroch Starwood Kiss Me Kate, who gave Alma Contrino (Gentry) her start, with three champions, and Maroch Go For It, purchased by Joan Huber (Blythewood), giving her five champions.

Another solid line of top producers stems from the Uproar son Ch. Jadee's Jump Up (40 Chs.), bred, owned and shown by Judy and Donald Smith (Jadee), and from their first homebred litter. Over a three-year span, Jump Up won five Specialties and four Groups. His breeding is intensely Ruffian, being out of a Colonel Dan daughter whose dam is by Harmony. Jump Up claims two top producing sons, Ch. Sky Rocket's Travel More (9 Chs.) and Ch. Repitition's Upcharge (5 Chs.), Carol and Kurt Garmaker's foundation sire. Upcharge is behind three more generations of top producers — a son, Ch. Repitition's Best Beau (6 Chs.), his son, Ch. Repitition's Rebel Warrior (17 Chs.), and his son, the black and silver Ch. Repitition's Darth Vader (6 Chs.).

Jump Up's best producing son, Ch. Sky Rocket's Travel More (9 Chs.), was purchased by the Moores (Travelmor), giving them a whole new approach with two daughters, Ch. Travelmor's Tartar (3 Chs.) and Ch. Travelmor's Tantrum (3 Chs.), the latter out of their Travelmor's Better Believe It (3 Chs.).

Jump Up is best known for his daughters, including BIS-winning Ch. Cyngar's Light Up (3 Chs.), the number one bitch in 1977, owned by Ruth and Douglas Dempster (Mariah). A Light Up son, Ch. Mariah's Forest Fire, by Blue Spruce, is the sire of Joan Williams's foundation bitch, Ch. Jolee Fire Stix Kandy Of Jadee, giving her four Jolee champions.

**Ch. Jadee's
Jump Up**

Ch. Mariah's I've Got A Secret **Ch. Haybrook's Son Rise**

This family was most effectively brought forward by the partnership of Robert Lashbrook and Steve Hayden (Haybrook) of Springfield, Illinois, who started with a Light Up daughter, Ch. Mariah's I've Got A Secret, that gave them four champions, including two top producing bitches, Ch. Haybrook's Sharpshooter (6 Chs.) and Ch. Haybrook's Pearl Of A Promise (3 Chs.). The Sharpshooter daughter Ch. Haybrook's Shooting Match brought honor to this family in 1987, as one of the few bitches to win the Montgomery County AMSC Specialty. She is the dam of the good producing bitch, Ch. Haybrook's Match Maker (3 Chs.), by Ch. Haybrook's Son Rise (5 Chs.).

The Jump Up get that proved most important came from his breedings to the Garmakers' Jobie (4 Chs.). She produced two of her champions by Jump Up, but more importantly, three nonchampion daughters that are top producers: Muffin XXIV (3 Chs.), Repitition's Kyssan Kismett (3 Chs.) and Repitition's Epitome (4 Chs.).

Muffin XXIV, like her dam Jobie, would seem unimpressive in a pedigree, lacking a title and even a prefix. Their producing ability, however, is undeniable. Muffin's champion get, linebred within this family, include Ch. Repitition's Renaissance (8 Chs.), foundation for Carole Weinberger's Bandsman family in Maryland (see CH. SKY ROCKET'S UPSWING line).

Repitition's Kyssan Kismett

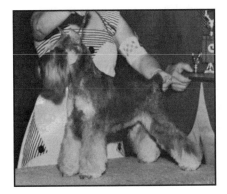

Repitition's Kyssan Kismett served as foundation for Jerry Oldham's Jerry O Kennel in Oregon, giving her second-generation top producers in a son, Ch. Jerry O's Secret Agent (9 Chs.), and a daughter, Ch. Jerry O's Kiss 'N Run (6 Chs.), by Ch. Jadee's Hush Up (11 Chs.). A nearly finished full sister, Jerry O's Kiss 'N Angel Jadee, is the dam of Ch. Jadee's Royal Supershot (16 Chs.), owned by Marge McClung (Wenmar). Handled by his breeder, Judy Smith, Supershot won a dozen Groups in 1985,

**Ch. Jadee's
Royal Supershot
with Judy Smith**

the same year in which his first five champions crossed the finish line. Kiss 'N Run brings this family forward as the dam of Ch. Jerry O's Future Shock (4 Chs.), which produced two formidable sons, Ch. Sumerwynd Bandsman Showoff (12 Chs.) and the B/S Ch. Bandsman's Newsprint (26 Chs.). Kiss 'N Run is also the dam of a B/S son Ch. Jerry O's Rain Check (14 Chs.), the sire of Newsprint, as well as the B/S Ch. Jerry O's Abiqua Frostfire, dam of three Abiqua champions. Rain Check is also the sire of the good producing salt and pepper sire, Ch. Carlyn's Check My Label (6 Chs.).

Repitition's Epitome has two top producing daughters. Repitition's Midnight Blue, by Ch. Sky Rocket's Upswing (15 Chs.), is the dam of Ch. Repitition's Best Beau (6 Chs.). Epitome, bred back to her sire Jump Up, produced Ch. Repitition's Rampage Brand (4 Chs.), foundation for many of the champions from Wisconsin bearing Janice Ramel's Rampage brand. Her champions, all by Ch. Irrenhaus Blueprint (19 Chs.), include the good producer Ch. Rampage's Kat Burglar (6 Chs.), sire of the very influential black and silver Ch. Rampage's Waco Kid (24 Chs.). Although Waco's impact on B/S exceeds all other modern sires, he heads an equally dynamic line of salt and pepper sires, beginning with his son, Ch. Rampage's Kid Moody, the sire of Ch. Rampage's Express Mail (33 Chs.), who stood number two in the ranking for 1986, when he won 38 Breed wins, including two Specialties, and also earned six Group Firsts, and a dozen additional placements.

Other top producing bitches at Rampage include the Blue Spruce daughter Ch. Rampage's Moody Blue (3 Chs.), and her daughter, Ch. Rampage's In The Mood (4 Chs.). The latter's sister, Ch. Rampage's Got The Mood, brought this prolific family forward through her daughter, Ch. Rampage's Positive Mood, dam of three champions, including the number one Schnauzer for 1993, her daughter, Ch. Rampage's Awesome Z. Positive Mood will be best remembered as the dam of the B/S Rampage's Positive Attitude (6 Chs.). Five of her champion get, all by Express Mail, were B/S, the exception being the number one

Ch. Rampage's Express Mail is Best in Sweepstakes at the 1985 Delaware Valley Specialty under breeder-judge Carol Weinberger, handled by Carol Garmaker.

Schnauzer for 1990 and 1991, Ch. Rampage's Representative. His stature was greatly enhanced by the fact that he became the number one sire for 1993, '94 and '95 (tied). Among the 45 champions produced in his first five years at stud is the outstanding winner, Awesome Z.

This extraordinary alliance was formed in 1989 — the 3 Rs (Rampage/Repitition/Ro-Sean), being joined by Hal and Jan Smith (Awesome) of Florida. They would sponsor both Representative and Awesome Z, to all but dominate the breed for the next four years. Representative served notice on the '89 Montgomery County weekend, scoring two five-pointers at Hatboro and Devon from the 9-12 puppy class. His record thereafter was phenomenal. Shown vigorously for two years, and on special occasions since, he topped 15 Specialties, including the 1996 Spring AMSC from the veterans class, and won four Bests in Show, over 200 BOBs, from which came over 150 Group placements, including 48 Group Firsts. His Knight point total of over 4,000 is unprecedented.

And then came Ch. Rampage's Awesome Z, earning 2,677 Knight points from over 150 BOBs, including 11 Specialties, plus a Best in Show, and over 100 Group placements, including 29 Group Firsts. Jan Ramel (Rampage), Carol Garmaker (Repitition), the late Sean O'Connor (Ro-Sean) and Hal and Jan Smith (Awesome) are to be congratulated.

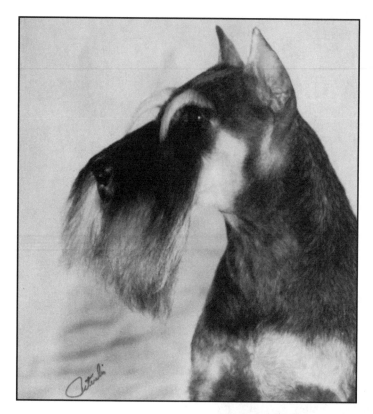

**Ch. Rampage's
Representative
with Carol Garmaker**

**Ch. Rampage's
Awesome Z
with Sean O'Connor**

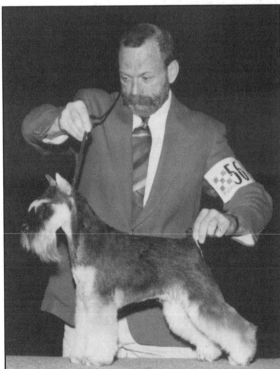

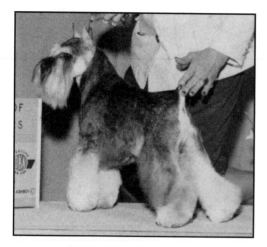

Ch. Meadoway Yankee Pedlar

An eastern branch of the 3 Rs family was founded in Massachusetts by Jane Gilbert (Meadoway). Her foundation, Ch. Repitition's Sparkle Plenty (7 Chs.), is given her due in the chapter on black and silver as this color variety's all-time top dam, with over 75 champion descendants, spread equally among S/P and B/S. One of these is the most dynamic show bitch of the 1990s, Ch. Das Feder's Drivin' Miss Daisy. There is also a strong salt and pepper branch being developed at Meadoway and being interwoven with the colored offspring from Sparkle. These are based on Ch. Rampage's Rebellion, a daughter of Moody Blue. She has produced well for Jane, giving her the 1989 Montgomery County Sweeps winner, Ch. Meadoway Sunshine, and being the great-granddam of the Sweeps winner in 1992, Ch. Meadoway Yankee Pedlar, the sire of six champions to date. Since 1982, Meadoway has bred or owned 22 champions, including three top producing sires, as well as the famed Sparkle Plenty.

Yet another Jump Up daughter, Ch. Twin Tree's Sky Jumper, would serve as foundation for Virginia Rice's Liebestraum Kennel in Florida. Bred to Ch. Shorlaine Dynamic Flash (20 Chs.), she produced Ch. Liebestraum's Bad Mamma Jamma — a 12 1/2 inch bitch that did it all! Jamma was Best in Sweepstakes at the Florida West Coast Specialty in 1983, and Best of Breed at the same show one year later, ending 1984 as number two bitch. She was the top producing bitch in 1988 and has since produced seven champions, including a multiple-Group-winning son, Ch. Liebestraum's Despirato (6 Chs.).

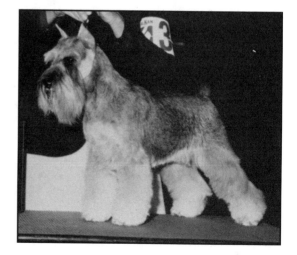

**Ch. Liebestraum's
Bad Mamma Jamma**

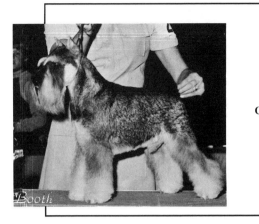

Ch. C-Ton's Bon Fire
Ch. Jay Dee's Sky Rocket
Oh By Jingo
Ch. Sky Rocket's First Stage
Ursafell Sandpiper
Miss Little Guys
Ursafell Niblet
CH. SKY ROCKET'S UPSWING
Ch. Jay Dee's Sky Rocket
Ch. Sky Rocket's First Stage
Miss Little Guys
Ch. Sky Rocket's Upstart
Ch. Wid's Von Kipper, CDX
Tessie Tigerlily
Martin's Countess Von Heidi

The CH. SKY ROCKET'S UPSWING line

The Smiths of Jadee had the pleasure of owning Ch. Sky Rocket's Upswing, in addition to Jump Up, blending their offspring with considerable success. Upswing maintained his Best in Show heritage into a fifth generation, also winning a Specialty Best, shown on only one coat in 1974. He produced well at home, nearly half of his 15 champion get bred at Jadee. Four of these were out of their foundation bitch, Heather's Windy Weather (6 Chs.), and included Ch. Jadee's Junebug (7 Chs.); three were out of the Windy daughter Ch. Jadee's Juju and include the good producing sire Ch. Jadee's Hush Up (11 Chs.).

Junebug was purchased as a puppy by David Owen Williams (Dow) of New York and proved an outstanding foundation. Among her offspring are three top producing daughters, as well as a son, Ch. Dow's Evergreen (10 Chs.).

Ch. Dow's Evergreen

The star of this family is the BIS-winning Junebug daughter, Ch. Dow's I Can't Smile Without You, by Peter Gunn. She is the dam of five champions, tightly linebred within the Ruffian branch. Bred to Blue Spruce, Junebug produced Evergreen and Ch. Dow's Lady Sings The Blues (6 Chs.). David was one of the first to combine lines from the significant sires—Peter Gunn and Blue Spruce.

Williams combined efforts with Margo Klingler (Dimensions) in Texas, so several winners bear both their prefixes. In 1985, Ch. Dimensions Over The Road (13 Chs.), from a Dimensions sire and a Dow dam (all linebred from Junebug), won one of the largest Best in Shows ever recorded by the breed, topping over 2,500 dogs in Arizona. Two weeks earlier, in February, he won the AMSC Specialty.

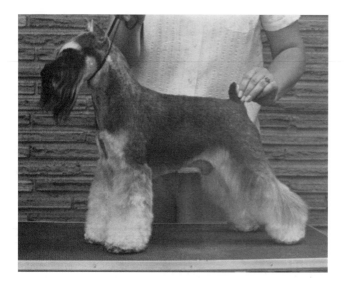

Ch. Jadee's
Hush Up

Ch. Jadee's Hush Up (11 Chs.) went to live in Idaho to head a breeding program already in progress. Wyoma and Owen Clouse (Wy-O) bought their first Miniature Schnauzer in 1974, and then her half sister two years later, both daughters of Ch. Hughcrest Hugh Hefner (15 Chs.). These were finished, followed by three of their children. The year 1979, when Hush Up joined them, marked the beginning of a whole new approach. He really hooked Wyoma on showing, as she handled him to several Group placements including two Firsts. His major contribution as a sire would come from the offspring he produced at Jerry'O, out of Repitition's Kyssan Kismet, previouly discussed.

His impact at Wy-O came as the result of purchasing a Hush Up daughter bred in Canada at Annfield. Ch. Annfield Justa Jiffy became their eighth champion and is behind everything that is new at Wy-O. She gave them four champions, that in turn are producing consistently in the next generation. Her daughter, Ch. Wy-O's Jiffy Pop, by Breakaway, produced three Champions from a breeding to Representative. Jiffy Pop's fourth, Ch. Wy-O's Shotgun, by Sharpshooter, won BOB at eleven months from the classes at Devon in 1991, and was also Best in Sweepstakes at AMSC Montgomery County. When bred to the two Representative-Poppy girls, Shotgun produced some very promising

Ch. Wy-O's Jiffy Pop
with Wyoma Clouss

children, including Ch. Wy-O's Barnburner, finishing at thirteen months with a BOS from the Bred-by-Exhibitor class at AMSC Montgomery County in 1994. Winning at AMSC Nationals has become a habit at Wy-O, with others scoring well at California AMSC Specialties.

One of the most important Upswing daughters has to be Ch. Repitition's Renaissance (8 Chs.), foundation for Carole Weinberger's Bandsman family. A very successful show bitch, Renaissance won over two dozen Breed wins and many Group placements before settling into her more important role as a producer. Renaissance is an intensely linebred bitch, with over a dozen crosses to Ruffian. She carries three lines to Ch. Sky Rocket's First Stage (8 Chs.) and boasts three of the breed's most influential sires closeup in her pedigree.

Renaissance was bred five times. The five surviving puppies from two trouble-filled litters were all sold as pets. It was her two litters sired by Ch. Dardane Wagonmaster

**Ch. Repitition's Renaissance
with Carol Garmaker**

(9 Chs.), and the one by Ch. R-Bo's Victory Flash (30 Chs.) that proved her worth. Her offspring included BIS-winning Ch. Bandsman's Legacy. It was the Renaissance daughter Ch. Bandsman's Bouquet, by Victory Flash, that proved to be the most valuable. Bouquet's first litter in 1984, produced four champions — all finished as puppies. These include the Sweepstakes winner at AMSC Montgomery County, Ch. Bandsman's Talisman. Most importantly, the three bitches each became top producers: Ch. Bandsman's Cookie

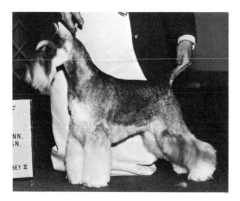

**Ch. Bandsman's
Bouquet**

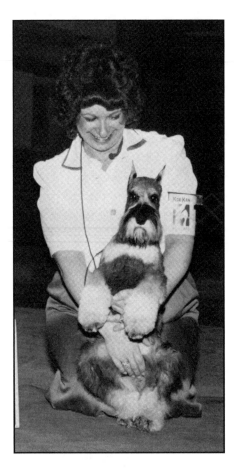

**Ch. Bandsman's Cookie Bouquet
with Carole Weinberger**

Bouquet (6 Chs.), Ch. Bandsman's Free Spirit (11 Chs.), shared with Sumerwynd, and Ch. Bandsman's PostScript (5 Chs.), the latter serving as foundation for Dr. Paula Steele's PostScript Kennel in Georgia.

Paula had already finished a pair of R-Bo champions before PostScript was purchased in 1985 as a four-month-old puppy. She became the top bitch — all systems — in 1986, handled by Sue Baines (Irrenhaus). Bred twice to her grandsire, Victory Flash, she produced five champions, from which have come two more generations of good winners and producers. Dr. Steele and Mrs. Ellis co-owned the good producing sire Ch. R-Bo's Devil's Advocate (9 Chs.). The working relationship between Dr. Steele, Mrs. Ellis and Mrs. Weinberger continues to keep the breed to the fore in the Southeast.

Several other breeders would add Bandsman bitches to their families. These include Janet Taylor's Pip'N's, based on Ch. Bandsman Free N Easy (4 Chs.), Paddy Skinder's Tammy's, based on Ch. Bandsman's Tammy of Laird (4 Chs.), and Jerry Oldham's Jerry O's helped by Bandsman N'Jerry O's Flirt (4 Chs.).

It was Carole's association with Jerry Oldham that resulted in Bandsman's top producing sire, Ch. Bandsman's Newsprint (26 Chs.). That he is black and silver makes it all the more unique. When Carole purchased the dark salt and pepper, Ch. Jerry O's Future Shock (4 Chs.), and bred her to half brother, Ch. Jerry O's Rain Check (14 Chs.), she could not have possibly known how great an effect Future Shock would have on the black and silver variety, as the dam of Newsprint. The key bitch in his background would be Repitition's foundation bitch, Jobie, as Newsprint carries lines to each of her previously mentioned top producing daughters, Muffin XXIV, Repitition's Kyssan Kismett and Repitition's Epitome. When Newsprint's 25th champion crossed the finish line in 1995, he replaced his famous grandsire, Waco, as the all-time top producing black and silver sire. Newsprint's impact extends north of the border, too, as his B/S son, Can. Ch. Bandsman's Imprint, owned by Hazel Whelan, is the sire of 15 Canadian (and two AKC) champions to date.

There is so much more to the Bandsman story, some of which is best told by Carole:

Mae Dickenson (Delfin) told me before I ever bred a litter that the way to make myself a breeder was to purchase the best bitch I could find, breed her right, and the rest would follow. Poppy (Renaissance) filled that requirement admirably, as all but the first Bandsman champion descend from her.

I don't know if the things I value in a Miniature Schnauzer were always there — and Poppy expressed them — or if because she looked and acted the way she did made me look for those qualities in succeeding generations. I only know that the Bandsman dogs are uniquely Poppy — they have that look.

Her legacy is all around me. She is so genetically dominant for the things that made her unique, that three, four, and even five generations later, they are still evident.

The greatest impact that Upswing would have came from his litter out of Ch. Skyline's Silver Lining. Foundation bitch—par excellence—Silver Lining, whelped January 12, 1971, is from the first litter bred by Carol Parker (Skyline), originally in California and more recently in Arizona. Seven generations of homebred champions emerged, all based on this one good bitch. And good she was, finishing from the Bred-by-Exhibitor class with several Best of Breeds, and eventually producing six champions from three different sires—all from the Ruffian branch. Five became multiple champion producers, headed by her most famous son, Ch. Skyline's Blue Spruce (55 Chs.). Mrs. Parker's formula for success was based entirely on Silver Lining offspring:

Three of these offspring became the nucleus of our breeding program. Ch. Skyline's Blue Spruce (by Ch. Sky Rocket's Upswing), Ch. Skyline's Little Britches (by Ch. Sky Rocket's Uproar) and Ch. Skyline's Summertime (by Ch. Jadee's Jump Up) head the three branches of descendency from Silver Lining which have been meshed and intermeshed in succeeding generations, so that now the name of Ch. Skyline's Silver Lining appears five times in the pedigree of our latest multiple AMSC Specialty winner.

The prepotent influence of balance, substance and movement that "Sparkle" stamped on her offspring has combined with the refinement and elegance of the Sky Rocket bloodlines to create animals of a type we consider exclusively Skyline.

**Ch. Skyline's
Silver Lining**

Ch. Jay Dee's Sky Rocket
Ch. Sky Rocket's First Stage
Miss Little Guys
Ch. Sky Rocket's Upswing
Ch. Sky Rocket's First Stage
Ch. Sky Rocket's Upstart
Tessie Tigerlily
CH. SKYLINE'S BLUE SPRUCE
Ch. Gandalf of Arador
Ch. Laddin of Arador
Ch. Faerwynd of Arador
Ch. Skyline's Silver Lining
Ch. Orbit's Time Traveler
Ch. Orbit's Lift Off, CDX
Ch. Janhof's Bon-Bon of Adford

The CH. SKYLINE'S BLUE SPRUCE line

As a breed historian, one hopes to see firsthand those individuals that will have an impact on the future. It was my good fortune to see Ch. Skyline's Blue Spruce in his ring debut at six months and one day old. To say that I was impressed is putting it mildly, indeed. The judge was similarly move. Doris Wear carried him through to Best of Breed over one of that year's leading champions. I marveled at her foresight as the first to recognize his potential.

This was fully realized in short order from coast to coast, with stopovers in the Midwest. His title quest was on the highest level, earning four Sweepstakes Bests, two of them AMSC. Spruce never took less than Reserve at any Specialty, and twice scored Best of Winners, including Montgomery County in 1974. Two breeder judges gave their stamp of approval: Dale Miller (Barclay Square) made him Best in Sweepstakes over forty-six puppies, and Jinx Gunville (Merry Makers) made him best of the 106 class dogs, bowing for Best of Breed to his cousin, Ch. Sky Rocket's Bound To Win (25 Chs.), enjoying a repeat win.

Blue Spruce returned the next year and topped them all at the AMSC under Olive Moore (Travelmor) and the next weekend at Mount Vernon under Gene Simmonds (Handful). He would go on to win four more Specialties over a two-year span, and was number one (Knight System) in 1976. His worth as a sire was just beginning to be realized, his closest competitor that year being his BIS-winning son, Ch. Skyline's Star Spangled Banner from his first litter.

Ch. Skyline's Blue Spruce was a first-class Miniature Schnauzer — one of the best that ever drew breath! Well off for make and shape, he was square and right, no question about it. He had an exquisite head-piece and a free-flowing way of going, and was well named for his unusual dark "blue" coloring. Carol described him once as having "that added look and attitude of a real stud dog . . . in short, 'sex appeal'!"

Spruce proved to be not only a splendid individual but an extraordinary sire. In his ten years at stud, he produced 55 champions, including six top producing daughters and four sons, with the line continuing to expand.

Ch. Skyline's Blue Spruce with Carol Parker

Ch. Daree's Pretty In Pink is BOS in Sweepstakes at the 1987 AMSC Specialty at Montgomery County under breeder-judge Jennifer Moore, handled by Chris Levy; Ted Bierman presenting trophy.

He figures prominently in the successes achieved at Irrenhaus through his record-setting daughter, Ch. Irrenhaus Flights of Fancy (8 Chs.), and equally successful son, Ch. Irrenhaus Blueprint (19 Chs.).

Spruce set the mood at Rampage, starting with his daughter Ch. Rampage's Moody Blue, whose three champions were all multiple champion producers. Several generations of leading winners and producers would follow.

Spruce was a leading factor in the successes at Dow and Dimensions, giving them their best produing sire and dam, Ch. Dow's Evergreen (10 Chs.) and Ch. Dow's Lady Sings The Blues (6 Chs.).

Margo Heiden founded her Sycamore Kennel on Ch. Aramis Sycamore So Blue, CD, by Spruce, out of a Bound To Win daughter. She produced six champions from five litters, two of which were by B/S sires. Several more generations of champions of both colors descend from So Blue.

Tom and Chris Levy (Abiqua) in Oregon gained two top producing daughters by Spruce, and have since bred more than twenty champions, virtually all of them owner-conditioned and-handled. Their foundation bitch, Paddle Wheel's Up Anchor, is his half sister. Abiqua Dare To Be Different (Blue Spruce - Up Anchor) is the dam of five Abiqua champions, most notably Ch. Abiqua Naughty Marietta, foundation dam for Gwen Mulheron (Daree), also of Oregon, giving her three champions, including Ch. Daree's Pretty In Pink (3 Chs.) and

**Ch. Skyline's
Storm Signal**

Ch. Daree's Serendipity. The latter was used to develop a family of Daree blacks that continue to thrive. Ch. Abiqua's Silk Stockings (Blue Spruce - Up Anchor) is the dam of three Neusky champions, including the Best in Show winner Ch. Neusky's Blue Is My World, by half brother Blueprint.

Built on superiority, the Skyline breeding program enjoyed continued success in succeeding generations, until it ceased operations in the mid-1980s. Their superstar was clearly Ch. Skyline's Storm Signal, number one (Knight System) 1983. He virtually skyrocketed to fame, gaining his status that year in two short months. He was the first Miniature Schnauzer to win the breed four consecutive days on the Montgomery County weekend, earning over 400 Knight points for his efforts. Storm Signal would score well again in 1984, adding two more AMSC Specialties in a row, repeating again at Montgomery County. Mrs. Parker has summed up her entire breeding program in this individual, and describes it appropriately:

The real purpose of dog shows is not to compile spectacular winning records, but instead to advance the development of a breed by pinpointing those individuals most valuable for breeding purposes. A student of pedigrees will immediately recognize that Storm Signal's background contains the entire history of Skyline. For the first time in six generations of breeding, we were able to combine in one pedigree the three outcross breedings of Silver Lining that formed the foundation of our entire breeding program. Three crosses go back to Blue Spruce and five to Silver Lining. In addition, the great producing bitch Ch. Faerwynd of Arador appears nine times, and the influential sire Ch. Sky Rocket's First Stage appears ten times. The outstanding DISPLAY son Ch. Meldon's Ruffian is represented well over a hundred times!

Spruce clearly heads the Skyline dynasty, beginning with the successes of Banner in the show ring and his sister Ch. Skyline's Fern of Winrush as a producer. She is the dam of three champions, including Ch. Skyline's Everlasting (5 Chs.). Bred back to Spruce, Everlasting produced one champion. She had four champions when bred to the Spruce double grandson — and heir apparent — Ch. Regency's Right On Target (78 Chs.).

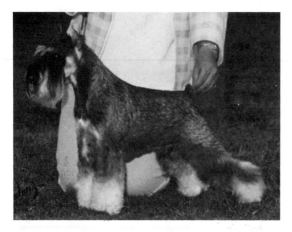

**Ch. Regency's
Right On**

Regardless of how successful a breeding program may be, unless bitches are advantageously placed in the hands of newcomers, the family will not progress. How fortunate that Beverly Verna (Regency) was able to secure not only foundation stock but the wisdom that was Skyline in her first years with the breed.

Blue Spruce would figure prominently, as the sire of seven champions out of Regency's foundation bitch Jana PD. From this breeding came two top producing daughters, Ch. Regency's Reward and Ch. Regency's Rosy Glow, both with four champion get. Their brother, Ch. Regency's Right On, proved to be Spruce's best producing son with 34 champions.

In addition to the firm foundation provided by Right On at Regency, he is behind virtually all the twenty-five champions bred in Northern California by Maxine Roster (Jax). Both of her foundation bitches, Shady Babe and Jax Casey, gave her a pair of champions by Right On. One of these, Ch. Jax Regency Renascent (3 Chs.), is the dam of two top producing daughters, Ch. Jax Honig (3 Chs.) and Ch. Jax Susse (3 Chs.), the latter by Ch. Tomei Super Star (30 Chs.), who also is the sire of her Jax Allways, another dam with three champions. Susse leaves a top producing son in Ch. Jax Landmark (5 Chs.), co-owned with Dan Durigan, who got his first three Fairwind champions from him. Few can claim as many top producing bitches in so limited a breeding program. That several are black and silver came as a bit of a surprise, but Max continues to develop her Jax family to include both color varieties, using Ruedesheim sires, and continues to average a champion each year.

Ch. Jax Susse

Also in the San Francisco area, Right On gave Amelia Baltrusaitis (Schneflock) three champions, most notably Am. and

Can. Ch. Schneflock's Timbuckto (5 Chs.), who sired the good producing Ch. Schneflock Rockette's Rocket (7 Chs.) and his sister Schneflock Rockette's Magic, dam of six champions, four in one litter, sired by Ch. Blythewood Shooting Sparks (53 Chs.). Rocket had a big year in 1992, handled by Clay Coady to 60 Bests of Breed, including two Specialties, making him the number one male with 850 Knight points. Amelia has averaged a champion each year since the first finished just over a decade ago. Her interest was sparked by a first pet purchased in 1958.

In 1980 Mrs. Verna took a calculated risk when she bred Right On to his litter sister Rosy Glow—and hit the jackpot! Bev remembers that particular whelping:

Ch. Schneflock Rockette's Rocket with Clay Coady

Target was different right from birth. He was almost totally black, with a head as long as his body. I thought — this one is either all wrong or we really have something special.

Bev brought Target and his sisters for me to see at eight weeks — and how well I remember it. Although they were like peas in a pod, all tall, dark and handsome, it was Target who stood out — a finished product in miniature — everything right, and in all the right places. He could best be described as an outline dog, squarelymade, with a little extra neck and a bang-on tailset. Seeing him a month later, he hadn't changed a bit; and again at five months, still looking and acting just right. He remained this way throughout his puppyhood, looking so finished all along the way, it was scary.

Target finished with a Group First at nine months of age, in just twenty-three days, shown entirely from the Bred-by-Exhibitor class. He won the Sweepstakes and was Best of Winners at the June 1981 AMSC Specialty in Los Angeles. For the next four years the name Target would become a byword, as he was exhibited from coast to coast with great success. His best year was 1982 when he tied for number one (Knight System), earning a BIS, three Specialties, 14 Group placements and 30 Bests of Breed. Two years later, he was still winning Specialties and Groups, along with unprecedented recognition as a sire.

Ch. Regency's Rosy Glow

Bev reminds us:

I sometimes wish that he had not come along until I had learned more. I felt that my inexperience in showing him often was to his detrement. I know that he could have done more had an experienced professional been showing him.

Target did not become the winningest Miniature Schnauzer in history, but in the five years he was used a stud, he did set a type and style that is distinctly his. The popular all-rounder, Michele Billings, made a point of telling me that no matter where she judged, she could always pick out the Target offspring right away. And picked out they were! Target can be found in the pedigrees of nearly all the nation's top-winning breeding programs. Of his 78 champions, only nine carry the Regency name. His success as a sire was not made by any one kennel, which gives me much gratification.

Perhaps it was his genetic strength, being from a brother-sister mating; perhaps it was the fact that he nicked so well with the bitches of the time, but whatever it was it seemed as if Target studied the bitch and pulled the appropriate gene out of a hat to improve on her shortcomings. In 1984 he established a new

---

Ch. Regency's Right On Target is Best of Breed at the 1983 AMSC Specialty at Great Western under judge Richard Hensel, handled by Beverly Verna; Barbara Schulenberg presenting trophy.

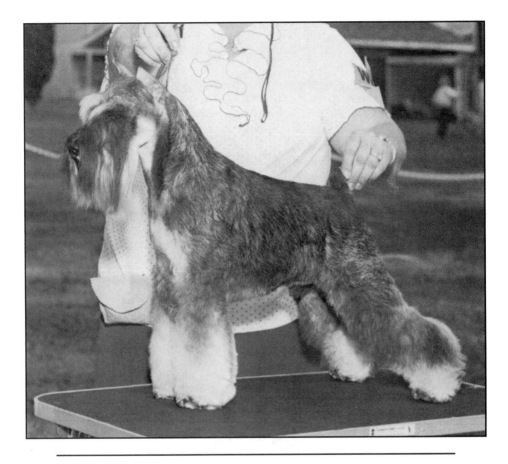

	Ch. Sky Rocket's Upswing	Ch. Sky Rocket's First Stage
Ch. Skyline's Blue Spruce		Ch. Sky Rocket's Upstart
	Ch. Skyline's Silver Lining	Ch. Laddin Of Arador
		Ch. Orbit's Lift Off, CDX

Ch. Regency's Right On
  Ch. Marcheim Poppin' Fresh   Ch. Mankit's Yo Ho
Jana PD   Ch. Miranda Von Brittanhof
  Jana Paulette   Ch. Howtwo's Hijacker
    Jana Agatha Paulette

CH. REGENCY'S RIGHT ON TARGET
  Ch. Sky Rocket's Upswing   Ch. Sky Rocket's First Stage
  Ch. Skyline's Blue Spruce   Ch. Sky Rocket's Upstart
  Ch. Skyline's Silver Lining   Ch. Laddin Of Arador
    Ch. Orbit's Lift Off, CDX

Ch. Regency's Rosy Glow
  Ch. Marcheim Poppin' Fresh   Ch. Mankit's Yo Ho
Jana PD   Ch. Miranda Von Brittanhof
  Jana Paulette   Ch. Howtwo's Hijacker
    Jana Agatha Paulette

Ch. Jerry O's Sharpshooter O'Daree with David Kirkland

one-year siring record, with 19 champion get, and duplicated the effort as the leading sire again in 1985 with 19 more. Although retired from stud at an early age, his record of 78 American and 23 Canadian champions (several with both titles) remains unchallenged.

When Target passed away in 1994, he could already claim over 600 champion descendents — many carrying him two or three times in their pedigree. Not since DISPLAY has there been a sire that could claim six top producing sons — Ch. Sathgate Breakaway (25 Chs.), Ch. Jadee's Royal Supershot (16 Chs.), Ch. Jubilee's Joker's Wild (B) (9 Chs.), Ch. B-Majer King of Swing (6 Chs.), Ch. Regency's Shot In The Dark (B) (5 Chs.) and the unfinished Jerry O's Target Practice, CDX (7 Chs.). That two are black makes his record all the more extraordinary. His impact on the black variety is unprecedented, as he has over

100 champion descendents — more than half the blacks finished in the last decade (see Black Chapter).

As for his salt and pepper sons and daughters, none have had a greater impact than those bred at Sathgate. Besides the multiple-champion Breakaway litters bred at Regency, Markworth, Far Hills, Abiqua, Wy-O and Sathgate, he has produced multiple-champion litters in Canada at Bowser and Jena.

Extraordinary results have been achieved by descendants of the best producing nonchampion sire in several decades, the Target son Jerry O's Target Practice, CDX. He produced a bonanza litter of four champions for Jerry Oldham (Jerry O) out of the intensely line-bred Bandsman 'N Jerry O's Flirt. The star among them was Ch. Jerry O's Sharpshooter O'Daree, co-owned with Gwen Mulheron (Daree) and Kathy Arnold. Handled by Bev Verna (Regency) in the West and by David Kirkland (Daland) in the East, he enjoyed being among the top show dogs for 1990, '91 and '92, and is the sire to date of 18 champions, including the all-time top winning bitch, Ch. Das Feder's Drivin' Miss Daisy.

Ch. Das Feder's Drivin' Miss Daisy with Beverly Verna

**Ch. Regency's Cream
Of Tar-Tar**

That Daisy was special, goes without saying. Bev Verna was fortunate to be asked to grade a Sharpshooter litter out of the black and silver Ch. Repitition's PB Production (4 Chs.) bred by Brad Spring (Das Feder) , and came away with a dog and bitch pup purchased for Larry and Georgia Drivon. They stayed with Bev, and Daisy was brought out as an open bitch on the 1992 Montgomery County weekend, with only limited success. I thought she was a stick out, except that her rolled coat, which was very dark, had not yet cleared into the beautiful salt and pepper coloring she would eventually enjoy. She began to come into her own by the following spring, ending 1993 as the number two Schnauzer (behind the awesome winning bitch, Ch. Rampage's Awesome Z), with a record of 60 Bests of Breed, including her first five Specialties, a Best in Show and five Group Firsts in top-class western terrier competition.

The next year was hers, earning the best one-year statistics ever achieved by a bitch — two Bests, 15 Group Firsts and 24 additional placements from 67 Breed wins, 11 of them Specialties. She earned 1,703 Knight System points for her effort — all of these "records" for bitches. But she was not through yet! On the June 1995 AMSC Specialty weekend, she established new breed records, earning her fifteenth Regional Specialty Best (five consecutive wins at the Northern California MSC), and sixth AMSC Specialty Best, for a record-setting total of twenty-one Specialty wins.

That year was great for Sharpshooter offspring, as his son, Ch. Adamis Cocked And Loaded (9 Chs.), tied for top sire.

Target's Canadian legacy, through daughters bred at Annfield, has prospered so that nearly 100 champions carry lines to him (see Canadian Chapter). His son, Am. and Jap. Ch. Regency's Cream Of Tar-Tar, owned by Sumiko Ikeda, has served the breed well in Japan, with over 20 champion get.

And, lest you forget, Target's dam, Ch. Regency's Rosy Glow, left other champion get besides Target. She is the dam of the good producing bitch Ch. Regency's Dusty Rose (3 Chs.), and more importantly a nonchampion daughter by Ch. Valharra's Extra Allaruth (6 Chs.) that was retained by Regency, doing much to bring this bitch line forward. Regency's Bonny Rose is the dam of six Regency champions, including Ch. Regency's Right On Time, who went

Ch. Time's Man Of The Hour is Best of Breed at the 1989 Cincinnati Specialty under judge Jon Cole, handled by Lisa Grames.

east to Joan Glenn (Time) to give her three champions, including a Montgomery County AMSC winning son, Ch. Time's Man Of The Hour (6 Chs.).

As one looks through current show catalogs, many familiar kennel prefixes catch the eye, along with a host of those yet to be recognized. Some of these will undoubtedly make their mark on future breed progress. We might well consider at this point the sage advice that concluded a similar section in Mrs. Eskrigge's 1960 breed "classic," *The Complete Miniature Schnauzer* (Howell Book House):

A lucky mating or two does not establish a strain, but only lays the foundation for it. All too often a breeder produces a few excellent dogs but does not know how to continue from this beginning and build upon it. Instead of seeking out suitable studs for his good bitches, or suitable bitches for a potentially excellent sire, he is too apt to breed to a big name of the wrong bloodlines or to something easily available. Or he may shy away from the bogey of too much inbreeding and dissipate a valuable line by indiscriminate crosses based on no definite plan instead of holding what he has and building further upon it. To establish a successful strain and maintain it over any extended period requires good foundation stock plus careful study of individuals and pedigrees. It involves a lot of hard work, and when it is accomplished is indeed no small achievement.

201

11

The History of Black Miniature Schnauzers

BLACK MINIATURE SCHNAUZERS have been a major factor in the breed since its inception. Peter v. Westerburg, whelped in Germany in 1902, is one of the three main pillars of the breed. All modern blacks (and all other color varieties) trace to Peter thousands of times over.

Blacks were imported into the United States in the mid-1920's, but not nearly on the scale of their salt and pepper cousins. Why blacks attracted so little attention in the early days is hard to justify, as their progress in Germany always equalled, and even exceeded that of the salt and peppers.

It was not until 1936 that the first black AKC champion would be recorded. Ch. Cunning Asta of Bambivin lived well over 16 years as the companion of her breeder, Willia Maguire of California, but leaves no modern descendants.

The next to finish, and first male, was the German import, Ch. Hupp von Schonhardt of Crystal in 1942. The third, Ch. Dirndl v. Schloss Helmstadt, also from Germany, completed her title in 1950, and would be the last German import of any color to finish. Dirndl left Champion descendants from her American breedings, but her historical significance traces to her German-bred daughters, who can be found in the pedigree of the important Italian-bred black sire, Eng. Ch. Jovinus Malya Swanee.

It was more than a decade before the next black would finish. This fourth AKC champion would mark a new beginning, as she would be the first to carry lines to the salt and pepper super sire, CH. DOREM DISPLAY. This renaissance would have an international flavor, based principally on imports. The three key dogs, in order of their impact, were Jovinus Rodin of Anfiger, from England, Italian Ch. Malya Gunter from Italy, and Koniglich The Groom from Australia. Rodin and Groom are very similarly bred, from English Jovinus and Italian Malya lines, while Gunter is intensely black-bred from German and Italian lines.

Every post-war black champion carries many lines to DISPLAY, even those descending from Gunter, who has essentially European breeding. Jovinus Risotto, as the dam of Rodin, brought nine lines from DISPLAY. Groom, doubly bred on Risotto, has more than twice as many.

Int. Ch. Ivo v.d. Heinrichsburg (B)
Frodi v. Rekelhof (B)
Olga v.d. Heinrichsburg (B)
Eng. Ch. Jovinus Malya Swanee (B)
Ital. Ch. Arno v.d. Walkmuhle (B)
Ital. Ch. Nixi dei Diavoli Neri (B)
Nitty dei Diavoli Neri (B)
JOVINUS RODIN OF ANFIGER
Eng. Ch. Wilkern Tony From American (S/P)
Eng. Ch. Jovinus Roxburgh (S/P)
Eng. Ch. Deltone Delsanta Barbara (S/P)
Jovinus Risotto (B)
Amerway Pirate (B)
Jovinus Ravenna (B)
Redenhall Hella (B)

The JOVINUS RODIN OF ANFIGER line

In the spring of 1964, Anne Eskrigge (Anfiger) of Massachusetts imported Jovinus Rodin of Anfiger. He enjoyed limited success as a show dog, acquiring five points in the United States during a period when blacks received scant consideration. His principal achievement was as the sire of a litter bred by Alice Gough of Minnesota. She bred the salt and pepper Gough's Pickwick Silver Belle, CD to Rodin in 1965. Intensely line-bred within the Ruffian branch, Belle represented the most modern type in salt and pepper. The Rodin-Belle breeding produced three blacks: a male, Gough's Ebony Royal Guardsman, and two bitches, Gough's Ebony Guardian Angel and Gough's Ebony Gay Gidget, all with champion descendants.

The Guardsman daughter, Ch. Johnson's Ebony Kwicksilver, became the first black champion in 20 years, finishing in December 1969. Her title quest included Winners Bitch at the Paul Revere Specialty - the first Specialty win for a black.

The next to finish was Ch. Woodhaven's Black Gough Drops, sired by the Guardsman son, Gough's Ebony Knight Longleat, CD. Although based in Minnesota, Gough Drops was given coast to coast exposure by his owners Harry, Helen and Dan Smith. In an extensive show career he accumulated several "firsts" for blacks, including two Group Firsts. This exposure opened the door for blacks at a critical period.

Gough Drops became a cornerstone sire, the first to produce four black

Gough's Ebony Royal Guardsman

Ch. Woodhaven's Black Gough Drops

champions. The principal breeders in the east, midwest and west used Gough Drops, each developing their own family of blacks. Alice and Wayne Gough, as the breeders of both Kwicksilver and Gough Drops, really got the ball rolling. They took the Gough Drops daughter, Gough's Ebony Heavens To Betsy (doubly bred on Knight Longleat) back to Knight Longleat to get their star of 1982, Ch. Gough's Ebony Royal Knight, CD. His accomplishments include five Group Firsts, a Specialty Best, and the first AKC all-breed Best in Show for a black, all wins owner handled by Alice.

Dolores Walters was the first westerner to make use of Gough Drops. Mrs. Walters' California-based kennel produced champions in all three colors for over two decades, frequently exporting her best throughout the world with excellent results. Although no champions resulted from the Gough Drops breeding, there are seven Walters champions that are line-bred from him. Most of these descend from Ch. Walters' Black Bonus and his sons, Ch. Walters' Black Topper and Ch. Walters' Black Bandit.

Ch. Walters' Black Bonus

Ch. Gough's Ebony Royal Knight, CD wins Best in Show in 1982 at the Greeley (CO) Kennel Club under Bettie Krause to become the first black to achieve this honor. He was shown by his breeder-owner Alice Gough.

One of the last blacks bred by Mrs. Walters, the Black Bonus son, Walters' Just Black, has sired two black champions. One of these, Ch. Jebema's Night Stormin Norman, is the sire of Ch. Jebema's Model T Of Yasmar, a 1994 black champion, already with four champion get.

Joan Corpin (Sandcastle) has had excellent success in a breeding program based on a Black Bonus daughter, bred into the Peter Gunn line, giving her nearly a dozen champions of all three colors in succeeding generations. Her black Ch. Sandcastle's Merlin V Sole Baye has enjoyed considerable success both in the show ring and as a sire.

Geri and Dick Kelly of Massachusetts purchased their first Miniature Schnauzer in 1963, and have since bred champions in all three colors. They are the premier breeders of black champions, with over 50 homebreds. Virtually all are Gough Drops descendents, with the salt and pepper Kelly's Fancy Nancy being one of the first to go to him. This breeding produced Ch. Kelly's Black Onyx (3 Chs.) and Ch. Kelly's Cassandrea Xan (4 Chs.), and the Kellys began to weave their offspring with remarkable success. Geri's thoughts about those beginnings suggest their commitment.

Blacks at that time were extremely rare in this country. They lacked bone, substance and furnishings, and as a result were neither as appealing to the eye nor as successful in the ring as the salt and peppers. We became fascinated with

Ch. Kelly's Black Onyx

Ch. Kelly's Cassandrea Xan

Gough's Ebony Knight Longleat, CD (B)	Gough's Ebony Royal Guardsman (B)
Ch. Woodhaven's Black Gough Drops (B)	Sylva Sprite Megan of Longleat (B/S)
Gough's Ebony Echo (B)	Ch. Gough's Silver Franchise, CD (S/P)
	Wynncliff Blacque Bianca (B)

CH. KELLY'S BLACK ONYX
CH. KELLY'S CASSANDREA XAN

Tucker's Tobey (S/P)	Ch. Swinheim Salutation (S/P)
Kelly's Fancy Nancy (S/P)	Gruenhagen Twiggy (S/P)
Tucker's Tinker Bell (S/P)	Ch. Tiger Bo Von Riptide (B/S)
	Maggie Lou of Frerichs (S/P)

---

the possibility and challenge of breeding black show dogs that could successfully compete. We have been fortunate in meeting this challenge by breeding a sizable number of blacks, including National Specialty Best of Breed and Best of Opposite Sex winners, all-breed Best in Show winners, and consistent Specialty and Group winners. In addition, our blacks have gained comparative success in Europe, Asia and Australia.

The Kelly's blacks claim most of the records for this color variety. Am. Can. and Bda. Ch. Kelly's K.E. Ebony Show Stopper, an Onyx son, was the first to gain titles in three countries. Whelped May 21, 1978, he was a star on several levels, being the first to gain a Canadian Best in Show. Most importantly, Show Stopper was a multiple Specialty winner, and the first black to win an AMSC Specialty, topping 56 entries including ten champions in New York, February 8, 1981. Before being exported to Japan, he sired two black champion daughters, plus a champion each in salt and pepper and black and silver.

Show Stopper was the maternal grandsire of the Kelly's next star, Ch. Kelly's Flamboyant Black — the top winning black bitch to date. I saw Flamboyant for the first time in New York where she showed herself to Best of Opposite Sex at the Specialty and Westminster. Along with the debut of one of her eventual mates, Ch. Tomei Super Star, they represented the two *"new good ones"* remembered from those events. Her quality and showmanship were well rewarded. Shown from January through June 1982, her show record consisted of 32 Bests of Breed, including the Centennial State Specialty, five Group Firsts and 13 additional placements.

That she would also become this color variety's all-time top dam comes as no surprise. Flamboyant was the dam of three litters by three different sires, resulting in one Canadian and ten AKC champions with extraordinary accomplishments. Her first litter, in-bred to Ch.Kelly's Imperial Black (5 Chs.), produced a record-setting four black champions, all Group winners. A daughter, Ch. Kelly's Ebony Top Of The Line, was not only a top winner, but became the dam of five champions, including a top producing son, Ch. Kelly's Magic Marker (7 Chs.).

Flamboyant's second litter, loosely line-bred to Ch. Jebema Rob-Hil Ebony Marquis, produced three champions, including the first black bitch to achieve a Best in Show - Ch. Kelly's Charwin's Bar None.

Her final litter, bred to the S/P Ch. Tomei Super Star (30 Chs.) also produced three champions.

In the mid-1980s, having already incorporated both Target and Peter Gunn to improve type, Geri Kelly made another salt and pepper cross, taking the black (with black and silver breeding) Kelly's Top Of The Line Ray-Zen to Ch. Meadoway's Solo Performance. The result was Ch. Kelly's Charwin's Spectular (8 Chs.) - about the darkest salt and pepper you can get. He is behind all that is new at Kelly's.

Ch. Kelly's Flamboyant Black
. . . on the move!

Ch. Kelly's Ebony Top Of The Line
with Geri Kelly

Ch. Kelly's Pebwin's Hallelujah winning Best in Show at the Tyler (TX) Kennel Club in 1990 under Raymond Fillburn, handled by breeder/co-owner Geri Kelly.

By the 1990s, the Kelly's breeding program was reaping great rewards, beginning with Am. Can. and Bda. Ch. Kelly's Pebwin's Hallelujah (17 Chs.), a Spectular son carrying three lines to Flamboyant. He was the leading winner on an all-breed basis in 1990 and '91, earning a record of three Bests in Show, 23 Group First and 49 additional placements, from 94 Bests of Breed, including a Specialty. He also became the first black to win Best in Show in all three countries in which he was shown. He returned to the "Top" the following year, as the breed's top sire, with a dozen champions. And the best was yet to come!

Ch. Kelly's Right On The Money, a Hallelujah grandson, was a breed leader in 1994, achieving one of the best one-year records for a black - three Bests in Show, 33 Group Firsts (a one-year breed record), 35 additional placements from 91 Bests of Breed, including two Specialties. He did almost as well in 1995.

Kelly's blacks have provided a base for a number of successful breeding programs. Cheryl Coffman (Jacqueminot) in Ohio, started out with a Show Stopper daughter, Kelly's Ebony Sensation (3 Chs.), and carry her top producing heritage a generation further with the Sensation daughter, Jacqueminot Jet Black, also the dam of three Champions. Shelia Prather (Shegar) has enjoyed fielding the top winning black bitch for three consecutive years, first with Ch. Shegar's Bo-Daious Ta-Ta, a granddaughter of Ch. Kelly's Charwin's Top Victory, in 1992 and '93, and in '94 with Ch. Shegar's Class Action, a daughter of Ch. Classic Midnight Cowboy (5 Chs.), who is based in the Italian Ch. Malya Gunter line.

Ital. Ch. Malya Gunter (B)
  Ch. Aljamar Tommy Gun (B)
    Klingsor's Last Summer (S/P)
Aljamar Riot Gun (B)
    Ch. Amigo of Merry Makers (S/P)
  Aljamar Riot Act (B)
    Aljamar Raven Riot (B)
CH. ALJAMAR RABBIT PUNCH (B)
    Ital. Ch. Malya Gunter (B)
  Ch. Aljamar Tommy Gun (B)
    Klingsor's Last Summer (S/P)
Ch. Aljamar Honey Bunny (B)
    Ch. Windy Hill Rob Roy (S/P)
  Ch. Suelen Bit O'Honey (S/P)
    Rojo's Lisa Gold (S/P)

The ITALIAN CH. MALYA GUNTER line

Italian Ch. Malya Gunter was imported from Italy by Janice Rue (Suelen) and Marilyn Laschinski (Aljamar). Gunter was personally selected by Mrs. Rue in 1970, and immediately left his mark. The Gunter son, Ch. Aljamar Tommy Gun, was the first black to gain points at Westminster, and the Tommy Gun daughter, Ch. Aljamar Honey Bun, the first black bitch to win a Group. Honey Bun is the dam of Ch. Aljamar Rabbit Punch, the first black sire to produce five black champion. Three were bred by Galen and Carma Ewer of the Carmel Kennel in Texas. All are out of their salt and pepper Tommy Gun daughter, Aljamar Honey Delite, CD (4 Chs.). One of these, Specialty winning Ch. Carmel Cinnamon N Honey (4 Chs.), gave them two generations of top producing sires - Ch. Carmel Knight Rider (5 Chs.) and

Ch. Shegar's Class Action with Shelia Prather

**Ch. Carmel Cinnamon N Honey
with Galen Ewer**

his son, Ch. Classic Midnight Cowboy (5 Chs.), the latter bred by Jimmy and Bonnie Preslar (Classic) who have continued the line successfully. This family can claim a few records for blacks. In 1986 Ch. Carmel Nite Life (5 Chs.), a Cinnamon N Honey daughter, became the first black bitch to go Winners at an AMSC Specialty, and she went on to Best of Winners and Best of Opposite Sex over three champions that day, earning her second 5-point win, while still a puppy. In 1987, Ch. Classic Black Ink, a Knight Rider daughter bred by the Preslars, became the first black bitch to win an AMSC Sweepstakes, and the first black with multiple Sweeps wins. The Aljamar-Suelen and Carmel families continue to flourish, spawning other breeders who are also enjoying success.

Tommy Gun has also exerted an influence on black and silvers

Ch. Carmel Nite Life, as a 6 months puppy, wins Best Opposite Sex at the Spring 1986 AMSC Specialty under breeder-judge Robert Condon, handled by Priscilla Wells.

through his black and silver grandson, Ch. Aljamar Hot Ice, CD (5 Chs.), who has champions in all three colors (see Black and Silver Chapter).

Beverly Pfaff's California-based Jebema Kennel has combined lines from Rodin and Gunter to get Ch. Jebema-Hil Black Jammer, by Aljamar's Ebony Lad, and Ch. Jebema-Robhil Ebony Marquis, by Ch. Regency's Right On Target (78 Chs.), both out of her outstanding producer Pfaff-Hils Black Cameo (3 Chs.), a granddaughter of Ch. Kelly's Black Onyx. Cameo, as the granddam of the top winning and top producing Ch. Sibehil's Dark Shadows (22 Chs.) would bring many a breed record to this family.

Pfaff-Hils Black Cameo

The KONIGLICH THE GROOM line

Jackie Walsh (now Olson) of Illinois imported Koniglich The Groom in 1965 from Sylvia Cerini of the Koniglich Kennel in Australia. He is an inbred son of Australian Ch. Jovinus Rigoletto, a full brother to Rodin, out of one of his daughters. Although Groom sired no champions, he has champion descendants in all three colors. His primary influence would be on black and silver lines (see Black and Silver Chapter).

The first black champion to emerge from this line was bred by the partnership of Jill Cook and Lucille Kocher. Miss Cook imported three black bitches in 1968. One of these, the German-bred Helga v.d. Stadtmusikanten, produced Ch. Arbury Gay Uncle Sam, sired by Sharon Tomanica's Tammashann's Black Onyx, who is doubly bred on Groom. He would be the most intensely black-bred champion to date, with no salt and pepper and only one black and silver appearing in his three-generation pedigree.

There would be a three-generation gap before the next black champion would emerge from this line. The Kellys would be responsible for a pair of littermates, Ch. Kelly's K.E. Ebony Son Of A Gunn and Ch. Kelly's K.E. Ebony Star Attraction, sired by the salt and pepper super sire, Ch. Penlan Peter Gunn (73 Chs.). They were three-quarters salt and pepper breeding, gaining their color from their great-grandsire, Uncle Sam. The branch from The Groom continues to flourish, mainly through descendents of the Kelly's breeding.

BLACK PROGRESS IN THE LAST DECADE

By 1984, a new high in black activity was achieved when an even dozen black champions were finished. At this point a total of 65 blacks had been made up, since the first in 1935. The Rodin branch dominated, with nearly three-quarters of the total carrying from three to 15 lines to Rodin. The majority trace to his grandson, Ch. Woodhaven's Black Gough Drops. The Gunter and Groom branches continued to be evident, with a pair of the 1984 champions tracing to each. For the next ten years an average of 18 blacks per year would achieve AKC titles. By 1995, over 240 black champions had been made up.

Since the mid-1980s, blacks were competing on all levels with unusual success, and the breed's two all-time top sires have contributed greatly to these achievements. Geri Kelly used Ch. Penlan Peter Gunn (73 Chs.), and his best producing son, Ch. Tomei Super Star (30 Chs.), and also went to yet another salt and pepper line when she used Ch. Jebema-Robhil Ebony Marquis, a black son of the breed's all-time top sire, Ch. Regency's Right On Target (78 Chs.). The previously mentioned multiple-BIS winning Ch. Kelly's Pebwin's Hallelujah (17 Chs.) and Ch. Kelly's Right On The Money carry a line to Target.

Target has become this color variety's most influential sire, producing ten black champions, and being behind over a hundred more by the end of 1995. It all began with the Target son, Ch. Regency's Shot In The Dark (5 Chs.), who at six months of age became the first black to win an AMSC Sweepstakes. A few months later he finished with back-to-back five-point

**Ch. Regency's Shot In The Dark
with Beverly Verna**

Ch. Jubilee's Joker's Wild

wins at the June 1984 AMSC and Southern California Specialties - another "first" for blacks. In 1985 Shot In The Dark became the first black to achieve Top Schnauzer (Knight System). He was handled throughout his career by Beverly Verna (Regency) for owners Judy and Bill Sousa (Jubilee).

The same team would field another Target son, Ch. Jubilee's Joker's Wild (9 Chs.), who served notice in 1987 by finishing as Best of Winners and Best of Opposite Sex (over 5 Specials) at the June AMSC Specialty. He would be the leading black for the next two years, winning a Best in Show and several Group and Specialty wins.

Ch. Jebema-Hil Black Jammer (B)
Rob-Hil Mr. Merlyn's Black Magic (B)
Rob-Hils Ebony Belle (B)
Ch. Jebema's Midnight Maverick (B)
Ch. Valharra's Marcus (S/P)
Jebema's Black Aruba (B)
Kelly's KE Ebony Empress (B)
CH. SIBEHIL'S DARK SHADOWS
Ch. Regency's Right On (S/P)
Ch. Regency's Right On Target (S/P)
Ch. Regency's Rosy Glow (S/P)
Rob-Hils Blaque Ni-Coal (B)
Jebema's Back Be Nimble (B)
Pfaff-Hils Black Cameo (B)
Bonanza's Gwendolyn Kricket (B)

A host of records for blacks would be shattered with the emergence of Am. and Bda. Ch. Sibehil's Dark Shadows (22 Chs.), a Target grandson, who finished at 7 1/2 months of age to become the youngest black ever to complete an AKC title. In 1986 Dark Shadows, owned by Beverly Pfaff (Jebema), and David Wortham and Russell Weaver (Ardee), began a record-setting show career by not only earning Top Schnauzer (Knight System), but also accumulating the best one-year record ever achieved by a black to that date. He started the year by winning the Southern California Specialty, and added six more by year's end. He won 86 Bests of Breed and 45 Group placements, seven of them Firsts. That 1987 saw him top his own record-setting year to repeat as Top Schnauzer - all systems, only adds impetus to his phenomenal career. Shown fearlessly from coast to coast by Joan Huber (Blythewood), he was in attendance at most every important Specialty, winning more often than not, and establishing the record for blacks with 18 Specialty Bests, 11 in 1987. In addition to his three AKC Bests in Show, he set yet another record by winning three Bermuda Bests. That he should establish new records as a sire seemed to be an expectation - and was fulfilled. Dark Shadows is the top black sire of all-time, and the first black to lead the annual list of top producing sires (1989). He numbers among his get two top producing black sons - Ch. Beacon's The Shadow Knows (5 Chs.) and Ch. B-Majer Harlem Nocturne (5 Chs.), and a daughter, Branford's Black Magic (3 Chs.).

There has been far less blending of the three original black branches (Rodin-Gunter-Groom) than might have been expected, and most current breeders are choosing salt and pepper lines to improve type. If the successes of the past decade are any true indication of quality, breeders continue to be on the right track. Type has improved far beyond what might have been expected, but true black color seems to become more and more illusive.

214

Ch. Sibehil's Dark Shadows wins Best in Show in 1987 at the Williamette Valley (OR) Kennel Club under Frank Bilger, handled by Joan Huber.

Anne Eskrigge (Anfiger), who had done so much to promote black progess, gives sage advice in the 1976 edition of *The Complete Miniature Schnauzer* (Howell Book House):

When selecting foundation stock for breeding blacks, the best plan is to choose one or more black bitches. If they are from stock in which some color crossing has already been done, care should be taken to see that such crossing has resulted in improvement of type without serious loss of color quality.

After establishing a uniform type, with a number of individuals at hand for further breeding, emphasis in selection must then be shifted to color. The problem then becomes one of retaining the desired type while using the strongest colored individuals to improve the black color. If the type is sufficiently established . . . the problem from that point on is to maintain both type and color quality.

12
The History of Black and Silver Miniature Schnauzers

THE HISTORY OF THE BLACK AND SILVER (B/S) Miniature Schnauzer is less clear-cut than that of salt and peppers (S/P) or blacks. One of the very distinct differences between solid black and B/S is that the blacks are genetically dominant while the B/S are recessive. In simple terms this means that a black parent can pass on this color gene regardless of the other parent's color, whereas both parents must carry the B/S gene to produce a puppy of that color. Two B/S parents, each having two B/S genes, will produce only B/S and cannot transmit the dominant black or S/P (the latter is dominant over B/S, but is in turn recessive to solid black). Due, however, to modifying factors about which we know too little, the quality of the black portion of the coat may vary, and some sprinkling of salt and pepper or pure white hairs may be present, as well as undercoat that is less than pure black.

It appears that the original Marienhof import, Ch. Amsel v.d. Cyriaksburg, carried the B/S gene. Her dam, Peppi v. Hohndorf, was listed in the German stud book as "black and brown," while Amsel's daughter, Fiffi of Marlou, and the latter's daughter, Abigail of Marienhof, were registered as B/S. Abigail, as the granddam of Ch. T.M.G. of Marienhof, appears many times in the pedigree of CH. DOREM DISPLAY.

The T.M.G. son Ch. Inka of Aspin Hill finished in 1938, seems to be the first B/S champion recorded by the American Kennel Club. Ch. Gretchen v. Harter was the first B/S champion bitch. She finished in 1940 and according to her owner, kept good color throughout her life. If there were any postwar

Ch. Tiger Bo Von Riptide

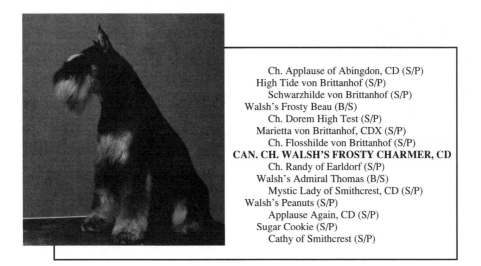

Ch. Applause of Abingdon, CD (S/P)
  High Tide von Brittanhof (S/P)
    Schwarzhilde von Brittanhof (S/P)
Walsh's Frosty Beau (B/S)
  Ch. Dorem High Test (S/P)
    Marietta von Brittanhof, CDX (S/P)
      Ch. Flosshilde von Brittanhof (S/P)
CAN. CH. WALSH'S FROSTY CHARMER, CD
  Ch. Randy of Earldorf (S/P)
Walsh's Admiral Thomas (B/S)
  Mystic Lady of Smithcrest, CD (S/P)
Walsh's Peanuts (S/P)
  Applause Again, CD (S/P)
Sugar Cookie (S/P)
  Cathy of Smithcrest (S/P)

champions of this color before 1967, the AKC has no record of them.

It was purely by chance that Ch. Tiger Bo Von Riptide emerged. His dark salt and pepper sire Ch. Melmar's Jack Frost clearly carried the B/S gene, also producing the B/S bitch Ch. Black Magic Of Mary-O. This pair when mated produced the first litter from champion B/S parents, and the first such combination to produce a pair of B/S champions.

Tiger Bo, owned in California by Sue Hendricks, did much to stimulate interest in this color through his success in the show ring. He was Best of Winners over forty-five class entries at the Southern California Specialty in 1967, and while still in the classes became the first B/S Group winner, topping a quality entry at the Kennel Club of Beverly Hills. Tiger Bo became the first B/S to sire three B/S champions, all from champion bitches linebred to Jack Frost.

The first serious attempt to develop a B/S line was begun in 1955 by Jackie Walsh (now Olsen) of Chicago. Her efforts were based on intense line-breeding from the S/P bitch Sugar Cookie, who carried twelve lines to DISPLAY. Cookie is the maternal granddam of the first B/S Canadian champion, Walsh's Frosty Charmer, CD. He, in turn, when inbred to a double Cookie granddaughter, produced the B/S Can. Ch. Walsh's Frosty Spaceman, who went to Sharon Tomanica (Tammashann) in Michigan, and Sylva Sprite Ceratina who, along with Charmer, was exported to Joanna Griggs (Sylva Sprite) in Canada.

Can. Ch. Walsh's Frosty Spaceman

Can. Ch. Eastwight Sea-Voyager, CD

**Am. & Can. Ch. Sylva Sprite
Snowy Mittens**

Mrs. Griggs began breeding B/S in 1964, importing Charmer and Ceratina from Mrs. Walsh. An additional import was made in 1968, but this time from England. Although British-bred for several generations, Can. Ch. Eastwight Sea-Voyager, CD, carries many lines to DISPLAY. Being uncropped, he became the first and only B/S Canadian champion with natural ears.

I saw Sea-Voyager on one of his rare showings in the United States. He was a first-class Miniature Schnauzer on all counts and had the best pair of natural ears I had ever seen. His coat and color were excellent and his attitude superb. He would have been easily finished in the United States had his owner persisted.

It was inevitable that Ceratina would be put to Sea-Voyager, and the result was all that could have been wanted, and more. Am. and Can. Ch. Sylva Sprite Snowy Mittens became the first B/S to earn both titles. He combined the substance and soundness of his dam with the refinement and showmanship of his sire. His success on the Montgomery County weekend in 1970, where he was Best of Winners at Devon, has yet be be duplicated by a B/S.

There were dozens of Sylva Sprite Canadian champions bred by Mrs. Griggs and her daughter, Dr. Dorothy Griggs, over the next few decades (see Canadian Chapter), and a series of exports to the Continent helped to establish this color variety long before it was accepted in the European show rings.

American B/S champions descending from Snowy Mittens trace mostly to his son Gough's Frosted Bonanza, who carries half solid black background. Bonanza is the sire of two B/S champions. One of these, Am. and Can. Ch. Britmor Sunnymeade Frost, Am. CDX and Can. CD. bred, owned and shown by Karen Brittan (Britmor) of Minnesota, owns several "firsts." He is the first B/S with both bench and obedience titles in two countries, as well as a C.G. (Certificate of Gameness). With his Canadian Best in Show win in 1983, he

**Gough's Frosted Bonanza
with Bob Berg**

**Ch. Aljamar Hot Ice, CD
with Dennis Kniola**

became the first B/S to achieve this honor in Canada.

Bob and Nancy Berg (Bo-Nanza) bred three generations of B/S champions descending from Frosted Bonanza. His daughter, Bo-Nanza's Delightful Delsey, was the first to claim three B/S champions. One of these was Ch. Bo-Nanza's Frosty Lone Ranger. He, in turn, sired Ch. Bo-Nanza's Frosty City Slicker who carries three lines to Frosted Bonanza.

Bonanza's greatest significance by far comes through his B/S great-grandson Ch. Aljamar Hot Ice, CD, the first of his color to sire five champions. For nearly three decades, the combined efforts of Janice Rue (Suelen) and Marilyn Laschinski (Aljamar) of Illinois, have resulted in many dozens of champions. They were the first to claim homebred champions in all three colors. In 1994, their B/S Ch. Suelen Ice Chips joined the ranks of top producers, with seven champions—again, in all three colors. Intensely linebred, Ice Chips carries six lines to Hot Ice.

The Aljamar/Suelen family is most noteworthy for having provided foundation stock for other successful breeding programs. Sean O'Connor (Ro-Sean) in Wisconsin began with the dark S/P, Aljamar Fanny May (4 Chs.). His first homebred, Ch. Ro-Sean's Maiden Warrior, finished at nine months, became the top winning B/S bitch. In 1982 she started out the year by winning the Milshore Specialty—the first B/S bitch to top a Specialty. For Jane Gilbert

Ch. Ro-Sean's Maiden Warrior shown going Best of Breed at the 1982 Milshore Specialty under breeder-judge Robert Condon, handled by Carol Garmaker.

(Meadoway), Fanny May produced Ch. Repitition's Sparkle Plenty, the all-time top producing B/S dam.

Jane's rememberances of "Sparkle" are sparkling:

Sparkle was eleven months old when we bought her. She arrived at my home like Rosalind Russell playing Auntie Mame— "Put my crate in the kitchen, I'll be sleeping upstairs with you guys." With her effervescent personality, she stood out in the crowd, anywhere, anytime.

Reflecting on this ten years later, it is hard to believe how lucky we were to connect with Sparkle and the Garmakers. In 1983 fewer than ten black and silver bitches had completed their championships. When Sparkle finished, we calculated that she was the thirteenth.

The number thirteen turned out to be anything but unlucky, as Sparkle proved to be an outstanding producer. Among her seven B/S champion get are two good producing sons: Ch. Meadoway Yankee Doodle Dandy (10 Chs.) and Ch. Meadoway's Southpaw (5 Chs.) Three more generations of top producers come down from Southpaw. An unshown Sparkle daughter, Meadoway's Funny

Ch. Repitition's Sparkle Plenty shown with Carol Garmaker winning a major as Winners Bitch and Best Opposite Sex at the 1983 Milshore Specialty under breeder-judge Lou Auslander.

Valentine, was the dam of Judy Sousa's B/S, Meadoway Prestige, giving her three American and one Japanese champion—all black.

Sparkle, in so many ways, assured fanciers that this family of black and silvers would blend well with what was to become the most prolific line of B/S yet to be developed.

Two decades ago, a salt and pepper bitch registered simply as Jobie became the foundation for Carol and Kurt Garmaker's Repitition Kennel in Nebraska and has had a marked effect on B/S as well as S/P. She has champion descendants numbering in the hundreds, and in all three colors. Their first B/S champion, Ch. Repitition's Midnight Cowboy, carrying three lines to Jobie, will best be remembered as the sire of Sparkle.

In the mid-1980s, there was formed a unique alliance between the Garmakers and Janice Ramel (Rampage), later joined by Sean O'Connor (Ro-Sean). I'm not sure just when I coined the phrase, "the 3 Rs" (Repititon/Rampage/Ro-Sean), but it soon came to represent the extraordinary accomplishments that resulted from their combined efforts. It was an extraordinary B/S

The CH. RAMPAGE'S WACO KID line

puppy that had much to do with initiating this alliance, and that dog turned into the most influential black and silver sire of all time—Ch. Rampage's Waco Kid.

As Carol remembers it:

Waco came into our lives purely by chance. Janice Ramel and Sean O'Connor were meeting us at a show in Wisconsin. Jan had this ten-week-old black and silver male sired by "Stealer" (Ch. Rampage's Kat Burglar), out of a "Sarge" (Ch. Repitition's Rebel Warrior) daughter she wanted us to see. At the time, Jan was not particularly fond of this color, and was not interested in keeping him.

As we were admiring the puppy, and there was so much about him to like, Doug Dempster (Mariah) and Judy Smith (Jadee) walked up and looked at the pup. Shortly after, Doug wrote out a blank check and gave it to Janice for Waco. Of course, she returned it and let me take him home.

Never have I known a dog with a more delightful personality. He was sure everyone was his friend. He lived with his ears and tail up—even in the bathtub! He never lost his sense of humor and was always ready to play.

He grew into a strikingly beautiful young dog with a long neck, wonderful shoulders and transition, and a short, short back. He had a shiny, deep black coat as hard as boar's bristles, and lots of silver white furnishings. Waco was only shown at eight shows, including two Specialties. He was Winners or better at six, including a Specialty, where he also won the Sweepstakes. Not shown beyond his title, few breeders saw his potential as we did.

The first crop of youngster, all bred by the 3 Rs, began to prove his worth. From Ch. Ro-Sean's Maiden Warrior came a son, Ch. Ro-Sean's Weekend Warrior, the first B/S to win an AKC Best in Show. His good producing B/S brother, Ch. Repitition's Mirror Man, CD (8 Chs.), although short-lived, left champions at Blackheath, Beucinder and C-Mark. For Repitition, Waco produced

Ch. Rampage's Kat Burglar

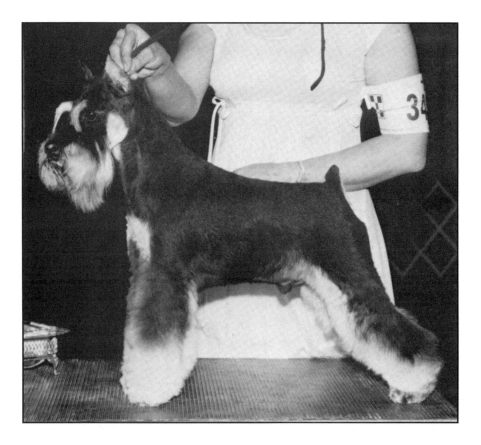

Ch. Skyline's Blue Spruce	Ch. Sky Rocket's Upswing
Ch. Irrenhaus Blueprint	Ch. Skyline's Silver Linning
Ch. Irrenhaus Fancy Finish	Ch. Sky Rocket's Bound To Win
	Ch. Winagin Showstopper
Ch. Rampage's Kat Burglar	
Ch. Jadee's Jump Up	Ch. Sky Rocket's Uproar
Ch. Reptitition's Rampage Brand	Heather's Windy Weather
Repitition's Epitome	Ch. Jadee's Jump Up
	Jobie
CH. RAMPAGE'S WACO KID [B/S]	
Ch. Repitition's Beau Beau	Ch. Repitition's Upcharge
Ch. Repitition's Rebel Warrior	Repitition's Midnight Blue
Ch. Repitition's Rojack's Reoccur	Ch. Jadee's Rebel Of Car-Bun
	Ch. Repitition's Sassafras
Rampage's Expression	
Ch. Valharra's Double Extra	Ch. Valharra's Extra
Kay-Jay's Rampage Express	Ch. Valharra's Touch Of Magic
Rampage's Kay-Jay Blue Angel	Ch. Skyline's Blue Spruce
	Rampage's Heads-A-Poppin'

Ch. Ro-Sean's Weekend Warrior winning Best in Show in 1984 under judge Alice Lane, handled by Sean O'Connor.

a B/S son, Ch. Repitition's Lover Boy (4 Chs.), and daughter, Ch. Repititon's Panda Bear (3 Chs.). The latter claims a special distinction, as the granddam of the record-setting Specialty winner and three-time Best in Show winner, the S/P Ch. Das Feder's Drivin' Miss Daisy. For Rampage, Waco's legacy was being passed on by his S/P son, Ch. Rampage's Kid Moody (4 Chs.), and B/S daughter, Rampage's Positive Attitude (5 Chs.).The latter, as the dam of the breed's all-time top winner, the S/P Ch. Rampage's Representative (45 Chs.), claims special recognition.That Representative carries three lines to Waco (two through Kid Moody) says it all!

By the time of his death in 1994, Waco had produced 24 champions and claimed over 350 champion descendants, including 120 black and silvers and sixteen blacks. The strongest B/S line develops from his son, Ch. Jerry O's Rain Check (14 Chs.), who in turn, sired this color variety's all-time top sire, Ch. Bandsman's Newsprint (26 Chs.). Extending yet another generation, Newsprint numbers among his get a top producing B/S son, Ch. Beucinder's Blackheath Brio (5 Chs.). When Sue Hersee (Blackheath) finished the Brio son Ch. Blackheath's Good Az Iam, he became the first B/S with natural ears to earn an AKC title.

Waco's extraordinary legacy extends far beyond his effect on the color varieties, as has been discussed previously (see RUFFIAN Chapter).

**Ch. Jerry O's
Rain Check
with Beverly Verna**

———————————

———————————

**Ch. Bandsman's
Newsprint**

Ch. Landmark's Masterpiece (S/P)
Ch. Skibo's Fancy Clancy (S/P)
Fancway's Carefree (S/P)
Ch. Glory's Eager Beaver (S/P)
Ch. Kugle's Cherokee Chief (S/P)
Lyon's Glory B (S/P)
Lyon's Winnie Too (B/S)
CH. SERCATEP'S STRUT N PROUD (B/S)
Can. Ch. Walsh's Frosty Spaceman (B/S)
Ch. Tammashann's Town Strutter (B/S)
Tammashann's Janlyn Frosteek (B/S)
Sercatep's Kismet (B/S)
Tammashann's Midnite Special (B/S)
Natasha XXXVII (S/P)
Mitzie Marie IX (S/P)

The CH. SERCATEP'S STRUT N PROUD line

The exclusively American-bred branch from the Charmer son Can. Ch. Walsh's Frosty Spaceman is brought forward principally through his B/S son (and great-grandson) Ch. Tammashann's Town Strutter. His only B/S champion offspring, Ch. Karma's Moonlight Shadow, is out of his B/S granddaughter, Ch. Sercatep's Frost N Flash, CD, who claims four other B/S champions, all bred, owned and shown by Karin and Mark Jaeger (Karma) of Michigan.

Debbie and Del Herrell (Sercatep), also in Michigan, have developed an extraordinary line of B/S, tightly linebred on Charmer. For many years, this color variety's top sire was their B/S Ch. Sercatep's Strut N Proud (14 Chs.). He is a half brother to Frost N Flash, both by the S/P Ch. Glory's Eager Beaver (4 Chs.). Through 1995,

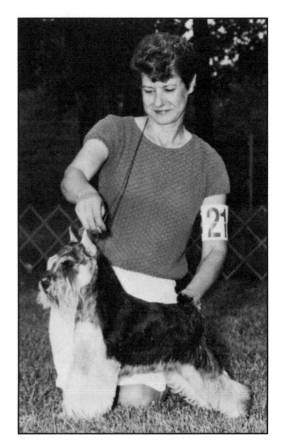

**Ch. Sycamore's
Sojourner
with Debbie Herrell**

fifty-two B/S and thirteen black champions carry one or more lines to Strut N Proud. These include two more generations of top producing B/S sires: the Strut N Proud son, Ch. Sycamore's Sojourner (9 Chs.) is the sire of Ch. Sercatep's Nite Flite (7 Chs.).

In 1994, the Herrells finished their first homebred black Ch. Sercatep's Kriss Kross, who carries two lines to Strut N Proud.

Several very successful breeders specializing in B/S have based their efforts on Sercatep bitches. The most successful by far is Carol Beagle (Blackwitch) in Michigan. More than two dozen champions have been made up in less than a decade, all descending from a pair of Strut N Proud daughters. The most influential was the S/P Sercatep's Strut Of Talisman, dam of six champions, four of these B/S. Carol has developed two distinct families,

**Ch. Sycamore's Solar Eclipse
with Richard Smith**

involving an S/P line based on Richlene sires and a B/S line based on Sercatep. Her best producing B/S bitch is Ch. Blackwitch Sweet-N-Sassy (3 Chs.).

In recent years, the Herrells have exported several outstanding youngsters to Sweden, where they have become champions and have produced champions.

The Charmer branch claims two additional top producing bitches. Pine Needles Sercatep Pride bred by Nancy DeCamp (Pine Needles) has four B/S champions, all by Strut N Proud. Margo Heiden (Sycamore) bred four B/S champions from her Charmer great-granddaughter Sycamore Sassafras, Am. and Can. CD. One of these is the record-setting Am. and Can. Ch. Sycamore Solar Eclipse (9 Chs.), whose AKC title quest included a Group First and a Best at the Columbus Specialty in Ohio—the first B/S to top a Specialty. In 1982, professionally handled by Richard and Arlene Smith (Richlene), his record-setting accomplishments included a repeat at Columbus, Best at the Chicago Specialty, plus three more Group Firsts.

Solar Eclipse carries lines to another key black and silver producer, the S/P Ch. Blythewood Winsome Lad (4 Chs.). Lad is the double grandsire of the champion B/S brothers, Ch. Eclipse Trethaway's Coaldust and Ch. Eclipse Shadow Of The Son, who numbers Solar Eclipse among his five champion get.

Ch. Sercatep's Truth Or Dare winning Best of Breed at the Holland Michigan Kennel Club under Margaret Patterson, who later gave him Group First. He is handled by his breeder-owner Debbra Herrell.

Ch. Blackwitch
Sweet-N-Sassy
with Carol Beagle

Ital. Ch. Malya Gunter (B)
Ch. Aljamar Tommy Gun (B)
Klingsor's Last Summer (S/P)
Ch. Suelen Ringleader (S/P)
Ch. Aljamar Hot Ice, CD (B/S)
Suelen Angel Puff (S/P)
Aljamar Diamond Lil (S/P)
CH. FELDMAR NIGHTSHADE (B/S)
Ch. Jo-Mar's Bric-A-Brac (S/P)
Jo-Mar's Magic Marker (B/S)
Jo-Mar's Jessica Too (S/P)
Suelen Snow Fantasy (B/S)
Ch. Aljamar Hot Ice, CD (B/S)
Feldmar Hopscotch (B/S)
Feld's Segelschlitten (S/P)

The CH. FELDMAR NIGHTSHADE line

In 1978, a little bitch registered as Feld's Segelschlitten (German for Scooter) was to become foundation for Marcia Feld's Feldmar Schnauzers, and her constant companion for over fourteen years. She described her as:

One of the best purchases I have ever made. She was an intelligent, sound little dog. Being short on leg, she stood 12 1/2 inches at the withers; bone was ample, no hint of toyishness; tailset good; front, wide but straight; rear, stong; eye, good; head, skully. Attitude she had with a capitol A. Scooter was every inch a terrier. She whelped six litters (including two CJC test litters) naturally, without a single abnormality or fatality. At twelve years of age, her eyes are clear, and her teeth are all still in her head.

In 1980, *Scooter* was to give Ch. Aljamar Hot Ice, CD, his first litter, and eventually his first champion—the B/S Ch. Suelen Show Flurry, CD, CG. The litter of six had four B/S and Marcia retained a bitch, Feldmar Hopscotch.

Hopscotch was very important to me. Already aware that I wanted to linebreed, and not wishing to ship an unproven bitch, I elected to use Aljamar Devil Dancer, a B/S son of Ch. Aljamar Tommy Gun (paternal great-grandsire to Hopscotch). This breeding produced Suelen Lady of Greentree who was bred to Flurry to produce Feldmar Snow Drop—dam of Ch. Feldmar Night Reveler. Hopscotch's second and last breeding was to her B/S paternal grandfather, Jo-Mar's Magic Marker. Two bitches from this litter were retained for breeding purposes—Feldmar Galewood Snow Storm, CDX, and Suelen Snow Fantasy; the latter, dam of Ch. Feldmar Nightshade.

Nightshade was whelped in May of 1984. With him came the desire to begin making all my own decisions by myself. Marilyn Laschinski had willingly and openly taught me everything from picking a puppy to handling a stud dog. Working at her elbow gave me the chance to learn much more rapidly than I ever could have on my own, but it was time for me to stand entirely alone.

Ch. Feldmar Night Reveler, in March of 1986, became the first black and silver to go Winners Dog at an AMSC Specialty, under breeder-judge Robert Condon, handled by Priscilla Wells; Ted Bierman presenting trophy.

That Marcia had a plan goes without saying, as the results have had a broad impact on black and silvers throughout the world (see the chapters on Schnauzers in other Countries). Nightshade is the sire of 17 champions, with his B/S son Ch. Feldmar Night Reveler (15 Chs.) by far the most significant. In 1986 Reveler became the first B/S to win points at an AMSC Specialty, and went on to lead this color variety that year and for the next two years. In 1988, he set a one-year record for B/S, winning 62 Bests of Breed, including two Specialties, and placing number two Knight System, the highest placing ever for a B/S. He continues to be the top winning B/S of all time.

Yet another first came to this family of B/S when in 1989 at Montgomery County, the Reveler daughter Ch. Blythewood Amara On The Move became the first B/S to

Ch. Blythewood Amara On The Move

win an AMSC Sweepstakes. The same year saw the Reveler son, Ch. Feldmar Casey At The Bat the leader among B/S. Casey is the sire of the good producing S/P stud, Ch. Blythewood Top Echelon, sire of six champions to date, five of them B/S.

Feldmar can claim yet another first — the first Miniature Schnauzer *ever* to come from frozen semen. The resulting singleton pup was the B/S Feldmar-Black Watch Brrrrrr, by Reveler out of Ch. Feldmar Finally.

When Marcia sent Ch. Feldmar Blaque Feathers to Delores and Karen Featherer in California, it helped considerably to reestablish B/S in the West. Bred to three different sires, she produced six champions, including the leading B/S winner of 1991, Ch. Feathers Moon River, a champion in just twenty-one days.

By the end of 1996, there were approximately 285 black and silvers that had earned their titles, over ninety percent of these during the last two decades. B/S have captured most of the possible top awards, but the one that still remains elusive is a Best of Breed win at an AMSC Specialty, or a B/S that can achieve Top Schnauzer honors. Both remain quite a challenge for breeders of this color variety.

Ch. Feldmar Blaque Feathers

**Ch. Feathers Moon River
with Beverly Verna**

13

The Miniature Schnauzer in Canada

Although MINIATURE SCHNAUZERS are among the more popular breeds in Canada, the numbers being bred continue to be small compared to activities in the United States. Canada now has a population of 30 million, and there are nearly 600 conformation shows being held annually. Breed activities can be divided into three areas: Ontario and Quebec in the East, British Columbia in the West, and the Prairies—Manitoba, Alberta and Saskatchewan. In 1994, approximately 2,400 Miniature Schnauzers were registered, and on average, eighty to ninety will become champions.

The first Canadian champion appears to be the German-bred Nette v. Mumlingtal, in 1933. Anne Eskrigge (Anfiger), American breed historian par excellence, claims this first. Nette descendants include the famed record-setting producer Am. and Can. Ch. Sorceress of Ledahof (12 Chs.).

The first homebred Canadian champion was Bendigo of Clearbrook, from an American-bred Wollaton sire and dam. It was a slow start, with only one other titlist, Am. and Can. Ch. Handful of Marienhof, finishing before World War II.

A small nucleus of breeders in Montreal and Toronto kept the breed alive before the war years brought a halt to their activity. Mr. Wylie's Strathburn establishment appears to have been the only really active breeding kennel during the 1940s, owning six Canadian champions, two of them also AKC champions. The first Miniature Schnauzer to win a Canadian Terrier Group was Mr. Wylie's homebred Ch. Strathburn JP Beta Misty in May 1948. In October that year, Mrs. Evashwick's famed Sorceress became the first to win Best in Show, and DISPLAY, in 1949, became the first male to attain this honor. From this point forward, the breed would depend exclusively on DISPLAY both here and in Canada.

Beginning with the formation of the Miniature Schnauzer Club of Ontario on September 26, 1951, the Toronto area became the center of breed activity. Mr. and Mrs. William Gottschalk were among the founders and served as club officers for several years. This club's first Specialty was won by their Am. and Can. Ch. Benrook Beau Brummell, and in 1952 by their Beau Brummell son, Am. and Can. Ch. Cosburn's Aristocrat—the first Canadian-bred AKC champion. Aristocrat duplicated the win two years later under the American breeder-judge Robert Kerns, Jr. (Wollaton).

Am. & Can. Ch. Cosburn's Aristocrat

In 1955 the club was renamed the Miniature Schnauzer Club of Canada, with Toronto continuing to be the center of activities. Mr. and Mrs. Gottschalk's Cosburn Kennel by this time had received broad recognition. As the breeders of Ch. Cosburn's Esquire, their influence is felt worldwide (see BEAU BRUMMELL line).

Several successful prefixes emerged during the 1960s, including Caldora, Rosehill, Sylva Sprite and Tannenbaum. The leading sire during this period was Am. and Can. Ch. Jonaire Pocono Gladiator with 15 champions. Gladiator is a triple great-grandson of Beau Brummell, and the dozens of Rosehill champions over the next four decades would extend this branch from DISPLAY to the present. Gladiator sons and daughters dominated the 1960s, the following gaining Top Schnauzer status: Ch. Rosehill Coco Chanel, Ch. Graham's Gladiator Trademark and Ch. Rosehill Poco's Impression, the latter the sire of seven champions.

One of Gladiator's first champion offspring was Jo-An-Alaur's Anastasia (ex Cosburn's Heide), foundation for Joan Morden's Tannenbaum Kennel in Ontario. Another breeder with nearly three decades of activity, Mrs. Morden claims a remarkable record of having finished one of every four puppies bred, all tracing to Anastasia. By the early 1970s, fourth generation Tannenbaums

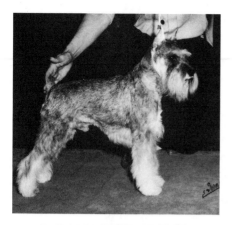

Am. & Can. Ch. Jonaire Pocono Gladiator

were enjoying successful show careers.

Best known perhaps is Ch. Tannenbaum Purse Snatcher, Top Schnauzer in 1972 and the first of the breed to win three Bests in Show in Canada. Having earned his Bermuda title at six months and four days of age, he is believed to be the world's youngest champion. Ch. Tannenbaum Sunday Punch kept the ball rolling as Top Schnauzer for the next two years. The kennel ceased operations in the mid-1980s with the death of Mrs. Morden.

Doris Hayes of Caldora Kennel was the first to bring Miniature Schnauzers into prominence in Western Canada, in the mid-1950s. The most famous of the dozens of Caldora homebreds was Am. and Can. Ch. Caldora Returning Ace, who held the honor of being Canada's Top Schnauzer for four years, and became the sire of 15 champions.

Dollie Ramsey's Sayblain Kennel in Surrey, British Columbia is the only current breeder with bloodlines that link to the Caldora dogs, finishing Ch. Sayblain Silver Shamus in the 1990s. Of particular interest is that he also is the only remaining male tracing in a direct line to the Beau Brummell line.

The Sylva Sprite Kennel was established in Ontario in 1959 by Joanna Griggs and her daughter Dr. Dorothy Griggs, and continues to the present. They have bred over ninety owner-handled champions to date, including some thirty black and silvers. Their most famous homebred, Am. and Can. Ch. Sylva Sprite Snowy Mittens, was Top Schnauzer in 1971, and became one of Canada's leading sires, with 15 champion get, the large majority black and silvers. No Canadian breeders have had a broader impact on bloodlines worldwide than Sylva Sprite. This influence is documented in the chapter on black and silvers, as well as on Great Britain and other countries.

In 1968, Cherrylane Kennel was formed by a young teenager named Martin DeForest, DVM. When Martin left home to attend university, breeding and showing were curtailed, but not his keen interest. Being an admirer of the Blythewood dogs, it was Joan Huber whom he contacted for a fresh start. He acquired a number of first-class animals, including Am. Can. and Bda. Ch. Blythewood National Newsman, one of eleven champions from matings of Valharra Prize of Blythewood to Ch. Blythewood National Anthem (25 AKC - 5 CKC Chs.). Newsman was the winner of four U.S. Speciaties in 1982, including AMSC Montgomery County, handled by Joan Huber — the only Canadian-owned dog to achieve this honor. He then finished his title in Bermuda with three straight Group Firsts. In 1983, Newsman was the Top Schnauzer in Canada, with a Best in Show and many Group wins, and in 1984, the top sire. With 15 Canadian and three AKC champion get that year, it was the best record ever achieved by a Canadian-owned sire. Newsman is the sire of seven AKC

**Am. & Can. Ch. Blythewood
National Newsman
with Joan Huber**

champions, including a top producing son, Ch. Sumerwynd Still Sizzlin (6 AKC - 5 CKC Chs.), and through him, the great-grandsire of Ch. Sumerwynd Bandsman Showoff (12 AKC - 8 CKC Chs.). Newsman is the sire of 38 Canadian Champions—a Canadian breed record—and several top producing daughters continue to influence the breed.

Newsman is the maternal grandsire of Canada's Top Schnauzer 1991, '92 and '93, Am. Can. and Bda. Ch. Moondreamer's Presumed Innocent. He is a son of Ch. Blythewood Shooting Sparks (53 AKC - 16 CKC Chs.). In a coast-to-coast campaign, he became Canada's all-time top winner, with a record of 32 Bests in Show and 134 Group Firsts, plus National and Regional Specialties. He completed his Bermudian title in 1994 at 5 1/2 years of age with four consecutive Group wins. Presumed Innocent is co-owned by Dr. DeForest, Jeffrey Reid, who handled him, and Donna Ralph (Moondreamer), his breeder. He is the sire of nine Canadian champions to date.

Blythewood would also figure prominently in Lynda Berar's Naibara Kennel in Alberta—breeder of over eighty Canadian champions. Mrs. Berar's foundation bitch carried several generations of Blythewood breeding. Naibara's first homebred champion, Naibara's Something Special, by Ch. Sky Rocket's Bound To Win (25 AKC - 12 CKC Chs.), was Top Bitch in 1976. Two years later her son Ch. Naibara's Midnight Special would lead the breed, and leaves 20 champions. Sires from the Ruffian branch would continue to be the mainstay in the Naibara breeding program to the present. In 1984, the Midnight Special son, Ch. Naibara's It's Hard To Be Humble, finished third in breed standings with a

Am. & Can. Ch. Moondreamer's Presumed Innocent with Jeffrey Reid

Group win and several placements. He is believed to be Canada's first homebred champion with natural ears! One of his ten champions, a son, Ch. Naibara's On The Move, won a Best in Show from the classes at eleven months of age. In 1994, Am. and Can. Ch. Naibara's Wizard of Awes, sired by Ch. Blythewood Ewok Von Der Stars (15 AKC - 15 CKC Chs.), topped the breed with three Bests in Show, and earned a fourth Best in '95. Ten Naibara bitches have become top producers, with three hitting double digits. Ch. Naibara's A Saint I Ain't (15 Chs.) leads all Canadian bitches, followed by her dam, Ch. Naibara's Almost An Angel (11 Chs.). Almost An Angel's older sister, Ch. Naibara's Be My Valentine produced ten champions for Minuteman in Saskatchewan.

Am. & Can. Ch. Naibara's Wizard of Awes with Lynda Berar

Catherine McMillan did right by Be My Valentine, beginning with her Best in Show-winning Ch. Minuteman's Go Dog Go, Canada's Top Schnauzer 1985. Close to forty Canadian and six American champions have emerged from a grand total of 65 puppies. Be My Valentine was the last bitch to be bred to Ch. Skyline's Star Spangled Banner, the first champion son of the famed sire, Ch. Skyline's Blue Spruce (55 AKC - 8 CKC Chs.). Banner holds a position of interest in Canadian lines, although never owned or shown in Canada. Five litters at Naibara and his last, at Minuteman (to Valentine, his double granddaughter), leave a legacy that traces through Naibara, Minuteman, Kaydees and Cestrian to Canadian champion descendants that number near the 200 mark. Banner's last son, Ch. Minuteman Bump In The Night, bred to only five

Ch. Skyline's Star Spangled Banner

**Am. & Can. Ch. Minuteman
Eleventh Hour
with Catherine McMillan**

bitches, claims seven CKC champions, plus fifty more in succeeding generation, including several AKC champions. Four Specialty winners descend from him, including two of the three bitches to win a Canadian National—Ch. Minuteman Conlar Busy Bein' Bad and Ch. Zetroepe Doz She Or Dozn't She. The latter was just 10 1/2 months of age when she topped the 1990 Specialty—the youngest ever to have achieved this honor. The Bump In The Night son, Am. and Can. Ch. Minuteman Eleventh Hour (4 AKC - 15 CKC Chs.), is still active.

Several Minuteman bitches have gone to breeders across North America. Am. and Can. Ch. Minuteman I Think I Can, Best in Specialty at the Chicago MSC in 1994 from the classes, is Kim Greenway's (Reggae) foundation in B.C. Am. and Can. Ch. Minuteman Not EZ Being Green went to Bev Verna (Regency) and Sumiko Ikeda (Sunshine Palace). Priscilla Wells (Aachen) acquired Am. and Can. Ch. Minuteman Brand New Set O'Lies. Am. and Can. Ch. Minuteman Wensday Addams was the first Canadian-bred bitch to win an AKC Group, which she did from the classes for her owner handler Mary Paisley of Wisconsin. Minuteman sires have played roles in breeding programs across Canada, and in 1995 the first traveled to Australia to Marilyne Woodhouse (Schonhardt). In 1994, Minuteman ventured into blacks, importing and finishing yet another record-setter, Ch. Sandcastle Good Guys Wear Black, the first black to win a Specialty. He is the sire Am. and Can. Ch. Benalta Batman, the first black to score

**Eleventh
Hour
on the move**

Winners Dog or better all three days on the Great Western weekend, which he did in 1996.

Massawippi Kennel, owned by Mr. and Mrs. S. I. Clark of Ontario, began breeding in the early 1970s and ceased in the mid-1980s. Their foundation bitch, Massawippi In For A Penny, gave them seven champions from three different sires. Penny's most successful offspring was her son Ch. Massawippi Troubadour, by Ch. Sky Rocket's Victory Bound (5 AKC Chs.). Troubadour was, until recently, Canada's top winning Miniature Schnauzer, with a record of 125 Bests of Breed. The Top Schnauzer for 1981 and 1982, he went on to win three Bests in Show, 35 Group Firsts and over 60 other Group placings. Troubadour sired ten champions including five Group winners and two Specialty winners. Ch. Massawippi The Ringbearer, by Ch. Regency's Right On Target (78 AKC - 23 CKC Chs.), was their best producing bitch, with seven champions.

Can. Ch. Massawippi Troubadour with Murray Clark

The Wheelwood Kennel was established in the mid-1970s by Irmgard Wheeler in Ontario, and continues to the present. She has the distinction of being Canada's first breeder of champions in all three colors. Based on a salt and pepper Rosehill bitch, Wheelwood has linebred tightly within the Diplomat branch. The blacks gain their color from Italian Ch. Malya Gunter, and the black and silvers from Snowy Mittens.

Ernie Sellers has worked exclusively with Penlan stock since 1980. He purchased Am. and Can. Ch. Penlan Penny Stock, getting his first two Jena champions from her breeding to Ch. Penlan Promissory (27 AKC - 5 CKC Chs.). Penny was next bred to Ch. Penlan Peter's Son (25 AKC Chs.), who came to Jena in 1984 to live out his retirement years as Sellers's companion. Ernie has shown little in recent years, but recently provided Claire Verner (Playground) of Quebec with Ch. Jena's Joanna, which produced her first three homebred champions. Claire is the owner of Am. and Can. Ch. Hobo 2nd, the National Specialty winner 1989, and the sire of six champions.

Kay DeVeyrac of Calgary founded her Kaydees Kennel in the early 1980s with a bitch of Brittanhof breeding. With a litter or two a year, breeding almost exclusively to Ruffian sires, there have been over thirty Kaydees champions, including several Best Puppy in Show and Group winners. Her first attempt to finish an AKC title was successful, Am. and Can. Ch. Kaydees Secret Weapon earning three majors on one weekend. He is by Ch. Jerry O's Secret Agent (9 Chs.), and out of a Bump In The Night daughter. His sister, Ch. Kaydees Renascent Rho's gave a good start for Rhoda Dease's Rho D breeding program, giving her five champions from two litters. Recent attention has been

Am. & Can. Ch. Cestrian's Court Jester

given to the agility ring, where the Kaydees are performing very well.

Cestrian Kennel in Ontario began in 1981 with the purchase of the linebred Naibara bitch, Koerad's Midnight Serenader. She became Pamela and Leslie Hallam's first champion and produced, by Ch. Massawippi Troubadour, five champions, including three Group and three Specialty winners. Her most notable offspring is Am. and Can. Ch. Cestrian's Court Jester, winner of four Bests in Show and 62 Group Firsts, including Group wins in the U.S.A. and Bermuda. He was Canada's Top Schnauzer 1988 and '89. Now ten years old, he continues to be a producer with 21 champions to date, including seven from breedings to Ch. Massawippi The Ring Bearer, and five from their Specialty winner, Ch. Cestrian's Gold Digger. Cestrian has bred nineteen champions, of which four were Specialty winners.

Armand and Jaclin Gratton (Frontenac) kept the breed to the fore in Quebec since the early 1970s, and only recently retired from breeding both Miniature Schnauzer and Pinschers, after celebrating their 100th champion— Ch. Frontenac's Priority Post. He traces several generations to their foundation, Ch. Postillion Pirate's Pearl. She proved to be a remarkable producer, with eight champion get, including Ch. Frontenac Franc Pirate, also the dam of eight champions. Pearl's most successful son is Am. and Can. Ch. Frontenac's Big Foot (8 Chs.).

Sensation Kennel was established in Ontario in 1981 by Irene Wessler, with Ch. Frontenac Cleopatra's Pearl, purchased as a puppy. Pearl gave her four champions, and is behind over thirty additional Sensation champions since produced. Infusion of the color varieteis came from the importation of a Suelen

Can. Ch. Sensation's Amanda C with Dr. Martin DeForest

bitch and breedings to the B/S Ch. Bandsman Newsprint (26 AKC - 6 CKC Chs.), and the black Am. and Can. Ch. Kelly's Pretty Boy Floyd, to produce champions in all three colors. Sensation can claim five top producing bitches, most notably Ch. Sensation Amanda C (8 Chs.)

Danielle Joncas and Paul LeRoy-Audy stayed in their home province of Quebec for their foundation bitch Ch. Frontenac's Heidi Ho. Since 1982 their limited

Am. & Can. Ch. Annfield Just One Like Me

breeding program has netted over thirty champions bearing their Audigny prefix. Four have also earned AKC titles. A later addition of Am. and Can. Ch. Annfield Just One Like Me has led to continued success giving them seven champions, with several Best Puppy in Show and Group winners among them.

Michelene Gosselin founded her small hobby kennel in Quebec with a pair of bitches of mostly Valharra background. Bred consistantly to Ruffian sires, she has produced eighteen champions. At the 1995 MSCC National, her Ch. Canton Allegra finished at the tender age of six months and six days—most likely the youngest black champion recorded in Canada.

Hazel Whalen and Vicki Cullis began their Jukebox breeding program in the late 1980s, and have produced nearly two dozen champions, most notably Ch. Jukebox 'N Spyglass Buckaroo, the 1995 National Specialty winner. He is a son of the B/S Ch. Bandsman's Imprint, brought to Canada by Hazel and currently the sire of 15 Canadian and two AKC champions.

The partnership of Tim Doxtater and Don Emslie (Annfield) in British Columbia is another venture founded on Blythewood imports: Ch. Blythewood National Sequence and Ch. Blythewood Shenna of Annfield. No other Canadian kennel has enjoyed as much American success as Annfield. Shenna, bred twice to "super sire", Ch. Regency's Right On Target (78 AKC - 23 CKC Chs.), produced six Canadian champions, three shown to AKC titles. Am. and Can. Ch. Annfield Ever Evident became the dominant of these through her son, Am. and Can. Ch. Annfield Ever Ready (1 CKC - 5 AKC Chs.), and daughter, Ch. Annfield Very Vogue (3 CKC - 2 AKC Chs.).

The Shenna son, Ch. Annfield Hitch Hiker (8 CKC - 4 AKC Chs.), sired by Ch. Bandsman's Talisman, has also played an important part in the Annfield breeding program.

Ch. Blythewood National Sequence, bred to Target, gave them Ch. Annfield Choral Cadenza (5 CKC - 4 AKC Chs.), which produced all her champions from two litters by Ch. Jadee's Hush Up (11 AKC - 5 CKC Chs.). Three champion daughters, Chs. Annfield Justa Jewel, Justa Jiffy and Just N Jest, as well as a son, Am. and Can. Ch. Annfield Secret Deal of Wy-O's all hold

**Am. & Can. Ch. Annfield Ever Evident
with Don Emslie**

strong position in today's pedigrees. Justa Jiffy went to Wyoma and Owen Clouss of Wy-O's Kennel in Idaho, giving them four AKC champions, including a top producer. Justa Jewel produced seven CKC and two AKC champions, including a son, Am. and Can. Ch. Annfield Yes Yes Yes (4 CKC - 2 AKC Chs.); a daughter, Ch. Annfield Rave Review O'Shantay, Top Schnauzer in Canada in 1990; and litter sister, Am. and Can. Ch. Annfield Rare Reflection who in the same year ranked number two bitch, SS System in the U.S.A. The third Choral Cadenza daughter, Just N Jest, is the dam of seven CKC and four AKC champions, and holds the record of top winning Canadian bitch. Her credits are four Bests in Show, two Specialty Bests as well as three Best of Opposite at U.S. Specialties, including the National at Great Western. She was number two in 1988 and number one in 1989, as well as being the top breeder-owner handled terrier in both those years.

Am. and Can. Ch. Annfield Just Top Dollar, a son of Just N Jest and Ch. Rampage's Representative (43 AKC - 13 CKC Chs.), was the 1992 Canadian

Can. Ch. Annfield
Hitch Hiker
winning the
Terrier Group
at the Alberni Valley
Canine Classic
Invitational in 1987
under judges
Lina Basquette
and Clay Coady,
handled by
Tim Doxtater.

Am. & Can. Ch. Annfield Just Top Dollar

National Specialty winner. Dollar (4 CKC - 3 AKC Chs.) is proving himself as a sire, his get including a son, Am. and Can. Ch. Annfield In Very Good Time, the 1994 Montgomery County AMSC Sweepstakes winner, and a daughter, Am. and Can. Ch. Annfield Oh So Very, Winners Bitch at Montgomery on the same day. Since the first Annfield dog appeared in the ring just a decade ago, there have been a total of fifty bred or co-bred dogs that have achieved a Canadian champion title. Sixteen of these have been Group winners, with an equal number winning Best Puppy in Show. Twenty Annfield dogs have added AKC titles to their name

Am. & Can.
Ch. Annfield
Rare Reflection
winning
Best of Breed
at the Portland
Specialty
in 1990 under
Seymour Weiss,
handled by
Brenda Combs.

since the first attained that status in 1987. Annfield has enjoyed many AMSC National Specialty wins and the bloodlines from this kennel are having a strong influence thoughout Canada in the kennels of Bowser, D'Audigny, Empire, Lynwil and Shantay, as well as the kennels of Theo Nass of the Netherlands.

Heather Dangelmaier's Bowser Kennel in Edmonton, Alberta, was already well established before the addition of Am. and Can. Ch. Annfield Rare Reflection, and has accounted for over thirty homebred champions, including several that have earned AKC titles. Bowser homebreds have been exported to the Pacific rim countries to finish there as well.

Shannon and Gerry Taylor recently founded their Shantay Kennel in Calgary, Alberta, with Ch. Annfield Head Over Heels and Ch. Annfield Rave Review O'Shantay, the latter dam of seven champions, some co-bred with Annfield.

Vicki and Greg Stephens of Surrey, British Columbia, also began with an Annfield-bred foundation—Am. and Can. Ch. Annfield Never Say Never, and have produced several champions, including the Best in Show winner Ch. Empire's Dorado. Empire has also followed the Annfield lead, exhibiting with success on both sides of the border, earning AKC titles on several homebreds. One of these, Am. and Can. Ch. Empire's Distant Galaxy, distinguished himself by winning the Delaware Valley Specialty on the Montgomery County weekend in 1995. He is one of three American and Canadian champions out of their

Am. and Can. Ch. Empire's Dark Angel. After producing three litters, Angel completed her American title at five years of age—a very rare accomplishment, indeed. The acquisition of Ch. Feldmar-Empire Edge of Night has brought in the B/S gene.

Blacks and black and silvers are clearly the specialty at Kathleen Todd's Stargazer Kennel in Manitoba. Founded on the all-color-bred black import, Ch. Suelen Evening Stargazer, she can claim the first Canadian-bred black to gain an AKC title—Am. and Can. Ch. Stargazer's Shoot The Moon.

Gail Wilford began her Scandal breeding program in Manitoba, based on the B/S Ch. Stargazer's Heaven Sent, and has finished over a dozen champions, including the black bitch, Ch. Scandal's Somethingotme Started, which scored several Group Firsts during 1994, as the year's top bitch.

Advocate Kennel in British Columbia is based on a partnership formed in 1988 by Bruce Fraser and Gary Cohen, and was founded on Am. and Can. Ch. Somerset Satin Doll, giving them five champions. Thereafter they also imported and finished the black Ch. Kelly's Devil's Advocate. The original pair are behind a dozen Advocate champions bred to date. They also enjoyed work in obedience, in 1995 completing a CD degree on the third-generation homebred black, Ch. Advocate's Black Gemstone, CD, a daughter of their Am. and Can. Ch. Advocate's Ben's Jessamine.

As American and Canadian bloodlines continue to overlap, the progress expected on both sides of the border should be comparable.

**Am. & Can. Ch. Empire's Dark Angel
with Vicki Stephens**

Am. & Can. Ch. Somerset Satin Doll

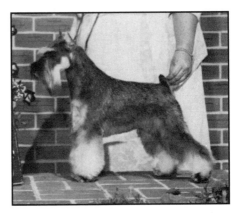

14

The Miniature Schnauzer in Other Countries

Virtually ever country in the world has had Miniature Schnauzers of which to be proud, and more than likely they will carry, somewhere deep in their pedigree, the name of the great American sire, CH. DOREM DISPLAY.

There is little doubt that the international dog show community has long accepted the fact that the best Miniature Schnauzer in the world are being bred in America, and every country in which the breed has progressed can divide its breed history into two catagories—before, and since DISPLAY.

• In Great Britain

The Miniature Schnauzer was introduced to Great Britain just a few years after the original Marienhof imports began to make their mark in the United States. British breeders faced several handicaps not experienced by their American counterparts, accounting for the breed's slower progress. The six-month quarantine required by British law added to the difficulty and expense of importing foundation stock. The most obvious handicap was the Kennel Club's rule forbidding the showing of dogs with cropped ears. Since virtually all the German stock imported were cropped, they could not be exhibited. This would have provided a strong base on which to educate both breeders and the public as to the correct type and charming qualities of the breed.

The history of the breed in Britain can be divided into three natural periods: prewar, postwar to the mid-1950s, and since DISPLAY. A select group of American imports, all DISPLAY descendents, would play a vital role in breed progress.

Douglas Appleton imported two American-breds which were to play an important part in bringing the breed forward. The first, Ch. Rannoch-Dune Randolph of Appeline, was a double grandson of Ch. Delegate of Ledahof (a son of DISPLAY). Uncropped, Randolph finished his championship in 1953 and won six CCs. In spite of his show successes, he sired only a few litters, but with significant results.

Bred to Doreen Crowe's Deltone Delilah, Randolph sired Ch. Deltone Appeline Doughboy, a cornerstone sire. Doughboy met with great success both in breed and all-breed competition, earning eight CCs. The next entire decade would be Doughboy's, as his offspring dominated the breed classes.

Between the years 1950 and 1972 the Deltone prefix was associated with eighteen champions, while twenty-seven English champions came from

Eng. Ch. Deltone Appeline Doughboy

either a Deltone sire or dam. The majority of present-day champions trace to Doughboy and the Deltone stock stemming from him. He is recognized as being one of the first to stamp his offspring with consistent and recognizable type.

American-bred dogs would continue to effect the breed through the 1960s. Mrs. Creasy of Roundway fame imported Ch. Wilkern Tony From America, adding to the concentration of DISPLAY blood. In 1954, Tony became the first Miniature Schnauzer to win a Group at a Championship show. Although Tony sired two champion sons, his line was brought forward to the present through daughters. Sonny and Sheila Dawe's Roundway Anklet, the all-time top producing dam with six champions, is intensely linebred to Tony.

Douglas Appleton imported from Canada Appeline Cosburn's Pickwick Peppers, linebred to DISPLAY and carrying Dorem, Benrook and Ledahof background. He proved to be a perfect tie-in for Pamela Morrison-Bell's developing Eastwights, founded on Deltone Delmanhatton, a Doughboy daughter out of Deltone Nevada, a Rudolph daughter.

Miss Morrison-Bell used a son of Tony with Delmanhatton, to get Ch. Eastwight Sea-Nymph. Peppers was used on Sea-Nymph, resulting in two champions. She produced a third when bred to yet another American-bred, Ch. Sternroc Sticky Wicket. More than two dozen homebred champions would follow, including a black and silver. The Eastwights obviously carried the black and silver recessive, as they would appear from time to time. The arrival of Eastwight Sea-Voyager in 1967 marked the recognizable advent of this color, but his effect had to be realized in America. Not until 1993 would the first Eastwight B/S champion be made up—Ch. Eastwight Sea-Mannikin.

Eng. Ch. Risepark Bon-Ell Taurus

Beginning in 1960, yet another line to DISPLAY was added when Pamela Cross-Stern returned to England from living in America. She brought with her the first American champion to be imported. The father-son brace, Ch. Nicomur Chasseur and Ch. Sternroc Sticky Wicket, produced some record-setting results. Wicket became the first to sire eight champions, four out of Audrey Dallison's Gosmore Peaches and Cream, a Doughboy great-granddaughter. These included Ch. Gosmore Wicket Keeper, the first Miniature Schnauzer to go to Australia, and Ch. Gosmore Opening Batsman, winner of twenty-four CCs, the breed record for nearly twenty years. Mrs. Dallison also bred Ch. Gosmore Hat Trick, by Wicket out of a double Tony granddaughter. Hat Trick was to hold the record for bitches with sixteen CCs for some twelve years.

Among those becoming interested in the breed around the middle 1950s was Peter Newman, starting with two Doughboy puppies, Deltone Delouisiana and Ch. Deltone Delaware. These two produced Risepark Ha'penny Breeze, the dam of two champions. Mr. Newman's Risepark prefix was to play a significant part in the breed's history, particularly through a series of American imports, beginning with Ch. Risepark Bon-Ell Taurus.

Bred in California, Taurus carried a concentration of DISPLAY, principally through Ch. Diplomat of Ledahof, full brother to Delegate. This provided yet another American branch from DISPLAY, and the resulting type, another variation on the theme. Taurus sired five champions, three out of Roundway Anklet. The most successful of the trio was Ch. Risepark Toreador, the sire of Pam Radford's and Dori Clark's first homebred Ch. Iccabod Chervil. He, in turn, sired seven champions, including Fred and Phyl Morley's Ch. Castilla Zambra, the dam of history-making Ch. Castilla Linajudo.

First shown in 1979 at eight months, Linajudo (his name means "blue blood") won his first CC and Best of Breed, and never looked back. Shown only once in 1982, he captured his thirty-first CC—a breed record. In between,

Eng. Ch. Castilla Linajudo

Linajudo became the first Miniature Schnauzer to win a Best in Show at Championship show level—and he won two! In addition he was three times Reserve BIS, including Crufts in 1980. He won the Utility Group nine times (another breed record) and was Reserve twice. These wins gave Miniature Schnauzers a tremendous nationwide boost, and set the stage for further top-level successes which quickly followed.

The Morley's Zambra would also produce Ch. Castilla Diamante, owned by the Ichabod partnership, the top winner of 1983 with 10 CCs and two Group wins. She was sired by yet another Risepark American-bred, Ch. Irrenhaus Impact At Risepark.

The impact made by Taurus is nothing short of phenomenal, with nearly half of the champions finished since 1970 being his descendants. The Taurus son, Toreador, is in charge of the largest percentage of champions descending from this line.

Eng. Ch. Risepark Toreador

Toreador daughters were highly prized by several new breeders during the 1970s. Tom Fennybough's Toreador daughter, Fernery Honeysuckle, gave him Ch. Fernery Fantastic, the sire of Linajudo. A trio of linebred sisters by Toreador were to have a significant place in the breed's development. The three Catalanta bitches, Catalanta Miss Lucy, Miss Lissette and Miss Sparkle, were bred by Sid and Gil Saville, and are out of a Taurus daughter.

Miss Lissette went over to Mrs. Furst-Danielson in Sweden, where she was mated to her American-bred Ch. Starfire Criterion Landmark. A dog from the litter was returned to Risepark where he became Ch. Jidjis Min Cato At Risepark, the sire of eight champions, including the good producer Ch. Catalanta True Luck of Risepark, out of Catalanta Miss Sparkle.

Malenda is the prefix of Glenys Allen, who started with Catalanta Miss Lucy and has bred several generations of champions since. Her Miss Lucy granddaughter, Ch. Malenda Mimosa, was Best of Breed at the Club Championship Show in 1978 under the American judge Olive Moore of Travelmor fame.

William, Olive and Jennifer Moore of Trenton, New Jersey, have had a far-reaching effect on contemporary British bloodlines. When Janet Price Callow returned home to England after spending several years with the Moores, she came with Ch. Travelmor's Fantazio and Riversedge Petite Pebbles. Fantazio brought with him yet another tail-male branch from the great DISPLAY. The pair, when mated in 1970, produced the aptly named Ch. Buffels All American Boy of Deansgate, the record-setting sire of nine champions.

All American Boy was owned by the Deansgate partnership of Pamela

Eng. Ch. Luke Lively At Deansgate

McLaren and Elisabeth Cooke, already well established with Roundway and Deltone stock. His major influence was through the Fernerys, Malendas and Eastwights, and subsequently, the Arbeys of Betty and Archie Fletcher. They started with the All American Boy daughter Ch. Short and Sweet of Deansgate, a Taurus granddaughter, giving them three champions by Eastwight sires.

More than two dozen champions emerged from Deansgate, many of them finished by new owners who have gone on to breed successfully from them. Miss Scott's Ch. Deansgate Hairs 'N' Graces was the first of the breed to win a Group. Mrs. Webster's Ch. Deansgate Truey Nuff was Best in Show at Blackpool's Golden Jubilee Show in 1983. The crowning achievement for Deansgate has to be Ch. Luke Lively At Deansgate, linebred on All American Boy. His show career spanned over six years, and he was the breed leader in 1987 and '88, and a Best in Show winner. He continued to win well, even as a veteran. His record-setting thirty-second CC was, in fact, won at a Specialty, from the Veterans class in 1990, and he was not through yet. Luke won his fortieth CC in 1992, giving any who wish to challenge the record a pretty stiff task.

The Travelmor people had for several years acted as host to American dog fanciers attending Crufts. They made many friends on their annual visits and have shared many experiences with their British counterparts. A particular friendship with the Iccabod partnership has reaped remarkable rewards. In the early 1980s, two cleverly named Travelmors were sent over to Iccabod. The first, Ch. Travelmor's From U.S. To You, had truly regal background. Her dam, Ch. Reflections Lively Image, is a top producer in the U.S. with seven American and two English

Eng. Ch. Travelmor's From U.S. To You

Eng. Ch. Samavai Steps Out

Eng. Ch. Maid For Gold With Armorique winning Best in Show at the Ladies Kennel Association in 1992, while still a puppy.

champions. She, in turn, is sired by the American "super sire", Ch. Penlan Peter Gunn (73 Chs.).

Breed history was made in 1982 when From U.S. To You became the first bitch to win Best in Show at a Championship event in Britain. She was to win nineteen CCs in just over a year to become the breed's top winning bitch to that date. She will best be remembered as the dam of Ch. Ichabod Mixed Herbs, the top sire for 1988 and '89, leaving a host of champion descendants in succeeding generations. He would, in fact, produce the bitch that would surpass his dam's record. At Crufts, in 1992, Tracy and Peter Slingsby's homebred Ch. Samavai Steps Out, earned her twentieth CC, but would hold the record ever so briefly, as she made room for the breed's all-time top winning bitch, Ch. Maid For Gold With Armorique. Her sire—Ch. Iccabod Olympic Gold.

Maid For Gold enjoyed a sensational career, giving her owners, Shaune Frost and David Bates, many a thrill. At the last show of 1992, while still a puppy, she won her fourth CC, won a round of the Pup of the Year contest, and ended the day winning the Utility Group enroute to Best in Show. The next year was hers—beginning with being named Pup Of The

Eng. Ch. Travelmor's U.S. Mail

Year in January, and ending as seventh among all breeds. She won a record-setting eighteen CCs (fifteen with BOB) in 1993, and established the record for bitches, with her twenty first CC.

The Moores later sent over Travelmor's U.S. Mail, personally selected as a ten-week-old puppy by Pam Radford. Another out of Lively Image, he also brought with him the top winning Skyline bloodlines, as the son of another American "super sire," Ch. Skyline's Blue Spruce (55 Chs.). U.S. Mail finished quickly and became a Best in Show winner, topping over ten thousand entries at Birmingham City and winning Best at the Group show and All-Schnauzer Specialty in 1984. An offspring of the Best in Show-winning Travelmor pair, Ch. Iccabod Travellers Tail quickly made his presence felt on all levels of competition. In addition, U.S. Mail continued to serve notice as a sire, and was runner-up for Top Sire - All Breeds in 1986. He eventually established a new record, with 14 champions to his credit. Of particular interest is the fact that U.S. Mail can be found twice in the pedigree of the 1992 Ch. Black Bijou At Jenmil, the first black male champion since 1964, when the Italian-bred Ch. Jovinus Malya Swanee became the first. Blacks in the British show rings continue to be a rarity.

The influence of the Iccabod Miniatures based on the Travelmor imports was graphically illustrated in 1990, when Radford and Clarke were the top breeders, U.S. Mail the top sire, Iccabod Jay Walker the top brood bitch (for the second consecutive year), Ch. Iccabod Olympic Gold the top winner, and his son, Daylorn Liberty Square the top puppy.

Philip and Suzanne Bagshaw's Brynmor prefix has yet another American-bred connection via Swedish Ch. Barclay Square

Eng. Ch. Iccabod Olympic Gold

Maximin Minx. Imported by Benny Blid, Minx produced two litters in England before returning to Sweden. Those breedings produced three champions. The first, by Brynsmor Joker, of Eastwight breeding, resulting in the brothers Ch. Maximin Isbyorn, owned by the Smedleys, and Ch. Maximin Graben of Deansgate, owned by Deansgate, both champion producers.

Eng. Ch. Irrenhaus Impact At Risepark

In England, 1986 marked the first year in which black and silvers achieved recognition. Pam and Dave Wick's Qassaba Tia Christel, by an Eastwight sire, became the first champion, finishing at the Miniature Club's Specialty, and ending the year as top bitch. She has since produced a B/S champion son.

A fourth "period" in British breed history emerged with the 1980s, based on a new influx of American breeding with related bloodlines. Ch. Skyline's Blue Spruce (55 Chs.), so intensely linebred within the Diplomat branch, already had a dominant position in these emerging bloodlines as the sire of U.S. Mail. Ch. Irrenhaus Impact At Risepark, imported by Peter Newman, carries three lines to Spruce and became the first sire to claim ten champion get, including the top winning Diamante and Ch. Risepark Here Comes Charlie. The latter produced a pair of champions in 1992, bred by Sheila and Sonny Dawe. One of these, Ch. Sonshea Call Me Mister Risepark, co-owned with Barry Day and Peter Newman, was a leading winner, with two Bests in Show, as well as a Reserve Best.

In 1985, yet another Irrenhaus import was made up by Peter Newman. Ch. Irrenhaus Aims to Please Risepark carries four lines to Spruce, being a daughter of the inbred Spruce double grandson, Ch. Regency's Right On Target (78 Chs.). Bred to U.S. Mail, she produced Ch. Risepark Maid To Order.

In 1994, the most recent American-bred to earn an English title was also imported by Mr. Newman. Smitten with the quality of America's top winner, Ch. Rampage's Representative (45 Chs.), he imported and finished a son, Ch. Repitition's Favorite Son For Risepark. He carries a half dozen lines to Spruce. It is hoped that he will impact the breed positively, as so many other Risepark imports have done over the last four decades.

The future holds promise for these emerging new American bloodlines. Only time will tell which will achieve prominence and play a significant part in the breed's future.

• In Australia

Any commentary on the Australian dog scene deserves a bit of a geography lesson as well. Australia is approximately the size of the United States, but has only one-twentieth the population. Sydney is the center of Australia's most populous state, New South Wales (N.S.W.), boasting 5,000,000 residents, and the most dog-related activities. The state of Victoria is next in population, and its center is Melbourne. The Melbourne Royal Show can be compared with our Westminster and England's Crufts. This spring event annually attracts over 6,000 dogs and lasts for ten days. Just before Melbourne Royal finishes, the Perth Royal starts. As it cost some $1,200 in 1995 to fly the 2,000 miles west, there are not too many people flitting cross-country to show dogs. Even the distance between Sydney and Melbourne seems to prohibit many fanciers from out-of-state exhibiting.

Miniature Schnauzers were first introduced to Australia in 1962, by Mrs. J. Rees of the Casa Verde Kennel in N.S.W. and Mrs. C. Cerini of the Koniglich Kennel in Victoria. England would supply the original stock, and continues to be the main source of new bloodlines. The key dog, however, would still be the "all-American" super sire, CH. DOREM DISPLAY.

Eng. Ch. Gosmore Wicket Keeper, from the famous Gosmore "Cricket Team" was the first to earn an Australian title. Mrs. Rees also imported a pair of bitches for his court, resulting in several Casa Verde champions.

Mrs. Cerini began with an English-bred, CC-winning Wicket Keeper son, Deltone Deldario. He became an Australian champion and was Best in Show at the first Schnauzer Club of Victoria Specialty in 1967. At seven years of age Deldario won the Breed at Melbourne Royal, and went on to further successes as a veteran. Blessed with the incredible longevity enjoyed by the breed, he died in 1980 at over eighteen years of age. The first bitch imported by Mrs. Cerini became Australian Ch. Deltone Delsanta Delia. She is behind virtually all the Koniglich champions. Other Deltones were added to the Koniglich roster, including Deltone Delsanta Doric, Deltone Deldaryl, and in 1972, Eng. Ch. Deltone Delduque—all becoming Australian champions and producers of champions.

Mrs. Cerini has been the main producer of blacks since the early 1960s. Virtually all black champions to date carry lines to her first black import from England, Jovinus Rigoletto. Here again, longevity was evident, as he lived to be over seventeen years of age. He became the first black to achieve an Australian title, and through his inbred son, Koniglich The Groom, has many black champion descendants in America. In Australia, Rigoletto descendants include the two-time Victoria Specialty winner Ch. Koniglich Jakreisel, CDX, and Ch. Koniglich Banjora, the Specialty winner in 1979.

Mr. and Mrs. J. Finn of the Elimbari prefix in N.S.W. took up the cause in 1979, importing from England the essentially American-bred Black Anfiger of Ripplevale, of Anfiger and Kelly breeding. He made up his championship and was Best in Show at the N.S.W. Specialty in 1982, only to die as a result of minor surgery a few weeks later. He did leave a champion son and daughter, and one

**Aust. Ch. Hi-Crest Schonhardt Hi-Spring,
the first American-bred to become an Australia champion.**

---

of his sons, Elimbari Benji Black, is the sire of Ch. Bastram Black Tacker and Ch. Manziller Black Onyx.

Although black and silvers were bred in Australia since the 1960s, as in England, they were not a recognized color for the show ring until the 1980s. Following the standard change in England, the Australian National Kennel Club also revised the Australian standard to include the color.

British-bred Eastwight imports can take credit for most of the black and silvers bred in Australia to date. They have been bred in N.S.W. by Schonhardt, Elimbari and Kolokov, in Queensland by Vabec and in South Australia by Guadala. A predominance of Eastwight breeding can be found in virtually all the areas "Down Under".

Mrs. E. Templeman started her Tempo Kennel in 1963 with the English import Sheenhart Honeysuckle, making her a champion. Her daughter, Ch. Tempo Dasheba, by Deldario, became the first Victorian-bred champion. Mrs. Templeman also imported Eng. Ch. Courtaud Pannyann Pampas, after he was Best of Breed at the Schnauzer Club of Great Britain Show in 1966. Mrs. Templeman later turned to Eastwight stock, importing and finishing Ch. Eastwight Sea-Cookie in 1977. He is a son of the important American-bred British sire, Eng. Ch. Buffels All American Boy of Deansgate (9 Chs.).

Mrs. Audrey Ralph of the Fernlands prefix in Victoria also started with Eastwight stock, importing Eng. Ch. Eastwight Sea-Lord and finishing him in 1974. These two Eastwight dogs played a prominent role in current breed development as both were used extensively, producing many champions. Mrs. Ralph, along with Lady Elizabeth Froggatt, imported Eng. Ch. Dengarse Take By Storm, who also traces in tail-male to All American Boy. He was Best in Show at the Schnauzer Club of N.S.W. in 1980, and became an important sire.

Aust. Ch. Starborne Brackens Boy

Until 1980, the only American bloodlines found in Australia came via British lines, due primarily to the stiff quarantine restrictions placed on all imports. Dogs entering Australia must do the full English quarantine, and then face a further two-month government kennel quarantine on their arrival. If they come in through Hawaii, they must do seven months there and then three months in Australia. All dogs from the American mainland must go through either England or Hawaii. It is an expensive and time-consuming process.

Alan Bracken of the Starborne prefix in N.S.W. was the first to bring in American dogs directly from the mainland. He imported a breeding pair from Blythewood, both sired by Ch. Blythewood National Acclaim (32 Chs.). They were cropped and unable to be shown, but a mating of the two produced excellent results. At the N.S.W. Specialty in 1981, under Vincent Mitchell, famed handler of the Gosmores in England, all three Starbornes from the Blythewood litter scored well. A year later, Anne Rogers Clark awarded Best of Breed at Sydney Royal to Starborne Brackens Boy and reserve to Starborne High Acclaim. During the remainder of the year the three Starborne dogs were to earn many top wins, each gaining their titles.

The offspring of the Blythewood imports have enjoyed continued success. A mating of High Acclaim to Ch. Vabec Sea Joletta resulted in Ch. Barbouze Hot Toddy and Ch. Barbouze Tia Maria. High Acclaim sired V. Fitzgerald's Ch. Varbruin Star Dynasty, Best in Show at the N.S.W. Specialty on two occasions. Brackens Boy was bred to B. Dennis and J. Lamping's Ch. Varbruin Love Flight, producing Ch. Barbouze Rockafella, CC winner at the Victoria Specialty at six and a half months of age.

The Schonhardt Kennel was established in 1974 by Marelyne MacLeod-

Am. & Aust.
Ch. Simon Say's
of Hansenhaus

Woodhouse in N.S.W. based on Eastwight stock already in Australia. Mr. N. Champion of Thornor Kennel provided Schonhardt with Ch. Thornor Kakak Kechil, dam of many champions, including Ch. Schonhardt Copy Boy, three-time CC winner at the Club Specialty, in addition to a host of top awards. Also a successful sire, Copy Boy claims two Best in Show winners among his six champion get, and has progeny in New Zealand, Hong Kong and Japan.

The American connection was further strengthened in 1983, when Schonhardt imported from Hawaii, and quickly finished Ch. Hi-Crest Schonhardt Hi-Spring and Ch. Hi-Crest Schonhardt Triumph-Hi, both sired by Ch. Sunshine Indigo. These were the first American imports to complete their Australian championships. Schonhardt also provided a retirement home for the record-holding Best in Show winner Ch. Hi-Charge of Hansenhaus (11 Chs.), nine years of age when he arrived in 1983. With him came yet another Hawaiian-bred, Hi-Crest Natural Eclectic-Hi, who quickly became the third American import to finish "Down Under". In 1988, Schonhardt would import the first American champion, Ch. Simon Say's of Hansenhaus. He finished his Australian title in just four weekends of showing, with multiple Group wins. He went on to win

Aust. Ch. Guadala Brunhilde

---

both Specialty and All-Breed Championship show Best in Shows, and has to date sired 14 champions. Simon carries two lines to Ch. Playboy's Block Buster (22 Chs.), the sire of Hi-Charge, and is intensely linebred within the Diplomat Branch from DISPLAY.

The Guadala Kennel of Steve & Jeanette Tiltman in South Australia was founded in 1980. Their foundation bitch, Ch. Eastdon Aurora Belle, bred by R. Ritzau, gave them three litters with champions in each, including two Best in Show winners. Bred to Ch. Schonhardt Copy Boy, Belle produced Guadala's most successful show bitch, Ch. Guadala Brunhilde. She was the breed leader in 1983, winning a Best in Show, once runner-up to Best in Show, and was Best South Australian Bitch at the Royal Adelaide Show. Two Skyline dogs were imported by Guadala in 1985. Both Skyline's Snap Judgement and Skyline's Silver Screen have American champion parents, the former by the famed cornerstone sire, Ch. Skyline's Blue Spruce (55 Chs.). Silver Screen, while in quarantine in England, was mated to the Blue Spruce son Eng. Ch. Travelmor's U.S. Mail. The Tiltmans latter purchased Regency's Thunder Down Under, by the Blue Spruce son Ch. Regency's Right On (32 Chs.). Their 1990 Best in Show winner, Ch. Guadala Typhoon Anne, is his daughter.

Guadala provided foundation stock for many new breeders, including Ruth and David Gardiner. They also decided to import, bringing over a Feldmar pair, including the B/S Feldmar Night Boss, a son of Ch. Feldmar Nightshade (17 Chs.) which they finished. Breeding him to their Ch. Guadala Supercharge gave them Ch. Mirazac Fatal Attraction. Breeding him to their Ch. Feldmar Starry Starry Night, also by Nightshade, gave them Ch. Mirazac Shadow Boxer, which in 1995 became the first B/S to finish in Western Australia.

In Victoria, Mrs. D. Williams and her talented daughters also got their start with a Guadala bitch, getting their first two champions from Ch. Guadala Double The Style. They also purchased Ch. Guadala Thunderbolt, a Brunhilde grandson, sired by Thunder Down Under, and made him one of the leading winners in 1989. The Williams have since made up several champions bearing their Cibach prefix.

Further American imports arrived in Australia throughout the 1980s. From the Skyline Kennel, the uncropped Skyline's Down Under and Ch. Skyline's Every Witch Way went to B. Dennis and J. Lamping. Down Under became the fourth American import to complete an Australian championship.

In the fall of 1987, I spent the most wonderful vacation I have ever enjoyed, having been invited to judge the breed (and others) in both Sydney and Adelaide, receiving a firsthand impression of Schnauzers in two widely separated states. The hospitality was overwhelming, the quality of the dogs well above what I had expected.

• In New Zealand

The first Miniature Schnauzers shown in New Zealand came from Mrs. Rees's Casa Verde Kennel in Australia. These were a combination of the basic English lines from Gosmore, Deltone and Eastwight stock. In time, further imports, mainly from Australia, introduced lines from Schonhardt, Fernland, Vabec, Starborne, Guadala and Elimari, and through them, added English lines from Risepark, Castilla and Iccabod.

The small nucleus of breeders during the 1970s and 1980s included Mr. K. Brown and Mr. R. Grey, working with British Deansgates. Mrs. V. Woodley and Mr. and Mrs. Berket developed their breeding program with additions from British Risepark and Courtaud lines.

For some time, all stock was salt and pepper, with the occasional black and silver cropping up. After the New Zealand Kennel Club recognized the color, a first B/S champion was made up by Mrs. Kath Grave. He was Ch. Woodsmor Bobbie Boy, of essentially Eastwight breeding.

Just as this striking color gained recognition, Michael Brick made the first direct import from the United States— a B/S dog and bitch, Feldmar Knight For Brickmark and Ruedesheim Maid of Brickmark, both earning their New Zealand titles in 1988. A few years later, these

Am. Ch. Feldmar Pistol Pete with Joan Huber

**New Zealand
Ch. Leecurt Silver Shimmer**

were joined by a pair of B/S American champions: Feldmar Night Reveler (15 Chs.) and Feldmar Pistol Pete. Since both were cropped, they were not allowed to be exhibited in New Zealand. At about the same time, Mr. Brick imported from England a trio from Leecurt, all of which were shown and finished. Ch. Leecurt Silver Shimmer, a Reveler daughter, was the most successful as a producer, giving him a pair of champions from Pistol Pete, a pair by yet another Britisher, Arbey Buffels Trouble Shooter, and a fifth by their Ch. Leecurt Night Rhythm, who also sired several other Brickmark champions. At the New Zealand National Dog Show, the Brickmark Schnauzers won Best of Breed in 1990, '91, '93 and '94.

The most recent import did not have such a long stay in quarantine, as Reverie's Maiden Kiwi Dream is Hawaiian-bred, introducing the Sole Baye line. She earned her title easily in 1994, handled by owner, Brent Philip.

The Miniature Schnauzers "Down Under" seem to have a great future with the introduction of so many new bloodlines, both from England and the United States.

• In Europe

The Federation Cynologique Internationale (FCI), located in Brussels, has been recognized as the governing body by dog clubs, first in Europe, and eventually throughout the world. Although each country has its own system for awarding a national title of champion, only the FCI can award the title of International Champion.

Each year the FCI sponsors a World Show, designating the best dog and bitch of each breed as that year's World Champion. In the last decade show sites were truly international—Mexico City, Tokyo, Brussels, and Dortmund, West Germany, the homeland of the breed, among others.

The site for the 1985 World Show was Amsterdam, featuring over 10,000 entries. Even here, close to the birthplace of the breed, all the major winners carried predominantly American bloodlines. There are, in fact, very few Miniature Schnauzers outside of their homeland that do not descend from America's super sire, CH. DOREM DISPLAY.

Ch. Tribute's Tuxedo Junction, Ch. Schnauzi's Sybil and Ch. Schnauzi Dinah, black and silver Swiss champions in the mid-1970s.

One of the first Europeans to import modern American stock was Frieda Steiger of the Schnauzi Kennel in Switzerland. Her original imports in the late 1960s were from Joanna Grigg's Sylva Sprite Kennel in Canada, and were principally black and silver. Frau Steiger was instrumental in bringing recognition to this color on the Continent of their birth. Until the mid-1970s, black and silvers could only be shown in the United States and Canada. Frieda had the honor of breeding the first B/S champion recognized by the Pinscher-Schnauzer Klub of Germany (PSK). In addition, Schnauzi's Pyewacket and Schnauzi's Nanette, in May 1976, became the first of their breed to be awarded the PSK Jahrsieger titles. Both were Swiss champions, as Switzerland was the one country on the Continent that recognized B/S right after their importation.

The foundation dam of the Schnauzi line is Swiss Ch. Schnauzi's Sybil, whelped in Switzerland but bred in Canada, as her dam, Can. Ch. Sylva Sprite Frills and Jade, arrived in whelp to Can. Ch. Eastwight Sea-Voyager, CD.

In 1977, the first year in which B/S could earn CACIB awards from FCI, the Pyewacket son, Schnauzi's King, owned by Peter Marx, won the B/S Bundessieger title in Essen, Germany. Frau Steiger's ten-month-old Pyewacket daughter, Schnauzi's Melissa, won the Youth Siegerin title, and her Israeli import, Chatifa Barluz, the Youth Sieger title. At three French shows that year, Schnauzi's Nanette became the first B/S to earn the FCI title of International Champion. Many more Schnauzi champions followed, all based on stock

**Int. Ch. Chatifa
Barluz**

descending from the B/S sires Sea-Voyager and Can. Ch. Walsh's Frosty Charmer, CD.

Oddly enough, Frau Steiger would find a needed outcross in Israel, where Izchak Schkedi had begun a black and silver line in the late 1960s based on Israeli Ch. Geelong Dandy, bred in New Jersey by Randolph Higgins. The Barluz B/S are essentially American breeding, but provided outcrosses to English Eastwight and Italian Barbanera lines. Mr. Schkedi also imported the B/S Gough's Frosted Black Jack from the well-established Gough's Kennel in Minnesota. The Barluz B/S, based on this pair of American-bred sires, is sufficiently established so that Barluz breeding is found throughout Europe and the Scandinavian countries.

The Klondaike Kennel of Nils and Bodil Jordal in Denmark, originally founded in 1974 on English Eastwights, had developed its own blend using the best from the Swiss Schnauzis, the Israeli Barluz and several American imports. From Janice Rue of Illinois came the highly successful B/S Best in Show winner Int. Ch. Aljamar Op Art of Klondaike—a champion of Denmark, Luxembourg and Germany. As a son of essentially Italian-bred Ch. Aljamar Tommy Gun, he owns a truly international pedigree. The Jordals, equally involved with salt and peppers, also turned to America for stock, importing Walters' Nugget of Klondaike in 1984, making her the first American-bred salt and pepper to earn a German title. Nugget also earned a Danish and International title. Further additions included the salt and pepper Carolane's Starfire, of essentially Penlan breeding, and their first venture in black, Skansen's Black Gem, both earning Danish titles. Gem is an inbred daughter of Ch. Walters' Black Bandit.

During the 1980s, Dolores Walters in California was foremost among breeders of all colors willing to export her best around the world. Walters dogs of all colors can be found throughout the Scandinavian countries, as well as Belgium, Italy, Japan and Taiwan. The salt and pepper Walters' One Shot, a half brother to Nugget, both by Ch. Ruedesheim's Landmark (5 Chs.), was imported by Grethe Hansen of Denmark, earning his Danish and International titles, and topped forty-six salt and peppers at the World Show in Amsterdam.

Sweden and Finland abound with Walters breeding. Mari Saari of Finland has imported four of them, in all three colors, making Swedish and Finnish champions of the black male Landmark's Raider and the B/S male,

**Int. Ch. Maximin
Smiling Yankee**

Greer's Dazzlin Frost, a son of Japanese Ch. Walters' Black Frost. In 1979, Christina Lundstrom exhibited her black American-bred male, Gough's Ebony Edge of Knight, to Swedish, Finnish and Norwegian titles. Millie Olsson of Sweden has also concentrated on blacks, enjoying success with Walters' Black Flash, Best in Show at the Swedish Jubilee Show in 1982.

In Finland, Soile Bister's Trixer Kennel, founded on English Deansgates and Swiss Schnauzis, added several American imports in the 1980s. From Bob and Nancy Berg's Minnesota-based Bo-Nanza Kennel came three black and silvers. Bo-Nanza's Trixer Frosty Pony earned Finnish and Swedish titles, and topped all colors at the Finnish Specialty in 1984. Already a successful sire, his son Trixer Voyager went to Frau Steiger and has CACIB wins in Switzerland, France and Germany. Bo-Nanza's Frosty Gambler and Bo-Nanza's Trixer Frosty Song, both by Ch. Bo-Nanza's Frosty R Jr., followed, Gambler earning his Finnish title. Mrs. Bister later added some salt and pepper Penlan breeding, gaining Swedish and Finnish titles on Penlan Princess of Trixer.

One of the most prolific producers of Scandinavian champions is the Maximin Kennel of Benny Blid in Sweden. Here again, the American influence is a dominant factor, as this kennel is based almost exclusively on a pair of salt and pepper imports from Barclay Square (see TRIBUTE chapter).

Barclay Square Maximin Midas and Barclay Square Maximin Minx were quarantined in England in 1978 before finally making their home in Sweden. Minx stayed on even longer, producing two litters from which came three English champions. Shown only four times in Sweden and Finland in 1980, Minx earned both titles, and then produced a final litter containing the Specialty winner, Ch. Maximin Super Trooper. Through her children and grandchildren, Minx has had a profound impact on English and Scandinavian breeding. Midas was shown ten times in Sweden, winning nine Bests of Breed, including a Specialty. As a sire, Midas produced eleven Swedish champions, six of these going on to produce another generation of champions. Most notable among the Midas sons is Int. Ch. Maximin Smiling Yankee, Sweden's first multiple Best in Show winner, and the sire of over twenty champions.

**Int. Ch. Sercatep
Falkendal Aces High**

During the early 1990s, Ewa-Marie and Leif Nackholm of Sweden, imported several young black and silvers from Debbra Herrell's Sercatep Kennel in Michigan. These included Sercatep's Nite Games and Sercatep Falkendal Aces High, both earning their Swedish titles in only three shows. Bred together they produced a pair of champions, Swed. Ch. Falkendal's Queen Of Diamonds, who they retained, and Falkendal's King Of Diamonds, who went to Fabio Ferrari of the Scedir Kennel in Italy. Mr. Ferrari, in turn, sent them Scedir Flamenco, which they are currently showing.

Belgium, home of the FCI, also has breed enthusiasts who have chosen American bloodlines. Madame and Monsieur Louis Huwaert of Brussels began with two Bo-Nanza black and silvers, earning a Dutch title on Bo-Nanza's Frosted Queen, a litter sister to the Bergs' Ch. Bo-Nanza's Frosty Lone Ranger. The Huwaerts then went to Dorothy and Ivan Mayberry's California-based Dorovan Kennel for their next B/S. Dorovan Midnite Star, sired by the B/S Ch. Valharra's Captain Midnite, offered an outcross to established European-American black and silver lines. He earned his International title in 1980.

In 1993, Vera Van Breusegem imported a pair of black and silvers to add to her Art Deco breeding program in Belgium. Both Bandsman's Chimney Sweep and Rampage's Rare Commodity have enjoyed considerable success in the show rings, the latter gaining both Dutch and International titles.

Int. Ch. Rampage's Rare Commodity

**Int. Ch. Ocus-Pocus
Van De Havenstad**

Cyriel De Meulenaer has been adding American lines to his well-established Havenstad Kennel, specializing in blacks. Skansen Playboy was the first to be imported, followed by Ch. Jebema's Black Debutante. She has given him his most successful winner to date, Int. Ch. Ocus-Pocus Van De Havenstad, with titles in Belgium, Holland, France, Denmark and Germany.

In Spain, Mr. A. Madueno of Madrid is recognized as the breed's founding father, bringing in breeding stock from Britain in the early 1970s. English Ch. Dengarse Pirates Treasure, and his Canadian-bred dam, Rosehill Pirates Silver, and later Eastwight Sea-Ballet and Eastwight Sea-Gem, all became Spanish champions. They formed the foundation for a host of Kilimanjaro champions, and are behind virtually all Spanish champions to the present.

Mr. F. Martinez Guijarro claims Spain's most successful winner and producer in International and Spanish Ch. Miky Kilimanjaro, the winner of fourteen Bests in Show. A Miky son, Ch. Tono del Escarambrujo, owned by Miss Saizar, was Best of Breed at the second Spanish Specialty in 1983.

The first Championship Show of the Schnauzer Club of Spain was held in 1982, judged by Heinz Holler, President of the German Pinscher-Schnauzer Klub. Best of Breed was Mr. Guijarro's homebred Ch. Beauty of Maidenhead. She is from the litter out of Pirates Silver, imported in whelp to Dengarse Yankee Spinoff. Tono and Beauty, bred together, produced Mr. J. Martinez Solano's Ch. Catalina de C'an Jack, a very successful winner.

The first Spaniard to import an American champion was Mr. A. Pons, in 1984, quickly making Marmac Pretorian a Spanish champion as well. Pretorian represents a viable outcross to the predominantly Dengarse, Eastwight and Risepark British lines currently in use. A few years later he imported another American champion, Sole Baye's John Henry, making him an international champion, as well as a Best in Show winner. Mr. Pons also bred Danish Ch. Chipirrusquis Captain Furillo, carrying two lines to John Henry. He was the breed leader in Denmark 1990 and '91.

A bit of international breed history was made in 1992, when Kari

Int. Ch. Blythewood Choice For L Y winning Best of Opposite Sex at the 1992 AMSC Specialty under breeder-judge Robert Moore, owner-handled by Carlos Mendez.

Wilberg's Ch. Chipirrusquis Chipa At Kanix, bred by Mr. Pons, made up his English title. He is a son of John Henry, and during his English visit he sired several litters from which two English champions emerged. Peter Newman and Barry Day of Risepark fame were the first to use him, finishing in the same year Ch. Risepark Remember Me To Armorique, bred by them and owned by Shaune Frost and David Bates.

Carlos Mendez of Madrid had the honor of handling his newly finished American Ch. Blythewood Choice For L Y to Best Opposite Sex at the 1992 A.M.S.C. Specialty at Montgomery County. This young son of Ch. Blythewood Shooting Sparks (53 Chs.) had finished his championship that same weekend with back-to-back five-point majors, returning with Carlos to Spain. He has enjoyed equal success in Europe, adding several titles.

Since 1985, the entire picture in Europe, and around the world for that matter, has been enormously affected by exports from Marcia Feld in Illinois, the large majority being black and silver. There are Feldmar Schnauzers in Sweden, Finland, Belgium, Denmark, France, Italy and Switzerland, as well as in South Africa, Australia and New Zealand.

Mrs. Feld had the pleasure of attending the World Dog Show in Copenhagen in 1989, and had to be overjoyed with the successes of her breeding program. Feldmar Scedir Midnite Dream, an Italian champion owned by Fabio and Grazia Ferrari of the Italian Scedir Schnauzers, was the World Youth Champion, while runner-up was his brother, Feldmar Night Shadow, a Danish champion and Belgium Best in Show winner, owned by Nils and Bodil Jordal of the long-established Klondaike Kennel. Midnite Dream has been a prolific producer with champion get throughout Europe.

The Feldmar dogs have had their greatest impact in Scandinavia, specifically Sweden, where Swed. and Int. Ch. Feldmar High Quickmix Quality was the first to be made up, by Eva Helmer. He is a full brother to Dolores Featherer's American top producer, Ch. Feldmar Blaque Feathers, dam of six champions.

By far the most successful exhibitors in

Int. Ch. Feldmar Scedir Midnite Dream

Sweden, if not the whole of Europe, are Lennart Bergqvist and Sune Hallblad of Backstreet Kennels. Mrs. Feld remembers how it all began:

Lennart purchased two bitches from me, and he came to get each of them. I will never forget going to the airport to meet this man—the stranger I now know so well. This was the same man who greeted me as I exited the plane in Copenhagen, when I attended the World Show. He was a wonderful escort for my friend Nancy Banas and myself through Denmark into Sweden.

Int. Ch. Feldmar Moonlit Night

Prior to his Feldmar black and silvers, this color was ignored in Scandinavia. They now have taken top honors for the past several years.

Lennart owns Swed. and Int. Ch. Feldmar Moonlit Night, a full sister to Ch. Feldmar Night Reveler (15 Chs.). She was Dog of the Year in 1988. They followed this with Swed. and Int. Ch. Feldmar Alice to Backstreet, Dog of the Year in 1989 and again in 1990. Of particular note is that both bitches earned the German Club Sieger (KBSG) titles.

Eva Helmer with Int. Ch. Feldmar High Quickmix Quality, and Sune Hallblad with Int. Ch. Backstreet's Light Roseanne

This outstanding pair was followed by Swed. and Int. Ch. Feldmar Son Of A Gun, Sweden's "winningest" Schnauzer ever! In just seven years, the Backstreet Schnauzers would earn over 100 champion titles on these dogs and their descendants. With the antidocking laws now in effect, all their homebred stock are shown completely natural—tails and all. These include their leading winner in 1993 and '94, Swed. and Int. Ch. Backstreet's Light Road Jack, by Son Of A Gun out of Moonlit Night, and his sister, Swed. and Int. Ch. Backstreet's Light Roseanne. Other Moonlit Night offspring have enjoyed success with their new owners in Finland and Norway.

What has to be Mrs. Feld's proudest export to date is Lux. Jgd. Ch. 1995 Feldmar Billy The Kid, puchased as a puppy by Werner and Martina Stamm of Frankfurt, Germany. He carries six lines to Nightshade and has been a wonderful ambassador for the breed in this, his country of origin.

There have obviously been many proud moments shared by new owners with Mrs. Feld, who wrote:

One of my biggest thrills came the day I picked up my phone and heard the familiar twang of the international call and then a voice saying,

Lux. Ch. Feldmar Billy The Kid

"Mrs. Feld, this is Signora Milia Pozzi-Tarlarini calling from Italy." Mrs. Pozzi! Gunter's mother! Italian Ch. Malya Gunter was an American import, and Tommy Gun's sire, therefore behind all my dogs. I couldn't believe that Mrs. Pozzi could possibly have any reason to be contacting me. But she was. Feldmar Malya Snow Crystal now happily resides with Milia at her lovely home in Italy, and quickly earned her Italian and International titles.

I am very proud to say she is now my friend.

Int. Ch. Feldmar Malya Snow Crystal with Milia Pozzi

When asked about her extraordinary success with exporting, Marcia explained:

I love working with the people. There is a definite respect on my part for their ideas and their needs. I make a sincere effort to understand the standard for the country involved and to find the dog to fit that standard. I detest the attitude of shipping the junk that can't be used here. I have no feeling of superiority, and in many cases find that I have much to learn from these people who have been working with my chosen color longer than I.

How can I explain the feeling of awe when I went to my front door and found a present of needlepoint from Frieda Steiger, a lady halfway around the world that I had never met nor even heard of except in the Schnauzer history books. But it happened.

The dogs and the people surrounding them, here and abroad, have given me much more in ten years than many people gain in an entire lifetime.

The 1994 World Show in Berne, Switzerland, was truly an international affair, bringing out a large and very representative entry of Miniature Schnauzers of all colors, from all over Europe. The effects of American breeding were very much in evidence, particularly among the black and silvers, where more than half the entry had recognizable American Schnauzers close up. The sires of the best of each of the colors were, in fact, American-bred. The World Champion B/S was Italian and Int. Ch. Scedir Charlie Brown, owned in Italy by Rosso Enrico. His sire is the Nightshade son Int. Ch. Feldmar Scedir Midnite Dream. In salt and peppers, the title was awarded to Quantro v.d. Spikke, a son of Int. Ch. Blythewood Wins A Blue Streak, owned in Holland by Jan Smienk, and from Belgium, Cyriel Meulenaer's nine-months-old Skansen Playboy son, Rolex Van De Havenstad, was the World Champion in blacks.

So. Afr. Ch. Feldmar-LoveJoy Trigger Happy At Tamarack

• In South Africa

For the most part, the Miniature Schnauzer has become established on a limited basis in Africa with stock imported from England. The first recorded Rhodesian champion, Liza of Albright, returned to England in 1967, winning the Veterans Class at the Schnauzer Club Open Show when nearly eight years of age.

More recently, South Africa has developed a nucleus of breeders. Johan and Edith Gallant, well established as successful breeders of Giant Schnauzers, began importing Miniature stock in the early 1980s, based on a blend of Eastwight from England, Schnauzi from Switzerland and Klondaike from Denmark—all essentially black and silvers carrying American lines. In 1984, Marcia Feld exported alternative bloodlines in the form of the B/S male Feldmar All-American Boy, linebred on the B/S Ch. Aljamar Hot Ice, CD (5 Chs.). At less than a year of age, he was second in the Utility Group, and thereafter made up his South African title. They next imported and made up So. Afr. Ch. Feldmar Mamzelle, a salt and pepper Reveler daughter, and then later imported the S/P Ch. Bejay's Bewitching Jambeau, who was in whelp to Ch. Feldmar Nightshade (17 Chs.) at the time she was shipped. These dogs were chosen to give the Van't Wareheim Kennel linebred dogs that were still genetically diverse enough to withstand generations of isolated breeding. The Nightshade-Jambeau breeding produced So. Afr. Ch. Van't Wareheim Felix, an S/P who was the leading winner from 1987 through 1990. Yet another export, from Marcia Feld and Nancy Banas, left for South Africa in 1993. So. Afr. Ch. Feldmar-LoveJoy Trigger Happy At Tamarack, carrying three lines to Nightshade, gave his owners, Mike and Bobbie Gale, many a thrill. He was Junior Dog of the Year in 1994, and South Africa's Top Miniature Schnauzer in '95, as well as a Best in Show winner. The Gales have already exported Trigger Happy get as far away as Czechoslovakia.

• In South America

Elsewhere in the western hemisphere, outside the United States and Canada, the breed is still relatively rare. American breeders continue to enjoy dog show vacations to Mexico and South America, taking along their current homebred to exhibit at these annual events. Usually three or four shows are strung together so that a title can be earned on a single trip.

Int. Ch. Karlshof King Of The Road

A small number of breeders in South America have imported American breeding stock, and have finished champions within their own country, and have even made up International (FCI) champions. The Schnauzer population, while admittedly small, consists mainly of dogs exported from the United States since 1980. Juan Aguilar of Medellin, Columbia imported Bandsman's Round-Up after he had won a Group and nine points as a yearling, shown by his breeder Carol Weinberger. He earned his Columbian title in 1980 with several Group placements.

The most recent American champion to score well throughout South America was exported to Graciela Miguel of Argentina by Dr. Karl Barth—a son of his top producing bitch, Ch. Karlshof Kornukopia (5 Chs.). Ch. Karlshof King Of The Road, in addition to earning titles in several countries, won Best in Show at SICALAM in 1994, the most prestigious show of the year.

Jose Machline of Sao Paulo, Brazil, enjoyed extraordinary success in 1982 with Am. and Braz. Ch. Sole Baye's Sound-Off, bred by Yvonne Phelps. In his first four Brazilian shows he won four Groups and two Bests in Show.

Sole Baye has more recently provided foundation stock for Claudia and Sebastion Torregrosa in Argentina, sending them Ch. Sole Baye's Broadside, while Vera Potiker added Sole Baye blood, sending the Ch. Sole Baye's T.J. Esquire (26 Chs.) sons Kelvercrest Main Event to the Torregrosas, and his brother Kelvercrest Curtain Call to Suzanne Blum in Brazil, where they both earned titles. Main Event was the top winning dog of all breeds in Argentina for 1991 with six Bests in Show. Also, Mrs. Phelps has the distinction of having bred Best in Show winning dogs in two hemispheres, having exported to Japan the BIS-winning bitch, Japanese Ch. Sole Baye's Sunbeam, owned by Dr. Nagatomo.

• In Japan

In 1982 the Japan Kennel Club hosted the first FCI meeting ever held in Asia. Following the meeting, the Tokyo World Show was held for three days, bringing out 1,860 dogs—sixty of them Miniature Schnauzers. Although the catalog shows only Japanese exhibitors participating, the entry was "All American." With the exception of a single entry sired by a British-bred Risepark

**Ch. Tomei Super Star
with Clay Coady**

dog, all others carried solid American backgrounds.

The 1970s saw a real boom in dog activities in Japan; the emphasis has been on smaller dogs, with Miniature Schnauzers among the most popular.

California breeders have been the initial suppliers of breeding stock, sending over several first-rate champions that have gone on to win Japanese titles and top awards on all levels. Such West Coast prefixes as Allaruth, Baws, Bokay, Hansenhaus, Skyline, Sole Baye and Walters are well represented.

For several years in the 1980s, the Watanabe family set up a breeding kennel in Southern California, based on stock from Baws, Hansenhaus, Ruedesheim, Sole Baye and Walters. The Watanabes were interested in all colors, and found that Dolores Walters could provide them with related stock that would produce them. They made Japanese champions of the black, Am., Can. and Mex. Ch. Walters' Dazzling Black and the B/S Walters' Ebony Snowman. Hichibei Kurashiki made up the salt and pepper Walters' Irish Treasure, thus making Mrs. Walters the first breeder of Japanese champions of all three colors.

Before returning to Japan the Watanabes finished several American champions, including Tomei homebreds. Foremost among them was the multiple Group and Specialty winner Ch. Tomei Super Star (30 Chs.). This Peter Gunn son was purchased by Carolane in 1984 and became a very influential sire.

On April 19, 1992, the first Miniature Schnauzer Specialty show was held in Tokyo. Judging this very special event was Jennifer Allen Moore of the famed Travelmor Schnauzers in New Jersey. She was honored with an entry of seventy-nine, including eighteeen Japanese champions, the largest group of Schnauzers ever assembled. Her ultimate winner came from the Bred-by-Exhibitor class—Terunoble's Miracle Ace, a second-generation homebred, but based entirely on American-bred stock. Of her winner, Jennifer wrote . . .

This dog is one the breeder can be proud to show. He is upstanding, of proper size, and has a dark harsh coat. He puts it all together with a lovely head and neck, smooth shoulders, solid short topline and excellent rear. His attitude was undeniable—truly a delight to judge.

Terunoble's Miracle Ace is selected Best of Breed by breeder-judge Jennifer Moore, at the first Tokyo, Japan Miniature Schnauzer Club Specialty Show.

The Winners Bitch was Terunoble's Jazzland Walz, a half sister to the Best of Breed winner. Ch. S. Joyful of Sunshine Island was selected Best Opposite Sex. She claims a Blythewood sire and a Regency dam. The catalog showed a host of American champions in the immediate background of this outstanding entry. Names like Ch. Blythewood Special Promise, Ch. Regency's Cream Of Tar-Tar, Ch. Jubilee's Joker's Wild, and Ch. Baws Lone-A-Ranger were among the sires; Ch. Belgar's Tequila Sunrise, Ch. Adamis First Class and Ch. Wyndwood Sunshine Report, among the dams.

Sumiko Ikeda, Secretary of the Tokyo Miniature Schnauzer Club, is one of the most successful breeders in Japan. Her Sunshine Palace S. prefix can

Jap. Ch. S. Joyful Of Sunshine Island is selected Best Opposite Sex by Ms. Moore.

273

Am. & Jap.
Ch. Sunshine
Palace S.
Super Star
shown winning
one of his five
Bests in Show,
handled by
Teruyoshi
Sugarhara.

be found on well over two dozen champions since 1984, including six that have achieved AKC titles. Sumiko has been making annual trips to the States, spending much of that time with her chosen mentor, Beverly Verna of Regency fame. Her Am. and Jap. Ch. Regency's Cream of Tar-Tar, a son of Ch. Regency's Right On Target (78 Chs.), is the leading sire in Japan with over two dozen champion get to date. Her most successful homebred has to be Am. and Jap. Ch. Sunshine Palace S. Super Star, Best of Winners at the AMSC Specialty at Montgomery County in 1988. After returning to Japan he earned five Bests in Show, and was the breed leader in 1990. In 1991 she had the honor of seeing her homebred, Sunshine Palace S. Skywalker complete his American title by going Best of Winners at the AMSC Specialty in California. That same year she returned to Japan with yet another American champion she had purchased as a puppy— Ch. Regency's Double Agent, showing him to Japanese and International titles. Sumiko came back to the United States two years later with a black Double Agent son, who became Am. Ch. Sunshine Palace S. Blue Blood— another first! Quality bitches from Travelmor and Wyndwood have been added in recent years. Sumiko must be justly proud to have authored the first Japanese book on the breed, published in 1995.

The Moustache J.P. Schnauzers of Hideo Takahashi have enjoyed extraordinary success on the highest levels. Hideo made several visits to the United States over the last

Am. & Jap. Ch. Regency's Double Agent with Beverly Verna

decade, not only learning the American style of grooming and handling, but also learning about the various types being exhibited. He made several purchases, principally of Bandsman and Sumerwynd stock. Bandsman's Printed Circuit is the sire of his Jap. Ch. Moustache J.P. Show Magic, top winning male in Japan in 1993, and Jap. Ch. Moustache J.P. Queen Circuit, the year's leading female.

• In Taiwan

The first Miniature Schnauzers to be introduced in Taiwan were a trio bred by Dolores Walters. In 1982 Dr. S.J. Shiow, Dean of Studies at the Chung Shan Medical College, imported the S/P Walters' Seeyouaround, a son of the B/S Japanese Ch. Walters' Ebony Snowman, along with two black females, one of which produced the first litter to be born in Taiwan.

Jap. Ch. Mustache J.P Show Magic with Hideo Takahashi

There are three breed clubs on the island: in Taipei, the capital; in the mid-island city of Taichung, apparently the largest club with around 150 members; and in Tainan, farthest south.

The 1990s have seen a tremendous influx of American breeding to Taiwan. Mr. George Chou Chi has been a major importer, bringing over the top producing sires, Ch. Adamis Cocked And Loaded (9 Chs.) and Ch. Regency's Born To Boogie (9 Chs.), in addition to the young males Ch. Blythewood Lightning Strikes, Ch. NickNack Good Time Charlie, and the B/S Ch. Rampage's Rebel Prince. Mr. Andy Shieh brought over a trio of bitches: Ch. Regency's Turned On, Ch. NickNack Party On Garth, and the Born to Boogie daughter, Regency's A Strut Above. Mr. Ryan Cheng Ming Weng has arranged to bring over Ch. Wy-O's Doc Holliday, after sponsoring his U.S. show career with Beverly Verna during 1996.

In 1994, while in her teens, Josephine Ching Wen served a considerable apprenticeship with Carol Garmaker, learning the skills of care, grooming and handling, besides taking home several Rampage-Repitition youngsters to start a breeding program.

In March 1994, Wyoma Clouss of the Wy-O Schnauzers in Idaho was invited to judge an entry of over fifty at the Taichung Specialty, selecting for Best of Breed Ch. Rampage's Rebel Prince.

Other countries have had Miniature Schnauzers of which to be proud, and more than likely they will carry, somewhere deep in their pedigree, the name of the great American sire, CH. DOREM DISPLAY.

15

The Miniature Schnauzer in Obedience and Agility

MINIATURE SCHNAUZERS have been outstanding performers in obedience competitions even before the AKC first established rules for such trials. Mrs. Slattery's Ch. Mussolini of Marienhof, after only ten days of training, won first in a Novice class of eleven in Philadelphia, November 3, 1935, showing all present that the breed was well suited for the sport. The *New York Times* came out with a full-page banner headline proclaiming, "Fine Performance Given by Marienhof Schnauzer in Taking Obedience Tests!" A two column story followed:

A Miniature Schnauzer, a bench show champion, opened the eyes of thousands of casual spectators today at the final session of the sixteenth annual exhibition of the Kennel Club of Philadelphia, which came to an interesting climax this evening.

Champion Mussolini of Marienhof, owned by the Marienhof Kennels of Captain and Mrs. Slattery of Edgewood, Maryland, displayed remarkable intelligence in passing through all the tests in the Novice obedience competition which was one of the most striking features of the closing day of the exhibition in Convention Hall.

Since the AKC did not award CD (Companion Dog) titles until the following year, Mussolini never officially gained the title. Perhaps an honorary CD should be his, as not only the breed's first obedience winner but also the first combined bench and obedience winner. Royally bred, Mussolini was from a litter of four champions,

Ch. Mussolini of Marienhof

The Gateway Miniature Schnauzer Club on May 31, 1985, was honored to have five Obedience Trial Champions at its Specialty. From left to right: Bill Oxandale and OTCh. Princess Pfeffer II, Eunice Revsdale and OTCh. Bo-Nanza's Miss Dark Shadow, Marilyn Oxandale and OTCh. Pepperhaus Pfiesty Pfritz, Phyllis Fleming and OTCh. Mistress Anne of Quancie, George Schilling and OTCh. Liebling Fritz Von Schilling.

including the prolific sire Ch. Marko of Marienhof (13 Chs.).

The trend for "beauty and brains" was officially initiated in 1936 by Ch. Shaw's Little Pepper, CD, trained and shown by his breeder-owner Marian Shaw. At the time, a perfect score was 100, and Pepper earned scores of 93 and 99, when just two qualifying scores were needed for the CD title. Pepper later became a bench champion, and so was the first of the breed to achieve dual titles.

World War II intervened during the next decade and there were just fourteen CD and two CDX titles awarded to the breed. The first CDX titles were gained by Dorem Extra and Playboy of Kenhoff, the latter eventually becoming the first Miniature Schnauzer to gain a Utility and Tracking title.

The versatility of the breed was impressively illustrated by the mid-1950s career of Ch. Mein Herr Schnapps, UD, the first to acquire championship and UD (Utility Dog) status. Mrs. Edward Getz recalls how it changed her life:

Schnapps was eight weeks old when we got him. How little we realized at that time how he would change the course of our lives. Our introduction to obedience was purely accidental. Until this time we had never participated in this satisfying endeavor. Before Schnapps was a year old, he had earned his CD and appeared on television to demonstrate the attributes of a well-trained dog.

At that time we decided to also show him in the breed ring. His recognition of the difference between the obedience and show collar is almost unbelieveable. While showing for his championship, Schnapps attained his CDX and UD titles. These titles were earned in three straight shows, his UD in four shows. All obedience training and handling was done by my husband, Edward Getz, who also occasionally showed him in the breed ring. At one show, Schnapps took the Terrier Group and tied for Highest Scoring Dog in Show. By the time he was two and a half years old Schnapps had completed his championship and UD titles. His average score for the three titles was 196 1/2.

In 1956, Schnapps appeared, by invitation, at Westminster as the highest scoring terrier in the nation for the previous year.

Schnapps was started in tracking but never finished, due to our negligence. But the training paid off. We were moving to a new home with a large ground area. In the process of clearing scrub trees, my husband lost the keys to the car. It was dusk. We started the impossible search for the keys. My husband gave Schnapps his scent and dispatched him to find the key case. In a very few minutes, Schnapps was back, keys barely showing from under his whiskers. Where he located them we will never know.

A trained dog is a joy.

An old misconception was that if you trained your dog in obedience it would not do well in conformation. It is still heard from time to time, but the facts prove otherwise, particularly with the versatile Miniature Schnauzer. This is not surprising considering their working inheritance from their larger cousins.

That age is not a factor is borne out by the achievements of Marilyn and Bill Oxandale's Ch. Pepperhaus Gunner's Fredrick, UD, earning the UD title at eight years of age. Shar Ways Michaela, UDX, owned by Sharon Bloss, finished her UDX title in 1995—at nine years of age!

The fact that first-class bloodlines continue to appear in the immediate background of most successful obedience dogs speaks highly for the breeders involved. This trend is clearly evident, beginning with Mussolini.

Since DISPLAY, several top-producing lines and families were equally involved in obedience work. DISPLAY, himself, sired a UD and four others with CDs. His sister, Ch. Dorem Shady Lady, CD, is the grand matriarch of the Phil-Mar family. DISPLAY descendants dominated in both rings from the 1950s to the present. His sons, Ch. Dorem High Test and Ch. Benrook Buckaroo, continued the trend, the former siring six obedience titlists, and the latter four. A few generations from them came Ch. Marwyck Brush Cliff, the new leader with seven. His record was short-lived, as eight obedience degree winners were sired by Ch. Applause of Abingdon, CD. It is interesting to note that Applause was sired by Brush Cliff's litter brother, Ch. Marwyck Scenery Road. All three are sires of five or more bench champions as well—a bright and beautiful family!

Applause's record stood for nearly two decades, broken in 1985 by Ch. Sim-Cal's Personality Plus, CD, sire of nine obedience winners: one UD, three CDX, one CD, TD and four CDs. Theresa Klemencic's Sim-Cal breeding program in Pennsylvania has for over two decades produced dogs that compete

Winemaker's Miranda, UD

successfully on all levels of competition, both bench and obedience. The foundation for Sim-Cal's success was Blythewood Naughty Kelly, who claims top producing parents: Ch. Blythewood Chief Bosun (11 Chs.) and Ch. Bon-Ell Sandstorm (3 Chs.). Linebred or outcrossed, Kelly produced pups with beauty and brains. Her son, Personality Plus, is by Ch. Blythewood His Majesty (11 Chs.). A daughter, Sim-Cal Lil Girl, from yet another top producing Blythewood sire, is the dam of a champion son, plus three CD dogs, bred to her half brother Personality Plus.

Winemaker's Miranda, UD, is far and away the leading dam of obedience winners, with seven offspring earning a CD. She is also the dam of two CDX, plus Ch. Ellar's Only Amos, UD. Bred by Cheryl Wine, Miranda was purchased as a four-month-old show prospect by Lynne Boone in 1973. She is a double great-granddaughter of Ch. Caradin Fancy That (9 Chs.), and is tightly linebred within the Diplomat branch. Her training for both conformation and obedience began almost immediately. She went High in Trial in her first outing and won her first point and second leg at her first show as an Open bitch. As Lynne tells it:

She went on to sparkle in the obedience ring and show her obvious boredom in conformation classes. She managed to accumulate seven points inspite of herself, and was High in Trial twice. A Dog World Award winner, she ranked as high as number two nationally in comparatively limited showing. She was also one of the first Miniature Schnauzers to earn OTCh. points, and at almost thirteen was still active enough to work, which she sometimes demands to do.

279

The Ellar breeding program in South Carolina has been more versatile than most, as Lynne has bred several champions, all descending from Miranda, and is the first and only breeder claiming two uncropped champions, including Ch. Ellar's Argonaut, the first male in half a century. He is a grandson of Miranda on one side of his pedigree, and a great-grandson on the other.

Since 1936, some 3,200 Miniature Schnauzers have gained their CD titles, and on the higher levels, over 630 CDXs and 200 UDs, and 7 UDXs. Many have gone on to compete at higher levels, and they are consistently among the top ten performing breeds. Since 1975, twenty-seven Miniature Schnauzers have qualified for the Tracking Dog (TD) title, with just three having gone on to achieve the Tracking Dog Excellent (TDX) title. They are Nikki V Lind, TDX, Aerides DeGard, TDX, and OTCh. Leslee's Blackberry Muffin, TDX. The latter is one very talented dog, having been awarded the combination of Obedience Trial Champion and Tracking Dog Excellent.

Beginning on July 1, 1977, a new obedience title was created by the American Kennel Club. Unlike the CD, CDX and UD titles, in which a dog is competing only for a perfect score, the new title measures the effectiveness of a dog against the others competing. To gain the title Obedience Trial Champion (OTCh.) a dog must place first at least three times under three different judges in Open B and Utility B, with at least one first place in each of the classes. A total of 100 points is required for the title. Points are awarded from two to 40 depending on the number of dogs competing in the class. Dogs placing second gain from one to seventeen points in the same manner. The title OTCh. is indeed a superior achievement.

Through August 1995, sixteen Miniature Schnauzers had passed this supreme test. They are listed below in the order of achievement:
1978 - OTCh. Princess Pfeffer II
1981 - OTCh. Bo-Nanza's Miss Dark Shadow
1983 - OTCh. Pepperhaus Pfeisty Pfritz
1985 - OTCh. Mistress Anne of Quancie
1985 - OTCh. Liebling Fritz Von Schilling
1985 - OTCh. Doug's Ms Laela Larissa
1986 - OTCh. Sycamore's Splash of Frost
1987 - OTCh. Baron
1988 - OTCh. Ajax VIII
1989 - OTCh. Leslee's Blackberry Muffin, TDX
1989 - OTCh. Sonny's Sir Magnum Brandt
1990 - OTCh. Schatzie
1991 - OTCh. Warchex Rant-N-Raven
1991 - OTCh. Sercatep's Storm Cloud
1993 - OTCh. Charles Von Slick
1994 - OTCh. Mandy Agapatos Shannon

OTCh. Princess Pfeffer II was the first, and her son, OTCh. Pepperhaus Pfeisty Pfritz, was the third. Both were trained and shown by Marilyn and Bill Oxandale of Missouri. Their Pepperhaus prefix can be found on both bench and obedience champions. Pfritz has two successful brothers, Pepperhaus Watch My Dust, UD, and Ch. Pepperhaus Karbon Kopy, CDX, the latter already the sire of several obedience winners, including a pair with advanced titles. Pfritz, Kopy and Dusty were sired by Ch. Penlan Paragon's Pride (30 Chs.), and owe much to the Phil-Mar heritage of quality and intelligence. It is Mr. Oxandale that we must thank for virtually all the obedience statistics made available to us.

The versatility of the Miniature Schnauzer is exemplified by the number of dogs that have achieved both bench championships and obedience titles. In the fifty years since trials have been recognized, over 120 Miniature Schnauzers have boasted titles in both rings. Of special note are those that have gained the dual titles of Champion and Utility Dog. Fifteen have achieved this goal:

Ch. Mein Herr Schnapps, UD
Am. and Mex. Ch. Marmeldon's Pacemaker, Am. and Mex. UD
Am. and Can. Ch. Jonaire Pocono Rough Rider, Am. and Can. UDT
Ch. Frevohly's Best Bon-Bon, UD
Ch. Ellar's Only Amos, UD
Ch. Dufferton Mack The Knight, UD
Ch. Adam v. Elfland, UD
Ch. Bobette's Bang Bang, UD
Ch. Pepperhaus Gunner's Fredrick, UD
Ch. Hillock Hocus Pocus, UD
Ch. Sercatep Curious Kassie, UD
Ch. Linden's Dynamic Domino, UD
Ch. Abralyn's Arisingstar V Barny, UD
Ch. Southcross Major Dimension, UD
Ch. Southcross Better Luv Nextym, UD

The Utility Dog Excellent (UDX) is a new title now offered by the AKC. To achieve it, a dog must have qualifying scores in both Open B and Utility B at the same show ten times. There are nine Miniature Schnauzers that have earned this title.

1994 - OTCh. Mandy Agapatos Shannon, UDX
1994 - OTCh. Sercatep's Storm Cloud, UDX
1994 - Image of Midnight Eclipse, UDX
1994 - Penlan Marquis Mercedes Benz, UDX
1995 - Black Bear III, UDX
1995 - Shar Way's Michaela, UDX
1995 - Aljamar's Silver Knight, UDX
1995 - Ch. Linden's Dynamic Domino, UDX—the first conformation champion to have also achieved the UDX title—owned and trained by Julia Wilson.
1996 - Ch. Abralyn's Arisingstar V Barny, UDX—bred, owned and trained by Marge Zarge.

OTCh. Sercatep's Storm Cloud

Blacks in Obedience

Obedience winners have come in all three colors right from the beginning, although the ones mentioned so far have nearly all been salt and pepper. The first black winner of an obedience title was Fred v. Schonhardt of Crystal, CD. Fred was also the first with imported parents to gain an obedience title. A quarter of a century later, in 1964, Hamann's Falla became the first black to earn a UD. His CD was achieved as a puppy, and his CDX shortly after his first birthday.

One of the most successful black lines in both bench and obedience stems from Gough's Ebony Knight Longleat, CD. He is the sire of the lone black Ch.-UD, Ch. Dufferton Mack The Knight, UD. The only other black to achieve Ch.-CDX, Ch. Gough's Bicentennial Black, CDX, also carries a line to Longleat. The Longleat son Ch. Woodhaven's Black Gough Drops (4 Chs.), although never shown in obedience, leads this color variety as a sire of obedience titlists with four CDX and five CD offspring.

Am. & Can Ch. Britmor Sunnymeade Frost, CG, Am. & Can. CDX

Perhaps the most successful dual champion is Alice Gough's Best in Show winner, Ch. Gough's Ebony Royal Knight, CD, the sire of two CDX and four CD winners, as well as bench champions. The chapters on blacks and black and silvers tell of further successes of the Gough's family, obviously bred for both beauty and brains.

Black and Silvers in Obedience

Virtually all the "beauty and brains" among B/S can be traced to Can. Ch. Walsh's Frosty Charmer, CD, and the British-bred Can. Ch. Eastwight Sea Voyager, Can. CD. All the dual champions of this color carry lines to one or both. Two generations of dual winners currently exist: Ch. Aljamar Hot Ice, CD, is the sire of Ch. Suelen Snow Flurry, CD, CG; Ch. Sercatep's Frost N Flash, CD, is the dam of Ch. Karma's Moonlight Shadow, CD, who in turn has a CD-winning offspring.

All the records among B/S dual champions fell in 1984 to Am. and Can. Ch. Britmor Sunnymeade Frost, Am. and Can. CDX, earning his CG (Certificate of Gameness). He became only the third Miniature Schnauzer to earn a CG through the auspices of the American Working Terrier Association. He is a third-generation black and silver CDX, being out of Britmor Sassafrost Teaberry, CDX, whose dam is Hi Ya Gret, CDX. The fact that Frost was the first B/S to win a Canadian Best in Show proves his quality as well as his versatility.

The first B/S to achieve the OTCh. is Am. and Can. OTCh. Sycamore's Splash of Frost, twice scoring High in Trial in 1985. He is a brother to the good producing B/S bitch, Sycamore's Sassafras, CD (4 Chs.).

Senior Citizens and Obedience

That obedience training can be a lifetime avocation is best borne out by Bill and Marilyn Oxandale, now sixty-four. They have achieved twenty-one titles between 1974 and 1995.

In the Des Moines Training Club, 1981 through 1985, four Miniature Schnauzers finished their UD degrees, trained and shown by senior citizens.

Arnie Arnold, at the age of sixty-four, put a UD on Ms. Fritz. It was his wife Edith who decided to try obedience and put Ms. Fritz through obedience classes and entered the shows at the age of sixty-two. Edith and Ms. Fritz went through the CD in three straight shows with scores averaging 196. Ms. Fritz at 3 1/2 years of age faced retirement, but Arnie would have none of it and took over her training, earning CDX and UD degrees in short order.

Arnie then took on another Miniature Schnauzer, a black, given to him as uncontrollable—a dog that could not be trained or even housebroken. That was a lot of "poppy-cock," said Arnold, and Arnie's Char Kol Imp, UD "took to training like a duck takes to water." Imp's granddam was Klein Schwarz Madchen, UD, the first black female to earn a UD.

Sam Beck, another senior citizen at sixty-four, has two UD girls, Mari Sam's Golden Girl and Mari Sam's Final Edition. Marilyn and Sam Beck enjoyed both aspects of the sport, Marilyn showing in conformation and Sam in obedience.

Why Formal Obedience Training?

Why, indeed, one might ask. And the reasons are many. Above all else, a well-trained dog is a pleasure to live with, a credit to the breed, and will constantly be a point of pride, whether on a pleasurable walk or when visiting or being visited. Equally important is that it serves as a safeguard for the dog itself.

A dog trained to obey his master will do so under any and all conditions. When an emergency does occur, whether on the street or in the home, a spoken command, readily obeyed, may be its salvation.

Shirley Willey, of Shirley's Schnauzers in California, has pioneered for bench and obedience, finishing several dogs to both titles. She relates an instance where training really paid off.

I found obedience to be an asset in the time of disaster more than once. While living in Florida we had a tornado. Our room was rapidly filling with water. I put Beau and Ginger's training collars and leads on and put them on down-stays on the bed while I went for help. They were still there when I returned.

Although obedience work is great fun, it requires time and patience. The Miniature Schnauzer is a highly intelligent breed which responds well to gentle, yet firm, training techniques. Under no circumstances should a dog be physically punished in the process. It will spoil his desire to work, and no dog that works out of fear will make the grade either as a companion or in competition. Training should not be laborious, with sessions lasting no more than fifteen minutes. Each time concentrate on a specific requirement. Should a particular session be less than fruitful, do not lose your temper—tomorrow will be better.

For those who wish to train a dog with the object of seeking titles, they would be well advised to seek out a training class where others are preparing for the same goals. Most cities have obedience training clubs or dog clubs which provide such classes throughout the year. Such classes provide experienced trainers in a group setting conducive to the socialization of the dogs.

Miniature Schnauzers Excel in Agility

Yet another very challenging activity was adopted in August 1994 by the United States Dog Agility Association (USDAA). Agility, a new performance event, consists of training the dog to traverse a series of obstacles (jumps, high walk, teeter-totter, A-frame, tunnels, etc.) in a timed competition. The USDAA's agility certification program offers three basic levels of competition with increasing levels of difficulty; Novice, Advanced and Masters. In the Novice level, a dog must demostrate performance of the basic obstacles on a course of fourteen to sixteen obstacles with relatively simple handling maneuvers. The Advanced level introduces more difficult maneuvers on a course of seventeen to twenty obstacles with time constraints. Dogs that are able to perform three courses at each level without penality are awarded the Agility Dog and Advanced Agility Dog title, respectively. The Masters level challenges a handler to manage a greater variety of maneuvers on a seventeen-to-twenty obstacle course, with even tighter time limits. Dogs that are able to perform three Master-level courses without penalty, and meet performance requirements in four different nonstandard classes are awarded the Master Agility Dog title.

Miniature Schnauzers have been involved in Agility since 1989, when the number two Agility Dog in the country was Callie, a salt and pepper owned

Nichol's Jumpin Jack Flash, CDX, OA

and trained by Sue Henry of Dallas, Texas. In 1990 this same dog was the number one Mini Agility Dog in the country. Continuing in Callie's tradition, every year at least one Miniature Schnauzer has attended the Grand Prix semifinals. The semifinals were held in San Antonio, Texas, in 1993 with a record number of four Miniature Schnauzers included. One of these progressed to the finals.

Sally Peterson's homebred, Nichol's Jumpin Jack Flash, CDX, OA, owns several firsts. She was the first black to attain the Novice and Open Agility titles, and the first of the breed to obtain dual AKC and USDAA Agility titles. "Whoopi" is also the dam of a black AKC champion, and has children and grandchildren competing in conformation, obedience and agility.

A new breed record was established in 1995 when Billie Rosen's Princess Kara, UDX, AX, completed the requirements for both the Utility Dog title and Agility Excellent title, the latter earned with three perfect scores of 100. She is the first Miniature Schnauzer to achieve both titles.

To date, Miniature Schnauzers have achieved eleven titles: eight Novice, two Advanced and one Masters.

This exciting sport can be a great complement to showing in either conformation or obedience. A dog and handler can master enough Agility in a month or two to have great fun. As with any other sport, competition-ready dogs do take longer to train.

The mechanics of obedience and/or agility training are not discussed here, since many excellent books are available which cover the subjects in depth. Rules and regulations for obedience trials, as well as those for USDAA events, are always available free through the offices of the American Kennel Club, 51 Madison Avenue, New York, NY 10010.

16
Breeding the
Miniature Schnauzer

IT HAS LONG BEEN SAID that "like begets like," and so selection remains the breeder's oldest tool. With bloodlines in Miniature Schnauzers being as tightly confined as they are to four main branches from a single individual, CH. DOREM DISPLAY, beginner's luck may find you have bred a top-flight puppy in your very first litter. This luck seldom lingers, however, as the ability to breed generation after generation of quality dogs comes only from careful planning and judicious selection.

A novice may feel that the study of genetics must enter into any thoughts of successful breeding. He would be surprised, however, at how little the subject of genetics is discussed. Wherever dog breeders get together to talk dogs, the discussion is more likely to turn to the various methods of breeding, such as inbreeding, linebreedng and outcrossing. These are the breeder's tools, and should be understood.

Inbreeding involves the breeding of closely related individuals: father to daughter, mother to son, brother to sister. Experience has indicated that inbreeding tends to set and perpetuate type. This explains the sudden appearance of a hidden recessive, and helps explain why inbreeding may have good and bad results. Inbreeding can, and does, produce wonderful results in skillful hands.

Most successful breeders will adapt a program based on various forms of linebreeding. The novice breeder would do well to follow their lead. The term linebreeding is generally applied to the mating of a dog and bitch sharing one or more common ancestors in the second or third generation. Grandsire to granddaughter or grandam to grandson is closely linebred, and may by some be called inbred. A more accurate definition of linebreeding is perhaps that it is a succession of matings of related animals with a long-range plan.

Yet another course available is the outcross—the mating of purebred animals that appear to be unrelated or, more realistically, only distantly related. Outcrossing in Miniature Schnauzers is virtually impossible, unless German imports should find their way into the North American gene pool in future. Finding a pedigree among current show stock that does not have a single common ancestor in five generations has become increasing unlikely.

Selection of Breeding Stock

In planning a breeding program that will be successful over a period of years, the first requirement is to have the type you want to produce clearly in mind. The shortest route to success would be to purchase a quality linebred bitch from an established breeder who is producing the type desired. Hopefully this breeder will also serve as mentor, and will be of help to you as you go on. Perhaps you have already purchased a bitch as a pet and have decided to breed her. Before blindly plunging in, give serious thought to the difficulties and problems you face, and be sure before you get involved.

The responsibilities of the breeder are many. The bitch during her pregnancy requires special care. There may be many anxious hours before, during and after whelping. Caring for puppies over an extended period is very time consuming, and must be a labor of love. Frequent trips to the veterinarian must be included: you must plan for tail docking and, probably, ear cropping. Then comes the most serious responsibility—placing the puppies in good homes.

If financial gain is a consideration, forget it! Few pet owners who raise a litter of puppies come close to breaking even, let alone coming out ahead. A long-range breeding program will require considerable expense, and more time and energy than you might ever imagine.

If you are certain, and want to embark on a Miniature Schnauzer breeding program, a mentor—someone with broad experience—is almost a must. You will need all the help you can get, and would be wise to trust only one mentor until you have your own experience and knowledge on which to draw.

First up is the selection of a stud. The breeder of your bitch should have had a plan, even before she was born. Her potential suitor would probably have been chosen, and if her virtues and faults are identified as not being uncomplimentary, that choice should be honored.

Many a novice, and even some experienced hands, breed their bitches to the latest top winner, so that the pedigree will reflect this famous champion. Little thought is given to whether the parents physically complement each other. The list of top winners of both sexes that have proven unsuccessful as producers suggests either misuse or disuse, and the reasons are many.

Hopefully your bitch will have common ancestors on both her sire's and her dam's side. Selection should be based on deciding which is the most outstanding and most prepotent for the qualities desired. Prepotency is too often loosely applied to animals less than deserving of this description. Only a broadly used individual with an outstanding record as a producer of consistent quality and type is truly prepotent. As a novice, you would do well to use such a sire for your first breeding. Chances are his fee will be only slightly higher than others that may be available, and perhaps more convenient.

The Bitch in Season

A Miniature Schnauzer bitch can be expected to come into season, or heat, for the first time between six and nine months of age. Some will wait until they are over a year old. Thereafter, they come in at roughly six-month intervals, although variations occur. A bitch should not be bred on her first season, and ideally, not until she is eighteen months of age.

The average heat cycle (estrus period) lasts from fourteen to twenty-one days. A bitch approaching her season may display a certain amount of restlessness as well as an increased appetite. The first real indication is the swelling of the vulva, along with a discharge which is light in color and flow. As the season progresses, the flow increases and the color deepens to a bright red. After the eighth or ninth day the discharge decreases, changing in color to a pale pink or straw color. The vaginal discharge may vary considerably. In some bitches it is quite heavy, while in others it is so slight that it may go unnoticed.

A bitch is normally receptive and ready to breed from the tenth to the fourteenth day. Here again, variations occur, with successful breedings resulting as early as the seventh and as late as the sixteenth day. Some can happen even later, when the bitch is thought to be well out of season. The importance of strict confinement during this period must be stressed.

If a mating has been planned, and the bitch is to go to an outside stud, arrangements must be made well in advance. As soon as the bitch is noticeably in season, notify the owner of the stud dog and set the date that the bitch will be shipped or brought to the stud for mating. If she is to be shipped, plan on sending her at least three or four days before the expected mating.

Airline regulations and fees are many and varied. Weather conditions must also be considered, as many carriers will not accept dogs if temperatures are too high or low. Be aware of health regulations, as most carriers require a veterinary health certificate, as well as an airline crate. A conscientious stud dog owner will request that your bitch be tested for brucellosis. This should be done as soon as the bitch comes in season. If she is due for booster shots, she should have them well before she is bred. Plan to leave your shipped bitch with the stud dog owner for several days after matings have been achieved.

That she should be in perfect health prior to mating is obvious. She should be neither too fat nor too thin, and completely free of internal or external parasites. Remember to avoid use of antimating products (pills, powders or sprays) at this time.

The Pregnant Bitch

Having achieved a breeding, your primary concern will be the health of the prospective mother, and this basically involves diet and exercise. On average, the gestation period is sixty-three days. Puppies born a week earlier, or more rarely a week later, can survive. Count the day after the first mating as the first day, even when two breedings were achieved. This way you are not left wondering whether the bitch is going past her due date.

Some bitches will reveal their condition early on while others keep you guessing. A marked personality change usually follows within two or three weeks. Your high-energy bitch may become far more sedate, and require a lot more lap time, soaking up all the affection you have time to give.

It is not uncommon for a bitch to go off her food for a day or two during this early period, so do not be alarmed. This is rather like "morning sickness" in women. You might try offering food at different times should this occur. However, refusing food for several days is not normal and should be investigated by your veterinarian. Her diet, however, will never be more important and should be of the highest quality. As a precaution against calcium deficiency while pregnant and while nursing, vitamin supplements should be used in quality and quantity advised by your mentor or veterinarian. The latter should see the bitch some time during the pregnancy, so that he will be familiar with her condition should his help or advice be needed during whelping.

Watch the bitch's weight closely during the entire pregnancy. As the pregnant bitch increases in size she will appreciate two or three smaller meals each day rather than a single large meal. A bowl of milk with a few dog biscuits before bedtime makes a good "nightcap."

Normal exercise and established routine are a must during pregnancy. She should be left to set the standard, and allowed plenty of free or controlled exercise, whichever has been her routine. There should be brisk and lengthy walks started as soon as she is bred. This will build up strength and stamina, both of which will be needed at whelping time.

Under no circumstances should you treat the pregnant bitch as an invalid, nor should you permit overexertion, particularly in the final weeks. She will slow up quite naturally as her condition warrants. Her favorite chair, or even the stairs, may become an obstacle, where help is required as the load increases.

During the last week she should never be unattended, even in a fenced yard. As her time approaches, she will be seeking out a nest, and unsupervised may find an unreachable hideout under a garage or shed.

Preparations for Whelping

At least a week before the due date, the whelping site should be prepared, and the bitch accustomed to it. Choose a quiet place outside the mainstream of activity. Needless to say, if you have other pets, the whelping area must be off-limits to them. The box itself should be square and sufficiently large for the bitch to stretch out fully in it, with several inches to spare. A box about thirty inches square with walls about fourteen inches high seems ideal for a Miniature Schnauzer.

About a week before the bitch is due to whelp she should be bathed, with special attention given to her breasts. Use a mild soap or shampoo containing no disinfectants, and rinse thoroughly. The average Schnauzer carries little belly coat, but whatever there is should be carefully trimmed to make the teats accessible to the puppies. The hair around the vulva and from the inside of the back legs should also be trimmed. After whelping, the bitch will have a discharge for several days, and shorter hair will be easier to keep clean.

Begin to accumulate other supplies that may prove useful during the actual whelping. A good supply of newspapers is a must. Layers of newspapers can best serve as bedding, being absorbent and easily disposable. The whelping box should be kept scrupulously clean, and the papers changed regularly. After the whelping, a rug or some other kind of sure-footed surface will be required so that the puppies can gain good traction while nursing.

Other needed supplies include clean towels, sterile blunt-nosed scissors, baby oil, cotton, Tincture of Merthiolate (or iodine), sterile string, a heating pad or hot water bottle, a small cardboard box (other than the whelping box), a bit of brandy, some alcohol for sterilization, and an eye dropper for stimulating a sluggish puppy. These supplies should be set out in the whelping area so they are immediately available when needed.

When Whelping Begins

The most reliable indication that whelping is imminent is a continuous drop in temperature. Normal temperature is 101.5 degrees. When the temperature drops below 99 degrees it is almost certain that there is not much longer to wait. Other common signs that whelping is about to commence are refusal of food, shivering, panting, digging, wide-eyed staring, and a slight, sticky vaginal discharge. Any or all of these symptoms are normal.

When the temperature has settled at the 99-to-98 degree range, and the bitch's appearance has changed to what can best be described as "lumped up," expect labor within twenty-four hours. Now is a good time to notify your veterinarian that you may be needing his assistance. Be sure you have also established contact with the breeder of your bitch. Ask the breeder if there are any unique idiosyncrasies that should be watched for, and what that breeder considers normal behavior.

The preliminary stages of labor—the panting and shivering, the digging and shredding of papers—can continue quite some time before the initial "breaking of water." The first puppy will be preceded by a water bag. If the bitch happens to be sitting as it is passed, you may not see the bag, only a spreading puddle. More likely it will appear from the vulva like a balloon. Allow it to break of its own accord. The first puppy should follow the expulsion of the water bag within four hours. More likely, you can expect the first born within a half hour. Note the time at which the first contraction occurs. If these hard contractions continue for more than an hour without producing a puppy, call for help.

Most likely a puppy will emerge after only two or three contractions, usually within ten to twenty minutes. Usually the puppy is presented headfirst in a sac surrounded by fluid. The puppy-filled sac will be followed by the cord and the placenta (afterbirth), all as a single unit. The placenta is a blackish mass, almost as large as the puppy. It is vital that there be an afterbirth accounted for each puppy that is born, as the retention of any may cause problems later.

Opinions differ as to how much assistance should be given from this point forward. Some bitches resent interference, preferring to deliver and care for their young unattended. If she immediately breaks the sac with her teeth, and begins licking and nuzzling the pup until it squeals, leave her a moment to also bite the cord and eat the placenta.

If none of this is accomplished almost immediately, be prepared to break the sac, cut the cord and remove the placenta. The cord should be cut about an inch from the puppy, and the end tied with sterile string and dabbed with Merthiolate. The new puppy should then be gently but firmly rubbed with a clean, warm towel until it squeals and is breathing clearly. Rubbed somewhat dry, it should then be given to the mother.

It is not uncommon for a new arrival to greet the world feet first! This is called a breech birth, and can cause some difficulty. Sometimes the sac ruptures during the passage down the birth canal and may be partially presented as two hind legs dangling from the vulva. If the rest of the body does not immediately follow with the next contraction, use a small towel or face cloth, dipped in warm water, and with gentle pressure, grasp the hindquarter, rotating the body very gently as the bitch strains. Pull in a downward direction if the puppy is coming tummy down; pull in an upward direction if the puppy is on his back. If you are not able to dislodge the puppy, and it slips back into the bitch, get her to the veterinarian quickly. Remember, however, that your efforts may save the puppy—waiting for help will surely limit its chances of survival.

Should a puppy arrive that appears lifeless, or nearly so, stimulate it with vigorous but gentle rubbing. If this accomplishes nothing, immerse the puppy, except for the head, first in cold (65-degree) water, then in hot (100-degree) water, and keep alternating until the shock stimulates the puppy to gasp or squeal. A drop or two of brandy placed on the tongue may also help.

When the bitch becomes restless and concerned with the next arrival, move the puppy to a small cardboard box in which there is a heating pad or hot water bottle, covered with a towel. The bottom of the box should feel warm to the touch—not hot. Keep the box within the mother's sight. There is no need to add to her anxiety.

The timing of successive puppies will vary. Often two pups will arrive a matter of moments apart, and then there may be a longer wait for the next. Between deliveries, remove the top layer of newspapers and replace them so that the box will have a clean surface to receive the next puppy. Should more than an hour elapse between puppies, when you are sure there are more, this is cause for only minor concern. If, however, the bitch is straining without success for more than twenty minutes, seek the advice of your veterinarian. She may require a Prituitrin shot to help speed up the process. Sluggish labor is usually due to uterine inertia or lack of muscle tone, encountered more often in older bitches. Sometimes a short walk around the room or yard (on leash) will stimulate labor.

A three-day-old litter of black and silver puppies after tail docking

Make certain that all puppies nurse as soon as possible, whether delivered normally or by cesarean section. It is also important that each puppy has an initial bowel movement. Watch for this black material to be passed by each puppy. Usually the mother stimulates this action by licking the genital area. Thereafter, she will continue to do so for several days, eating all of the stools. This is her instinctual way of keeping her nest clean, and is quite normal.

It is difficult to determine when a bitch has finished delivering a litter. The most obvious information comes from the bitch herself. Most often, a definite change occurs in her attitude and behavior. She will seem to relax, resting contentedly as she cleans and nurses her new family. If, however, another puppy arrives an hour later, don't be surprised—and above all, be there!

Once the whelping is over, she should be given the opportunity to relieve herself, and then given privacy and quiet. The whelping box should be freshly covered with newspapers, topped by a clean pad or towel to provide traction for the crawling puppies. This is not the time for visits from the children or neighbors. There is plenty of time for sharing later on.

After the Whelping

The new mother should be fed as soon after whelping as an interest in food is shown. Keep the meals light for the first day or so. Cereal and milk three or four times a day, adding a raw egg yolk to one of these will do nicely. Rice with cooked chicken is a good transition from the milky feeds to her more usual fare. Her appetite may lag for the first few days, and she may have a slightly elevated temperature—above 102 degrees. Take her temperature at least twice daily. It

A five-week-old litter of black and silver puppies before ear cropping

---

should be a normal 101.5 degrees within four days. She will soon be eating and drinking normally while her puppies grow chubby and contented. Fresh water should be available at all times.

Miniature Schnauzers are a docked breed and tail docking should be accomplished at between three and six days, if all the puppies are strong. Dewclaws should be removed at the same time. Examine all four feet as dewclaws are frequently found on the rear as well as the front feet. Docking and dewclaw removal should not be attempted by a novice. Consult your veterinarian on this. Check the puppies' toenails and cut them back when necessary. They can be as sharp as needles and can hurt the mother as the puppies nurse.

For the first few days your bitch may be reluctant to leave her new babies. If necessary, carry her out to relieve herself frequently, and clean her breasts with warm water after each trip.

The bitch's diet during the four or five weeks of nursing will depend on the size of the litter. She should be fed three or four times a day. For the first week she will need about one and one-half times her normal ration. By the second week it should be doubled, and with large litters it should be increased to three times the usual amount, and more, if necessary. Always offer more food if she quickly finishes a meal—she will know best if more food is required.

Puppy Size and Growth Rate

Puppies vary in size at birth and frequently in the rate of development. Five to seven ounces at birth appears to be average in Miniature Schnauzers. Weight charts compiled by Dale Miller (Barclay Square) indicate that puppies maturing at a correct size weigh from thirteen ounces to one pound, three ounces at two weeks old. At four weeks, puppies of correct size weighed one pound, nine ounces to two pounds, four ounces. At six weeks they should weigh from two pounds, eight ounces to three pounds, five ounces. The greatest uniformity seems to occur at eight weeks of age, with males ranging from four pounds, three ounces to four pounds, nine ounces, and females from four pounds to four pounds, six ounces. In keeping charts for future reference, be sure the time of weighing is consistent, always either before or after feeding.

Weaning the Puppies

Along with more than doubling in size after the first ten days, expect the eyes to begin opening. The lids open gradually, beginning with slits at the inside corners. Sometimes the eyes are stuck-up initially. When this happens, gently wipe them with warm water until they are clean and open. Although seeing very little, all eyes should be open and clear by fifteen days of age.

The third and fourth week in a puppy's life is considered the most crucial. Tests indicate that very rapid development occurs at this time. An excellent book on socialization of puppies is Clarence Pfaffenberger's *The New Knowledge of Dog Behavior* (Howell Book House, New York).

At twenty-one days of age the puppy not only can start to learn but will start whether he is taught or not. This change is so abrupt that whereas the puppy does not see (at least very little) or smell or hear at all on his twentieth day of age, within twenty-four hours he does all of these quite well. Naturally, he needs the security of his mother.

If the puppies are to be moved to new quarters in another section of the house, this should be accomplished before or after the critical twenty-one-to-twenty-eight day period. The bright lights, noise and confusion of family life may be fine for socializing older puppies, but not babies.

Weaning should not begin until after the puppies are twenty-eight days old under normal circumstances. If the mother has an inadequate milk supply, you will of course start weaning earlier. Teaching a puppy to eat from a dish is started only as a supplement to mother's milk. Weaning is a gradual procedure. Baby cereals with a spot of honey in warm milk provide a good beginning. Each puppy should be started individually. Put your finger, dipped in the milk, into the puppy's mouth. As he begins to suckle or lap, place him within reach of the food until he laps by himself. It is best to do this when the puppies are hungry. They will catch on to lapping up milky foods right away, and will happily share the same feed pan with their littermates for two or three weeks.

At the end of the sixth week, puppies should be checked for worms and given their first immunization shot. Virtually all puppies are born with round-worm (ascarids), and worming procedures should be followed on the advice of your veterinarian. A schedule for future immunizations should also be set.

About thirty days after whelping the mother will start making herself less available for nursing. Most bitches ask for time off before then, and will enjoy some of their more usual activities, like free exercise, longer walks, lap time with you—any change from the confines of the whelping box. The mother will want to stay with the puppies during the night, at least for the first six weeks. Thereafter, if she still has milk, she will only visit them periodically, mostly for play.

As the puppies depend less and less on mother for their supply of essential vitamins and minerals, these nutrients must be provided in the basic diet you are feeding. Seek advice from your mentor or veterinarian as to what supplements should be used.

Weaning should be complete by eight weeks of age, with no further nursing required. Separate feeding dishes should be used for each pup hereafter, not only to prevent squabbling but as a check that each pup is getting a full ration.

Uncropped, untended natural ears are just as likely to stand straight up as they are to hang houndlike.

Ears—To Crop or Not to Crop

Schnauzers of all sizes are among the dozen or so breeds that are more frequently seen with cropped rather than natural ears. Since this is accomplished most usually at ten to twelve weeks, the breeder must decide whether to accept the responsibility or leave this to the new owner. Most prefer the former, and place their pet puppies after ears are cropped and completely healed.

The history of cropping falls into the realm of folklore, beginning centuries ago. The justification for this essentially cosmetic procedure has for over a century been a matter of aesthetics and tradition. The fact that the large majority of Miniature Schnauzers are still being cropped speaks for the persisting desire to perpetuate this tradition.

Tail docking and ear cropping has an aesthetic objective. Both are thought to enhance the beauty of the individual by achieving a more distinctive look. As with length of tail, there are similar variations in the length and shape achieved in ear cropping. Each breed has its own style.

Several countries throughout the world have outlawed ear cropping, and in several of the United States, this procedure is illegal.

There is considerable risk and expense involved with ear cropping, and those who elect the procedure should be well informed. The decision should be made only after you are completely familiar with the entire process, including the after-care required. Above all, seek out a professional who has a reputation for excellence, one who specializes in the breed. Your local veterinarian may not have the skills, experience or desire to perform cosmetic surgery.

Natural Ears

Natural ears may not always do what you want "naturally." Uncropped, untended natural ears are just as likely to stand straight up as they are to hang houndlike. Getting them well placed, so that they break above the skull, may take a bit of doing.

Since the 1930s, only an occasional uncropped Schnauzer has appeared in the American show ring. Only a few (eight as of 1995) have earned championship status. There are more and more dogs with natural ears being sold as pets, and a few breeders are electing to leave all their homebreds uncropped.

Since little attention has been given to breeding correct natural ears, those of the Miniature Schnauzer are quite varied in size, shape, thickness of leather, as well as placement on the head. Dogs with large, houndy ears will have little chance in the show ring. Those who hope to exhibit an uncropped dog will be well advised to select a specimen with fairly small, well-placed ears that can be enhanced by "setting." Judges will expect ear carriage not unlike some of the other terrier breeds, breaking above the skull and held close to the cheeks.

On November 22, 1981, history was made when Jean Fancy (Fancway) gave Best of Breed to Ch. Regency's Equal Rights, making her the first uncropped Miniature Schnauzer to complete the requirements for an AKC title since 1934. She was conditioned and shown by her owner, Beverly Verna (Regency). A year later, Ch. Skyline's Seventh Heaven finished on one coat, handled by Clay Coady for owner Carol Parker (Skyline). Lynne Boone (Ellar) is the only breeder with a brace of uncropped champions. Ch. Ellar's Wildflower finished in 1984 and Ch. Ellar's Argonaut in 1985, both handled by Sue Baines. The most recent to finished uncropped is Ch. Abiqua The Divine Miss M, co-bred by Jerry Oldham and Chris and Tom Levy. Her record is extraordinary, winning at eight of the fourteen shows attended, handled by Chris Levy throughout. Miss M won three majors and four Bests of Breed and added a Group

Ch. Abiqua The Divine Miss M

Second and Group Fourth. In 1995, she became the first uncropped Miniature Schnauzer to achieve an Award of Merit at a National Specialty.

Most of these breeders took special pains to "set" the ears at various stages of puppyhood so that they would be well placed and carried.

Setting Ears

Setting ears is a fairly simple process and involves a minimum of materials. Needed will be a surgical adhesive, or any other glue that will hold fabric to fabric. Some wholesale pet suppliers carry a specialized glue produced specifically for setting ears. Tincture of Benzoin or mineral spirits are useful in properly cleansing the inner ear.

A conscientious breeder that sells a puppy with natural ears will have already begun the process at between six and eight weeks, and will be able to advise the new owner on the maintenance of the procedure. Several months with glued ears will not appeal to every new owner, but if a show career is in the future, it is almost a must!

To begin with, this is an entirely painless process, and the puppy will quickly become accustomed to the condition, and will enjoy the extra attention. Another pair of hands will be necessary in the beginning. Someone will have to hold the puppy's head to get the job done quickly and easily. With electric clippers, remove all the hair from the skull and ears, inside and out. The inner ear should be cleansed with dry cotton, and excess hair pulled from the ear canal. Repeat the procedure using Tincture of Benzoin or mineral spirits and allow to dry. Keeping the inner ear scrupulously clean at all times is imperative.

Keep a box of tissues handy as pasting can be messy. Study the diagram, noting the positions: A, B, C and D. Spread the glue on the underside of the ear flap from the tip (A) toward B and C. Lay the ear on the skull, the tip pointing toward the inside corner of the eye, and press. Hold the pup's head to prevent him from shaking the ear loose. Paste the other ear in a similar way. After both are clearly held fast, place a bit of surgical tape at position D, to hold the outer edge of the ears, at the fold. Check to see that there is ample space, unglued, to allow the ears to "breathe." Be sure the ears are placed symmetrically. The position can be changed by resetting. When you are satisfied with the set, hold the pup and brush him or otherwise distract him so that he does not shake his head until the glue is dry. This will take about five minutes. Should an ear come loose from the pup shaking or scratching, repeat the process.

The initial set will be maintained for three weeks, after which the hair on the ears and skull will have grown enough that the area can be easily cut loose. Carefully snip the hairs near the adhesive with the tips of the scissors until they are free. Clean the ears, inside and out, and clip the same areas as before. Reset within a day or two, unless some soreness or possible infection is found. In this case, correct completely before resetting.

At about five months, when the front permanent teeth are in, leave the ears loose for a few days to see if they are as you want them. Some will be ready at this time and will require no further setting. If they are lower than desired, or if an ear tends to "fly," reset them both. If an ear appears further away from the head than its mate, it should be pasted further onto the skull than its mate. This is the time when any corrections should be made. Ears that are not symmetrical in placement and carriage are a decided disadvantage in the show ring.

There is a simple technique for assisting the fold to crease at the desired position. Using a light oil (baby oil will do) between thumb and forefinger, gently press the fold as you would to crease paper. Press and rub the entire length of the fold. A few minutes of this from time to time will greatly increase your chances of achieving correct natural ears with a proper fold. This procedure can be done while the puppy is enjoying time in your lap. Use one hand for petting and the other for creasing an ear. The pup will love the extra attention. It should be relatively painless, but if you press too hard, the pup will let you know.

The skin may, on very rare occasions, become allergic to the glue. Take the ears down and dust the affected areas with a medicated powder, allowing them to dry and heal. Dust the area several times the first day. Allow them to completely heal, then repaste.

The setting and resetting process can be continued as long as necessary up to a year of age. If the ears are not as you wish by then, their chances of ever being correct are slim.

17
Grooming the Miniature Schnauzer

A WELL-GROOMED Miniature Schnauzer is a delight to the eye, and should be a point of pride to the owner. The breed loses much of its character and charm if the coat is not properly maintained.

The grooming instructions in this chapter are intended to educate the new owner in all facets of grooming and general coat management. The instructions may appear lengthy due to their detail, but once digested and experienced, you will want to know even more.

The first-time owner will probably be dealing with a three- to four month-old puppy, already with ears cropped and fully healed. If your puppy is uncropped, it is assumed that this is as you wish and the ears will remain natural.

The new puppy, purchased from a reliable and responsible breeder, will arrive with a multitude of instructions, hopefully even some on initial grooming. If you prove to be a worthy owner, that breeder may serve as mentor, providing a constant source for needed information and advice.

Purchased from a responsible breeder, your new puppy will have already had considerable experience, and will arrive in a neat and tidy condition. If it was agreed that yours is a "pet" puppy that will not be shown, chances are he will already be neatly clipped in a proper style, and maintenance thereafter will always involve electric clippers as your principal tool.

If there is to be a future in showing, be sure the puppy is not machine clipped early on, as this will make the required initial stripping process more difficult.

In either case, the grooming process should begin immediately. Proper training during puppyhood can mean the difference between an individual easily managed, leaving both hands for the grooming process, or one that leaves neither to do the job intended. Be kind, but firm. Keep the sessions brief in the beginning, and follow them with some reward, like a favorite tidbit or a brisk walk. There is much to be learned by you and the puppy during these first few months.

Tools and Equipment

Regardless of whether you intend to show or plan simply to maintain a well-groomed pet, certain basic tools and equipment are required. The advice of a mentor will prove invaluable in securing the best for the least. If this is not possible, another source may be a local grooming shop. The average pet store may not be equipped to handle your needs if you are planning to show your puppy. It may, however, be able to supply you with the address of, or catalogs from, wholesale pet supply houses. These are by far the best source for the sophisticated grooming gear needed. Another source may be at a local AKC sanctioned dog show, where suppliers and vendors have booths for direct sale. The selection may not be as complete, and the prices will surely be higher than those offered through wholesale catalogs. You will, however, be able to see first-hand the large assortment of grooming paraphernalia available.

Consider the grooming tools and equipment to be a lifetime investment and buy the best you can afford. A grooming table with a restraining arm, two combs, two brushes, two scissors, nail clippers, stripping knives and a hand and/or electric clipper are all required items.

The Grooming Table

Grooming tables are manufactured in a variety of styles, each suited to special needs. They are readily available through wholesale catalog suppliers as well as some national chain stores. Along with the required grooming arm or post, this may be your most costly investment. If you are planning to show your dog, you will need this equipment for working both at home and at the shows.

If you wish to improvise, the simplest solution would be to secure a piece of one-half to three-quarter-inch-thick plywood, approximately 18 inches wide and 30 inches long. This can be topped with rubber matting, and a clamp-on post can be purchased or even improvised if you are handy with plumbing supplies.

Grooming Tools

Combs

You will need two metal combs. One is the combination comb, like the Greyhound®, with both coarse and medium teeth. The points are sharp and go through leg and face hair without tearing them. The other comb should have fine metal teeth—from ten to 15 teeth per inch. It may be with or without a handle. This comb will have duller points and is used on the body coat, principally for removing undercoat.

Brushes

Two brushes are needed, each having a particular purpose, while a third, called a palm pad, might be a welcomed addition. The most important for general use is a wooden or rubber-backed pin brush—Safari #442'® is a favorite with Schnauzer fanciers. This brush is excellent for daily brushing, removing a minimum of undercoat. You will need a slicker brush for the undercoat as well as for brushing leg hair and face furnishings. This is a small rectangular brush, approximately 2" x 4", with bent metal bristles and an angled handle. It must be used with caution as it can easily remove more undercoat or furnishings than desired.

Scissors

Two pairs are needed, one for straight trimming and the other for thinning. Straight-edged barber scissors, with at least three-inch blades, should be snub-nosed for safety. Thinning scissors come in two types—single or double serrated. I prefer the former, as it cuts half as much hair. However, the Skipper® "double duck" is excellent, having three-inch blades with 30 teeth on each blade. Carbon steel scissors are recommended rather than stainless, as they work better on dog hair and retain their sharpness far longer.

Nail Clippers

Guillotine nail clippers are best suited to the task—the Resco® clippers being most popular. A small metal nail file will also prove useful, between clippings and to soften edges immediately after clipping.

Stripping Knives

At least two stripping knives will be needed. One should be a coarse or medium knife having 12 to 18 teeth, for body work. A fine stripper with 20 to 30 teeth is necessary for working on areas which must be kept particularly short, like the head, ears and chest. Bowsprite®, MacKnyfe®, McClellan®, and Pearson® make excellent knives in fine, medium and coarse grades. Each produces a knife specifically suited to removing undercoat.

Clippers

Although there are several varieties of hand clippers available—the type the barber uses for trimming—you will eventually want to invest in electric clippers manufactured by Oster®. Model A2 is the older design, while Model A5 is a more recent innovation. Both are excellent machines. The principal difference is in the A5's "snap-in" blade feature. If a pet trim is desired, this is a must. Even with show trims, it will come in handy in dealing with the throat, ears and belly. Most dogs after enjoying their show careers will eventually be maintained by clipping instead of stripping the body coat. Two or three blades will be needed—a #8 or #10 will handle body work most easily, while a #15 is used for areas to be kept shorter.

Miscellaneous Supplies

As you become more involved in the grooming process, several items will prove useful—actually necessary if you intend to show. Grooming chalk or powder comes in a variety of types; the choice is best left to individual taste. Cornstarch from the pantry shelf will suffice until you are familiar with other products. Working chalk or powder into the coat during the stripping process makes the hair easier to grasp. Baby oil can be used on tender, over-worked areas to avert burning or drying out.

The waterless-rinseless type of shampoos are best suited to cleaning the dog in part, rather than giving a full bath, which is seldom necessary.

Add a spray bottle to your paraphernalia. Filled with water, it can be used in a variety of ways. Cotton swab sticks also are useful, as are tweezers. Various hair products, such as cream conditioners, are also likely to be found in the tack boxes of most exhibitors.

The Miniature Schnauzer Coat

The Miniature Schnauzer has a double coat: the hard, wiry outer coat and the soft, dense undercoat. The recognized colors are salt and pepper, solid black and black and silver. The same basic grooming is used for all three colors.

The more popular salt and pepper color is distinctive and unique to the breed. Although the overall color is gray, it is produced as a result of "banded" hair. Banding occurs when an individual hair has one color at the root which changes to a lighter color, and to dark again at the tip. A properly banded salt and pepper coat can only be achieved by stripping or plucking the hair. This is also the only way harsh texture and correct color can be maintained. If the coat is cut or clipped, the main body coloring becomes an overall slate gray, varying in tone from light to dark, with the true salt and pepper color being lost.

The Stripping Process

The process of stripping, or pulling the hair out from the roots, may seem abhorrent to the uninformed. It is, however, quite natural to strip out the coat of a Miniature Schnauzer. If left to its normal cycle, the hair would eventually reach a length of two to four inches and die. Rather than shedding, the dead hair tends to linger half-heartedly. It does not break off, but eventually falls from the roots. The stripping process is only assisting the natural cycle, and can be relatively painless.

The finger method of stripping is best for beginners, as you learn the process. If the coat is blown (dead, and ready to be plucked), it will come out easily. Grasp the strands of hair between thumb and index finger. Pull in the direction of the lay of the coat. Repeat the process until one or two square inches have been removed. Then take a coarse or medium stripping knife and attempt to repeat the procedure. Instead of gripping the hairs between thumb and bent forefinger, grasp them between your thumb and the knife. Hold the knife perpendicular to the dog and grasp the hair as close to the roots as possible, softer

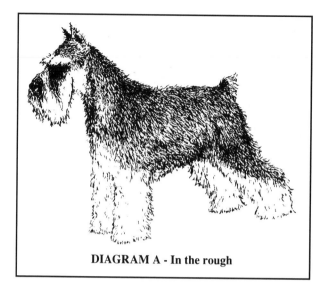

DIAGRAM A - In the rough

pulling in the direction of the lay of the coat. Use an arm-and-shoulder pulling movement, not a wrist action. If you flex your wrist, you will cut rather than pull the hairs with the knife. Compare the hairs being removed from the finger stripping and knife stripping. If you are plucking, the hair is of uneven length. If you are cutting, the hair will be even in length. Remember to work a small area at a time until all the outer coat has been removed.

Stripping is a tedious chore—partly manual labor and partly an art. The cliché "practice makes perfect" definitely applies. The length of time consumed in hand stripping depends on three factors: proper tools and equipment, the cooperation received from the dog, and your own skills.

There is only one correct grooming pattern for a Miniature Schnauzer, but there are two distinctly different ways to achieve it. Whether hand-stripping, which is necessary if you wish to show, or machine-clipping, the overall look will be the same—only coat texture and color will differ.

Basically there are two approaches to stripping. One involves dealing with the entire body in one or two sessions, as would be done in clipping the pet. The other requires stripping in "sections" over a period of weeks. Artful "sectioning" is one of the basic requirements in bringing the Miniature Schnauzer into "show" coat.

The "One Strip" Method

The "one strip" method is clearly shown in DIAGRAM A and B. Essentially, all the areas that appear to be clean are removed within a week to ten days. A longer period will result in obvious strip lines and too much variation in coat length. No amount of skillful blending of the areas is very successful.

In handling the body section, begin at the base of the tail, but not the tail itself. Go up the back to the withers (base of neck), taking out the sides or rib section, but leaving the underbody fringe to be scissored later.

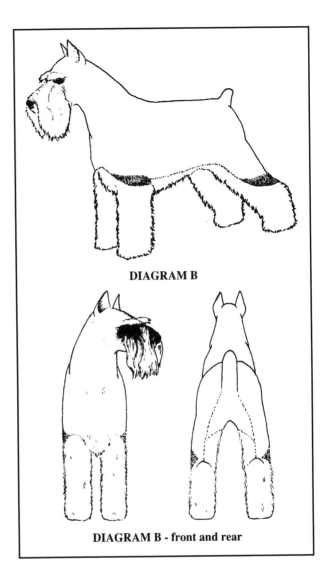

DIAGRAM B

DIAGRAM B - front and rear

After completing the back and sides, strip the hind legs to about an inch above the hocks. Never strip into the indentation of the hock joint.

At this point, the dog is half stripped, and if you are unable to complete the forward section at this time, it can be picked up in a few days. In completing the "one strip" method, you would continue to remove the forward section: neck, shoulders and head, as well as the tail.

In order to make these instructions as thorough as possible, time will now be given to some of the more professional methods used in preparing the body section for show purposes.

DIAGRAM C

Stripping in Sections
Stripping in sections is the exhibitor's way of achieving the most desirable outline, based on variations of coat lengths. This process involves between eight and ten weeks, depending on the individual coat quality of your dog. No two dogs grow their coats at exactly the same rate, and it is not unusual for a dog to grow coat faster on one stripping than the next. Be sure that the period between sections does not exceed ten days, or the blending of the coat later will prove more difficult.

These steps should be followed over a six-week period.

WEEK 1 - Remove all the body hair from behind the withers on the back and sides and on the hind legs as described in the "One Strip" Method. DIAGRAM C illustrates the completed process achieved in the first week.

WEEK 2-Beginning at the base of the skull, strip out an inverted V, starting out with a width of about one inch. Gradually widen the strip as you work down the back of the neck until you join the section of the back previously stripped. DIAGRAM D shows the desired result.

WEEK 3-Take out the remaining hair on the sides of the neck and shoulders, down to an inch above the elbows. See DIAGRAMS E and F. Be sure you do not strip or trim into the indentation at the elbow. This small area of hair just above the elbows is trimmed later in a process to be described.

WEEK 4-Study DIAGRAMS G and H before beginning the work on head and ears. Study both the profile and top of the head as it should look when stripping is completed. A medium or fine knife will do the job, although frequent use of thumb and forefinger will give the best result. Remove all the hair in this area, including the undercoat. Start stripping from the back of the skull forward. As you bring your work to where the eyebrows begin, take considerable care in forming this line. With thumb and forefinger, strip out the area between the eyes, but not as deeply as on the skull. Strip out the sides of the skull from the outer corner of the eyes to the outer corner of the ears, leaving the sides of the cheeks and under throat for later.

Strip or clip the ears at this time, using scissors to finish off the edges. The beginner will find ear stripping difficult as the area is particularly sensitive.

306

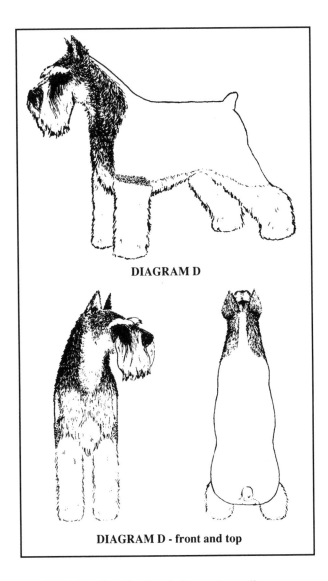

DIAGRAM D

DIAGRAM D - front and top

Use a fine knife for these more difficult-to-handle short hairs, and use clippers if you must.

Whether cropped or natural, the inner ear should look neat and clean. This is a sensitive area and using only thumb and forefinger can be very time consuming. A pair of tweezers will help, and a fastidious groomer will quickly learn their function.

WEEK 5-At this point, the cheeks, throat and chest must be dealt with. The amount that is stripped and that which is clipped is a matter of personal pride. These areas must be kept neat throughout the weeks of showing—as short, in fact, as the head. These areas will need constant maintenance during the show period, whether stripping or clipping. Be reminded that clipping will produce a

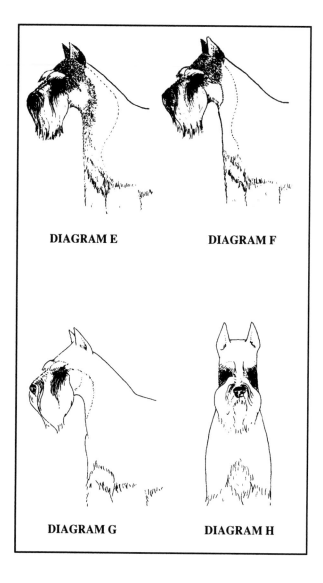

DIAGRAM E

DIAGRAM F

DIAGRAM G

DIAGRAM H

softer texture, and a loss of true salt and pepper color.

Using clippers, take out the hair under the throat. Before proceeding, comb the whiskers (beard) carefully forward and then grasp the beard and muzzle before bringing the clipping to within one and a half inches of the corners of the mouth. When in doubt, remove less rather than more—chin whiskers take a long time to grow.

With stripping knife or clippers, remove the hair on the chest to the point of the shoulders, leaving a small inverted V shape as shown in DIAGRAM H. Thinning scissors may be used to blend the joining line between shoulders and chest, and between neck and throat.

WEEK 6-At this point the undercoat will begin to show prominently. This should all be completely removed over the next two or three weeks, using a fine stripping knife or comb, and following the same pattern used for the outer coat. This process can do some damage to the new growth of hard hair if not done correctly. You may wish to use a fine (flea) comb first in order to learn the skills involved. The knife or comb should be held at a forty-five-degree angle, and with slight pressure, working in the direction of the natural lay of the coat.

This weeding out process must be continued as the new coat grows, otherwise the ingrowing coat will lift and separate quicker than it otherwise would.

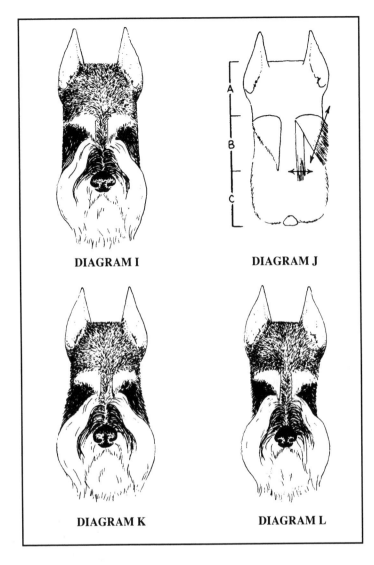

DIAGRAM I

DIAGRAM J

DIAGRAM K

DIAGRAM L

Trimming Head, Beard and Eyebrows

The Miniature Schnauzer's head should give the appearance of being *brick-shaped* as illustrated in DIAGRAM I. All trimming is done to achieve this look, aiming at length and flatness of skull, cleanness of cheeks, as well as a keen and alert expression.

There is a tendency to leave an overabundance of whiskers, both in length and thickness, as in DIAGRAM K. This detracts from the overall rectangular look which is desired. DIAGRAM L shows a dished-out look, where too much hair has been removed from under the eyes.

Before proceeding, be sure the beard and eyebrows are freshly washed

309

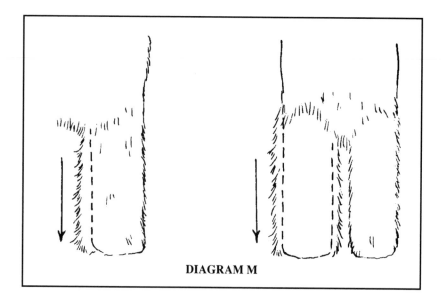

DIAGRAM M

and chalked. Facing the dog, comb the beard forward and with barber scissors cut a straight line to the outer corner of the eye. Where the clipping of the cheeks and the cutting of the beard meet, blending should be done with thinning scissors. The area under the eyes and at the bridge of the nose should be carefully hand plucked should there be any "fuzzy" quality here. The darker mask, so desirable in the salt and peppers, should be carefully maintained. Finger-strip when it begins to look untidy.

Trimming the eyebrows takes special skills, and the process should be studied firsthand before any attempt is made. A word of caution: take off less rather than more, and give yourself some time to look at your work. More can always be removed.

Facing the dog, comb the eyebrows forward, but slightly outward. Trim close at the outer corners of the eyes. The length of hair left on the inside will depend on several factors. If the foreface is short, a little less eyebrow will give the effect of more length. If the foreface is longer than the skull, leave the eyebrows slightly longer. Longer brows are often left to disguise light, round or large eyes, reducing the amount of eye seen. Follow the pattern illustrated in DIAGRAM J for the basic technique.

Trimming Front Legs and Feet

The aim in grooming the front legs is to have them look solid, full and straight viewed from any angle. All Schnauzers are not blessed with heavy leg furnishings, therefore they should be kept as dense as possible. The texture of leg hair may vary from soft and silky to hard and brittle. But in each type, cleanliness and careful grooming will prevent loss of furnishings.

Dry clean and comb out the legs before beginning. Add chalk and back

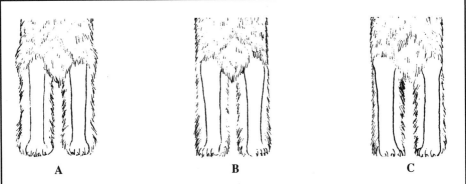

A - Straight front spoiled by excessive hair at the elbows and near feet.
B - Toeing-out minimized by leaving more hair on the inside of the feet while trimming closely at the outside.
C - Toeing-in minimized by leaving more hair on the outside of the feet while trimming closely at the inside.

comb the leg hair and then lightly comb downward with a palm pad. Before trimming, make sure the dog is standing in its natural show stance.

An honest appraisal of the front will pay off here, as you will want to minimize any fault that is present. Avoid creating a fault that isn't there! Poor blending at the elbows can create a pinched-in front or an out-at-elbow effect. Study DIAGRAM M before proceeding.

Standing directly over the dog and looking down onto the front legs, use straight scissors, pointing straight down. Trim in a circular manner all the way around each leg. This is called "posting," as the aim is to achieve a straight-as-a-post look.

The hair around the feet should be trimmed in a similar fashion, aiming at a round rather than pointed look. Lift each paw so that the pads are visible as shown in DIAGRAM N. Remove mats or any excess hair between the toes. Be careful not to carry your trimming to the top of the toes. The hair on top of the feet should be left full so that it can be blended evenly with the lower leg hair.

If your dog is not blessed with full furnishings, you will want to do some trimming during (or before) the first week of body stripping. Sparse, thin or brittle furnishings can be improved by limited stripping, using thumb and finger. Applying a light oil or lanolin preparation will help prevent brittle hair from breaking, and seems to encourage growth.

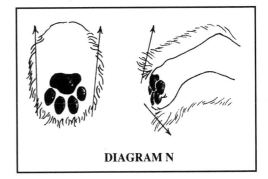

DIAGRAM N

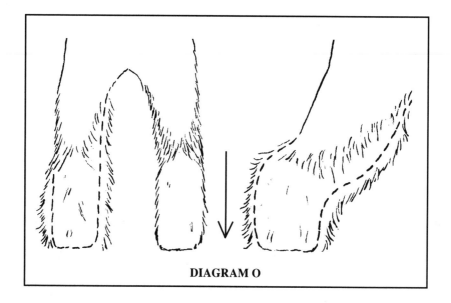

DIAGRAM O

Trimming Hindquarters and Feet

The hind legs are prepared and trimmed in much the same manner as the front legs. Here again, be sure the dog is in its natural show stance, and assess its qualities and faults. Study DIAGRAM O and see what technique may be used to create the best possible look.

Back comb the furnishings and then comb downward with the palm pad or comb. In trimming the hocks, begin in the same manner, standing over the dog with the scissors pointing straight down. You want to achieve that straight-as-a-post look, and will trim the hocks in the same circular motion. The hair on the rear feet should be trimmed in the same manner, remembering that the rear feet are slightly smaller, and will be left a little fuller.

On the inside of the stifle, from the breech to the inside of the hock, trim any wispy hairs. On the outside of the stifle, trim along the natural contour of the stifle to blend into the hock. Make sure the finished scissoring of the rear is in balance with what you have accomplished on the front legs.

The true test of your trimming occurs when you move your dog. What efforts you have made to minimize faults while in stance may not be adequate on the trot. More work may be necessary, but extreme care should be taken. It takes some time to grow an inch of leg hair.

Trimming the Underbody Fringe

Comb the underbody fringe and then use the palm pad to box it out a bit. Using straight scissors, trim the hair at the tuck-up near the rear legs to about a half inch in length. Trim toward the front legs, gently tapering your line, so that the hair is longer at the chest than at the tuck-up or loin. The chest hair should

312

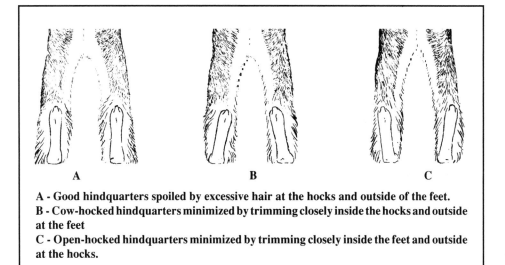

A - Good hindquarters spoiled by excessive hair at the hocks and outside of the feet.
B - Cow-hocked hindquarters minimized by trimming closely inside the hocks and outside at the feet
C - Open-hocked hindquarters minimized by trimming closely inside the feet and outside at the hocks.

reach only to the elbow and should not appear to be overabundant.

Trimming the Tail

The tail and the area below the tail will need periodic trimming. This area should always be kept neat and close by topping with either a stripping knife or thinning scissors. The tail itself should be rounded at the end, not pointed, and the length of hair kept in balance as further growth occurs.

Maintaining the Show Coat

Bringing your Miniature Schnauzer into show coat is only the beginning. To keep a show coat going longer requires considerable time and effort. The hair will constantly grow, and continued adjustments are required. The head, cheeks, ears and front section, as well as under the tail, will need to be stripped or clipped almost weekly. The shoulders will need occasional blending and thinning, using the stripping knife. After the dog has been in full coat for a month, begin weekly thinning of the neck and body by finger-stripping longer hairs as they appear. Hair between the pads and inside the ears should be cleaned out at all times.

Before each and every grooming session, reassess your dog, both standing and moving. Become more and more aware of his virtues and faults, and always trim with these in mind. Each grooming session is a learning experience, and often a revelation, as you discover some new way of providing a better balanced and more finished product.

There are no shortcuts to good grooming. Experience is the best teacher. No, experience is the only teacher!

18
Showing the
Miniature Schnauzer

IF YOU ARE LOOKING for a sport that offers good fellowship as well as boundless competition, showing your Miniature Schnauzer may be just the thing. This challenging activity has been enjoyed by young and old throughout the world for over a century. It knows no barriers—class, color or creed.

It is a sport for all seasons—and all reasons. Showing dogs offers enjoyment and involvement for the single person as well as the whole family, and creates friendships that last a lifetime. Whatever your reasons, there is a great deal of pleasure and satisfaction in showing a well-bred dog, beautifully groomed and thoughtfully trained.

Providing your dog has been sensibly raised, and has typical temperament, there is no real reason why you cannot succeed to some degree right from the beginning. Like all sports, there are levels on which success can be measured. If your immediate goals are realistic, they are within reach. Only the chosen few become Olympians, Derby winners—or Best in Show at Westminster. Reaching the top in any endeavor takes talent, effort and, above all, perseverance.

Dog Shows

The conformation, or breed classes, at a dog show are essentially a series of beauty contests—a process of elimination that ultimately results in one dog being selected as Best in Show. The level of competition will vary, depending on the type of show. On the highest level, Best in Show at the Westminster Kennel Club's annual all-breed dog show can be compared with victory at the Kentucky Derby. The 1941 winners of these events are known to this day. Ch. My Own Brucie is as famous a Cocker Spaniel as there ever was, and who has not heard of the great Whirlaway. Their breeders achieved a pinnacle that few realize, and that success represented decades of serious involvement.

Match Shows

Matches are held in many urban areas nearly every weekend, and most are open to all ages and all breeds. The match show is intended as a training ground for the dogs, the exhibitors and even the judges. Experienced breeders take their puppies to match shows for ring education, as well as to see how they

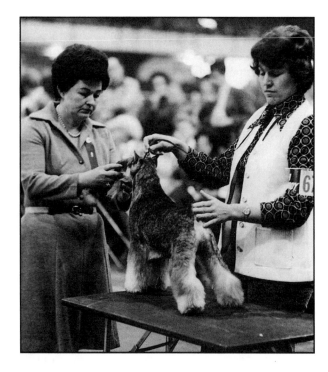

Jean Fancy examines Ch. Skyline's Blue Spruce while his breeder-owner Carol Parker keeps him under control, looking his best, without interfering with the examination.

react to the experience. Here is where you and your dog can learn the procedure as well as benefit by watching those more experienced. Many of the more seasoned exhibitors will be helpful to newcomers and will readily share their knowledge.

Most entry fees at match shows are very reasonable and entries can be made on the day of the match. The form and procedure is very much like that of an AKC licensed show where championship points are offered.

AKC Licensed Shows

In 1995 the American Kennel Club licensed over 800 all-breed shows and an additional 1,200 independent single breed (Specialty) shows. Entry fees for most shows range from sixteen to twenty-six dollars, and must be included along with a properly filled out official entry form. All must be received by the show superintendent before the posted closing date, usually two to three weeks before the actual show.

When your entry is acknowledged, the excitement begins. The program will tell you what time your breed will be judged and in which ring. It will also show the number of dogs in each breed. It lists the breed, followed by four numbers. For example, it may read: *Miniature Schnauzers 12-14-3-2*. This means that there are twelve dogs (males) competing for the championship points and fourteen for the points in bitches. The last two figures indicate that three champion males and two champion females are entered for Best of Breed competition, and are not competing for championship points. On the other hand, it may read: *Miniature Schnauzers 1-0-0-0,* which means that only your dog has been entered, and there will be no championship points offered.

Getting Started

The best way for a complete beginner to start is to enter a local match show where there is some assurance that other Miniature Schnauzers will be shown. If your first effort can be in the company of an experienced exhibitor you have already met, that would be most helpful. If not, seek out other Schnauzer exhibitors as soon as you arrive, and set up near them as there is much to be gained by observing their procedure.

From the moment you enter the show grounds you are creating the circumstance for making your dog show or not show. Above all else, you must make the entire experience as pleasurable as possible. A day at the dog show should be a joyful experience, not something to be dreaded.

If you have done your homework, your dog will take examinations, both on the table and on the ground, in his stride. He will be lead trained and prepared to perform as expected in the show ring. Most judges follow the same pattern in ring procedure, so it would be wise to watch earlier classes under the same judge if at all possible.

Exhibiting may appear simple on the surface, but it takes a great deal of time and effort to have a dog looking and showing competitively. It is a competition, and to seasoned exhibitors the show ring is their "moment of truth." Here is where fanciers evaluate and compare the progress of their breeding programs with those of fellow breeders.

The chapter on grooming will give you all the needed instructions on bringing your Miniature Schnauzer to the show looking his best. What follows is advice about training, handling and ring procedure.

Show Training

Start posing the future show dog on the table each time he is groomed. Teach him to allow you to place his four feet just the way you want them and to keep them that way. Then hold his head and his tail up and tell him to "stay" or "hold it," giving the command in a firm voice. If he does not obey and keeps moving, start all over from the beginning and keep at it until he understands just what you want. It will not take him long.

Open his lips and examine his front teeth and encourage members of the household to do so; then later, friends and strangers. Always be gentle. Have people lift up his front feet, run their hands along his spine and handle his hindquarters and hocks. Soon he will take this all as a matter of course.

You must start training your puppy to the show lead early. A soft slip lead is all that is necessary. He will soon learn that this lead requires a particular response. Hold the lead straight and fairly tight in your left hand, and train your Schnauzer always to walk on your left side. Never allow him to walk on the right side, and teach him not to cross in front of you.

You should attend as many dog shows as possible to learn the procedure in the show ring in order to teach your Miniature Schnauzer exactly what to do. If your dog knows in detail just what you require of him and thoroughly understands the routine, he will do his utmost to please without any uncertainty or bewilderment. You must, in turn, remain calm and collected and have confidence in yourself and in your dog. Most Schnauzers enter into the game of showing with zest and enjoyment and give of their best. They seem to sense that the other dogs are rivals and, with confidence in and affection for their handler, do their best to outshow their competitors. You must do your best as well.

Watch the professional handlers at the dog shows. See what they do and how they do it. Learn as much as possible of ring technique. Observe, for instance, that a good handler never comes between his dog and the judge but always allows the judge a clear and uninterrupted field of vision. Standing or moving, you must always keep your dog in the judge's eye in the most advantageous manner.

Before you show your Miniature Schnauzer, make up your mind that you will meet other very good dogs in the ring. A knowledge of your dog's faults and virtues helps you to keep a balanced point of view. Study him against others in your own mind, study the printed Standard, study pictures of the best. Know just where your dog stands. Although your affections are involved, and you are justly proud of him, all the other exhibitors feel exactly the same way about their dogs. These natural sentiments have nothing to do with your Schnauzer's points as a show dog.

You may be sure, if you keep on showing, your Schnauzer will find his rightful level. If he is really good, and well presented, nothing can keep him down; if not, nothing can bring him up. In the course of a long show career, you will be knocked down at times unjustly, and, on the other hand, you may also win unjustly. Unless you can cheerfully take whatever comes, showing dogs may not be for you. Be a modest winner and a good loser. It pays.

Show Procedure

If you have entered an AKC licensed show, you will receive the Schedule of Judging and your exhibitor's pass in the mail. It is your responsibility to have your dog groomed and ready at ringside when your class is called. A few minutes before the scheduled time, check in with the ring steward who will give you an armband with your dog's catalogue number printed on it. If you have entered the 6 months to 9 months puppy dog class, you will be among the first of the breed to enter the ring. When your class is called you enter the ring with the dog on your left and line up as the steward or judge directs. If you are a beginner or novice, try not to be first in line. This gives a little extra time to observe the judge's procedure.

Most judges follow a basic pattern in ring procedure. The first direction will usually involve the entire class being asked to move counterclockwise around the ring once or twice. Hold the lead in your left hand, always keeping your dog between you and the judge. When the judge signals the class to stop, stack your dog, or use bait to keep him alert and in control until it is your turn to be examined. Miniature Schnauzers are usually examined on a table. After placing your dog on the table in a show pose, be prepared to have his teeth and bite examined. Some judges will ask you to show the mouth, others will do their own examination. While always having complete control of your dog, try to keep your hands out of the way during the entire examination.

Following this, the judge may ask you to move your dog, or he may go on and check the next dog, saving movement requirements for later. He will eventually want to see your dog gait in a pattern of his choice. He may ask you simply to take your dog "Down and Back"—straight away across the ring and straight back to the judge. Many judges will request various patterns: the "Triangle" in which the dog moves straight away down the ring, across to the opposite corner and back to the judge on a diagonal; the "T" pattern in which your dog moves straight down the ring, across to one side of the ring, back across to the other side of the ring, back to the center and then returning to the judge; the "L" pattern in which the dog moves straight down the ring, across to a corner, back to the center and back to the judge. He may want a second look and ask for a different pattern, so be prepared and listen carefully.

At the end of a requested movement pattern, stop a short distance from the judge, as he will want to see your dog standing free. He will be making a final check of ear-set and expression, as well as natural topline and tail-set. At this crucial point you will want your dog looking alert and showing his best. The name of the game is Dog *Show,* so teach your dog to show on command, either with bait (boiled liver is most commonly used) or with a ball or squeaky toy. When the judge has completed his individual examination of your dog, standing and moving, he will request that you take a position behind the other dogs already examined. If there are still others yet to be examined, take the time to work with your dog, straightening his beard and furnishings while also keeping him from getting bored. Here is where the bait or toy may again come in handy.

After all the dogs have been examined and gaited, the real competition begins, and a "third" eye would be helpful. Always keep an eye on the judge as well as your dog—and an extra eye on the competition if you can. The judge may ask the entire class to move again in unison, or he may ask only a few. Be ready! He may ask certain dogs to come together for further comparison. This is not a sparring match, and you must always have complete control of your dog. The judge will eventually make up his mind and send the first four placings to the designated markers and distribute the ribbons and any other awards offered.

If you win first in the class you must return for the judging of Winners Dog; if you are second, you may also be called for further judging for Reserve

Winners Dog, so stand by. After each class for males is judged, the steward will request that all first-place winners return to the ring for the judging of Winners Dog (WD). Here is where championship points are awarded, depending on the number of males in competition. If your 6-9 months puppy dog is selected WD, the second-place winner from that class is called to compete with the remaining class winners for Reserve Winners Dog (RWD). If the WD is disqualified for any infraction of the AKC rules, the RWD would then be credited with WD and awarded the points.

The classes for females follow in the same way, and after Winners Bitch (WB) and Reserve are selected the WD and WB compete further against champions for Best of Breed (BB). The judge will examine this class as he did all others. The final outcome will be a BB winner, a Best of Opposite Sex (BOS), as well as Best of Winners (BW). The BW award can be crucial, as there are frequently larger numbers in one sex. Example: in an entry of four dogs, eleven bitches, three male champions and four female champions, your 6-9 puppy dog might earn two points for WD, an extra point for BW (there are three points in bitches), and yet another point (four points total) for going BB. In defeating all fifteen bitches, he earns the scale of points (four) for the total number of bitches competing.

The Best of Breed Miniature Schnauzer is then eligible to compete in the Terrier Group. The best of each of the twenty-six terrier breeds are judged in much the same manner, with the emphasis being on which dog is closest to his own breed Standard. The best four will be given Group placements, and the Group First winner goes on to compete for Best in Show. If, by chance, your puppy is named Best Terrier, there may be an additional point awarded (total of five). If there was a five-point award made in any of the terrier breeds, your dog picks up the additional point by virtue of the superior win.

The final competition of the day will see seven finalists—the best Sporting, Hound, Working, Terrier, Toy, Non-Sporting and Herding dogs—the winner earning the coveted Red, White and Blue ribbon for Best Dog in Show.

How a Dog Becomes a Champion

Championship points (from zero to five) are awarded to the Winners Dog and Winners Bitch, with the possibility of additional points for defeating champions for the Best of Breed and Best of Opposite Sex. Further points may be earned by going on to Best Terrier or Best in Show. The maximum award possible at any single show is 5 points.

To become a champion, a dog or bitch must acquire fifteen points under at least three different judges, and two of these wins must be *majors*. A major win carries three, four or five points, and must be won under two different judges. A real "flyer" might earn three five-point majors on a three-show weekend, but most show quality Miniature Schnauzers compete in twenty-five or more shows in order to achieve enough wins to earn the AKC certificate naming the dog a "Champion of Record."

Epilogue

$\mathbf{Y}$OU HAVE READ the history of the Miniature Schnauzer in the United States and throughout the world. You have learned of and from the dedicated fanciers who have brought the breed to its present state. You can, with a minimum of time and effort, connect your own Miniature Schnauzers to their proper sire lines and learn more of their families through studying the text and photos which accompany the charts.

You have been given a visualization of breed perfection, and hopefully a clearer understanding of how these qualities may be achieved, not only through breeding but also through a higher degree of grooming and presentation.

The gallery of photos presented, both historic and contemporary, are intended for the pleasure of every reader, as well as to give a graphic record of breed progress.

In closing the pages of *THE NEW MINIATURE SCHNAUZER,* every effort has been made to touch on all facets of the breed that are important to dedicated fanciers, both old and new. The goal has been to combine all topics in print and picture that will have value in helping you better understand and appreciate this wonderful breed.